The Queen and the Mistress

The Queen and the Mistress

The Women of Edward III

GEMMA HOLLMAN

First published 2022

The History Press
97 St George's Place, Cheltenham,
Gloucestershire, GL50 3QB
www.thehistorypress.co.uk

British Library Cataloguing in Publication Data.
A catalogue record for this book is available from the British Library.

ISBN 978 0 7509 9369 2

Typesetting and origination by The History Press
Printed and bound in Great Britain by TJ Books Limited, Padstow, Cornwall.

MIX
Paper from
responsible sources
FSC® C013056

Trees for LYfe

To Mum and Dad,
for always supporting me in everything I wanted to do.

The most gentle Queen, most liberal, and most courteous that ever was Queen in her days

Jean Froissart on Queen Philippa of Hainault

There was in England ... an unchaste woman, a most shameless whore, named Alice Perrers ... but she was advanced by fortune, for she was neither noble nor beautiful

Thomas Walsingham on Alice Perrers

Contents

Acknowledgements

No book written during this time can fail to acknowledge the impact of the coronavirus pandemic on its production. This book was greatly delayed when access to resources shut down, but I would like to start by acknowledging the hard work of all the librarians and archivists across the country who endeavoured to open up new ways for historians to access their materials. A thank you, too, to the online journals and other source websites who opened up their digital resources for free, thus allowing the continuation of research despite the circumstances. My next thanks goes to Chrissy at The History Press for asking me to write this next book, and for helping me to shape my ideas when it was in its infancy. Thank you to Simon for ably taking over as commissioning editor when Chrissy moved on, and thank you to Jess for being such a fantastic publicist.

Thank you, too, to my parents for keeping me encouraged whilst writing, and for listening to me ramble random titbits at them over dinner. A special thanks to my mum for reading over early drafts and giving her opinion, and to my friends who did the same: Conor, Claudia, Desa, Glyn and Aaron. Thank you to my other friends, Cat, Fiona, Ella, Harriet and Michael B. for keeping me sane over the pandemic, with virtual birthday drinks and endless text messages. You kept me going so that I had the energy at the end of the day to sit and write all this. Thank you to Nick for always chatting to me about writing and our respective projects and to Jill for continuing to be my archive auntie – try not to put this one in the washing machine. And thank you Conor for staying by my side, for bringing a wonderful little cat into our lives and for being a great companion during lockdown. The days flew by with you. A final thank you to the wonderful historians who have done so much work on the reign of Edward III and the women in his life, so that I could learn about and fall in love with Philippa and Alice.

Genealogical Tables

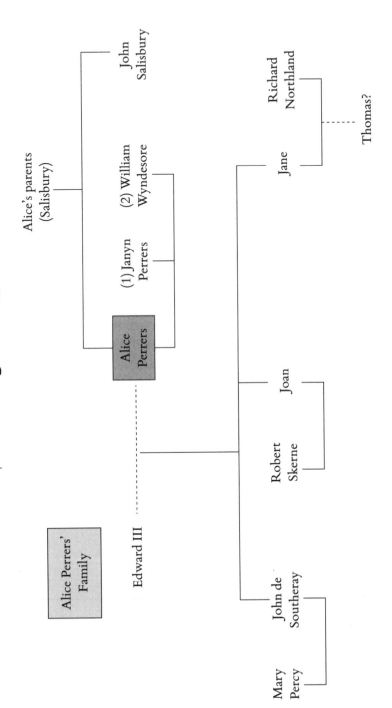

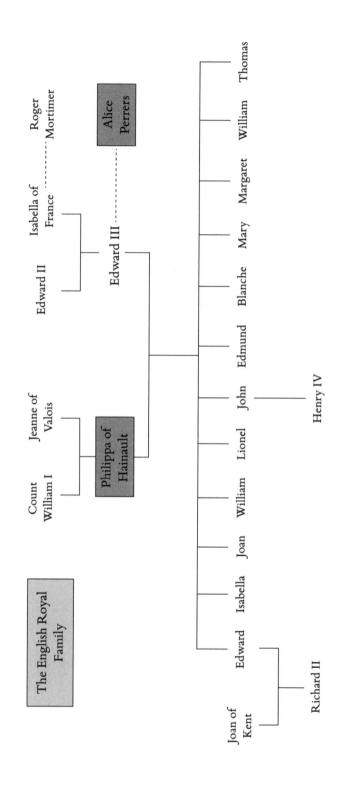

The English Royal Family

Introduction

'His like had not been seen since the days of King Arthur.'[1] So says the chronicler Jean Froissart of the great King Edward III of England. But behind every great man is a woman, and Edward was no exception.

Edward's mother was Isabella of France, daughter of King Philip IV of France and Queen Joan I of Navarre, and her later title of 'She-Wolf' was well deserved. In 1326 she deposed her husband, King Edward II of England, and ruled as regent with her lover for four years before her son took control of the kingdom as Edward III. Edward had a powerful role model in his mother, and she continued to influence him until her death.

The next most important woman in Edward's life was his wife, Queen Philippa of Hainault, who was the daughter of the Count and Countess of Hainault. Edward and Philippa's marriage had been a political one, but from the start the attraction between them was clear. Theirs was one of the most successful royal marriages in English history, lasting for forty-one years and producing twelve children. Philippa has been remembered as a pious, kind-hearted woman who excelled at being a wife and mother, and whose charity and mercy benefited not only the whole of the kingdom but also England's enemies; a tearful plea to Edward famously saved the lives of prisoners-of-war at Calais. Her death in 1369 broke the king's heart and, in the minds of many, marked the start of his downfall.

Philippa's death did not leave Edward completely alone. A few years previously he had begun a relationship with the final woman who was to exert great influence on his life and the kingdom of England: Alice Perrers. Alice's name has become synonymous with greed, immorality and cruelty. She became probably the richest woman in England through Edward's patronage, and she held more land than most of the male nobility too. For hundreds of years after she lived, writers told of the seductress who charmed an ageing, mourning king into loving her, then proceeded to wring him of his wealth, his friends and his kingship. This Alice Perrers was so heartless that after the poor king died she even stooped to steal the rings from his still-warm fingers.

As is so often the case with the history of women in the medieval period, this is not the whole story. The tales of these women's personalities and deeds have been twisted over the centuries, making each of them a caricature. This book focuses on the lives of the only two women Edward is known to have had romantic relationships with – Philippa of Hainault and Alice Perrers. At first glance these women seem like the angel and devil on Edward's shoulders. Dig a little deeper and the real women begin to come to the surface, showing very different characters. Philippa was indeed an exemplary queen who in so many ways fitted the model for a perfect ruler, and yet she had vices of her own. She was in debt for most of her life, with Edward – and the coffers of England – continually coming to her rescue. Often portrayed by modern historians as greedy and keen to exploit the monetary privileges given to her as queen, she adorned herself with luxurious fabrics and was always dripping with jewels.

It is true that Alice gathered as much land as she could, and at times she was unpleasant to her contemporaries. But underneath the sexist judgements laid upon her for centuries, an incredibly intelligent, shrewd and confident woman emerges. In a time where many women only had two paths in life – marriage or a nunnery – Alice chose to forge a path of her own: mistress. Previous kings, of course, had mistresses, but their names have been lost to history. Only the legendary Rosamund Clifford, mistress to Henry II, came close to Alice's fame before her. In a time when it was expected that only women from the nobility would be educated, Alice rose from obscurity and navigated complicated legal systems to build her empire, a feat which has astounded contemporaries and historians since. To be this astute, Alice was indeed a special woman. If she used her sexuality to her advantage, it was only to level the playing field with the wealthy, powerful men at court.

Though these two women dominated the court for most of the fourteenth century, significant parts of their lives remain in obscurity. Their dates of birth are not recorded, nor is Alice's death, and we can only make educated guesses. Both seem to have been beautiful, but the exact nature of their appearance is difficult to pin down. For the past 600 years Alice's family has been completely anonymous, with only the fantastic work of historians in the last decade or so starting to unravel her origins. Alice might have been infamous, but her contemporaries knew strikingly little about who she really was. So how does one begin to reveal the real women when so much has been lost or twisted?

There is a fine line between restoring the reputation of women of the past who have been unfairly judged, and going too far the other way to gloss over their failings. As with any person alive today, these women were complicated. They had good moments and bad, respectable qualities and those we may judge more harshly. It is important as well to look at them in the context of the time, where even for the nobility life could be harsh and one had to fight to stay afloat at court.

Alice Perrers has just one biography of her life, written in 1966 before new information came to light. Philippa was given her own modern biography in 2019, the only other one being published in 1910. This book is a contribution to this scholarship, and hopefully by placing these two remarkable women side by side, they can both be seen in a new light. The queen and the mistress, two women who loved and were loved by the same man.

I

The Count's Daughter

As the queen's coffin entered Westminster Abbey, accompanied by nearly thirty of her ladies dressed in black cloth and furs, the English nation reflected on her life. So greatly had she been loved and admired that the funeral procession had spanned six days, with thousands thronging to the capital to pay their respects. In churches across the kingdom, prayers were offered to God for her soul. Chroniclers would record their mournful eulogies, extolling her grace, virtue and gentleness. No one mourned her passing more than her devoted husband. Their marriage had lasted over forty years, and the king had promised her as she lay dying that they would be together in death, too. Within a decade this promise was fulfilled, and the old king was buried beside his queen.

Philippa of Hainault was medieval England's longest-reigning queen consort, but her birth is shrouded in mystery. Surviving records of births of children, even royal and noble children, are notoriously patchy in a time before concerted efforts to keep official records of such things, and this was even more the case for women. If Philippa was born in her father's territory of Hainault, as is very likely, then it follows that she was probably born in the principal town of Valenciennes, where her parents spent much of their time.

Philippa's father was the illustrious William, Count of Hainault, Holland and Zeeland, a variety of independent territories in north-western Europe that bordered the kingdom of France and covered areas of modern-day Belgium, France and the Netherlands. His territories were not the largest in western Europe, but they were particularly affluent due to the trading skills of their inhabitants and the sumptuous cloth that they produced which was highly desired. This wealth gave William quite a bit of political power when dealing with his English and French neighbours.

Philippa's mother was no less important, and in fact came from a higher bloodline. Countess Jeanne was part of the French royal family on her father's side, being the granddaughter of King Philip III of France; her brother also went on to become king. Jeanne's maternal grandfather was King Charles II of Naples, meaning she was related to rulers across Europe through her various aunts, uncles and cousins. Jeanne passed this royal blood down to her daughter Philippa, whose noble connections were to prove an invaluable asset later in her life.

The date of Philippa's birth has been hotly debated by historians. The chronicler Jean Froissart – who was employed by Philippa for many years as a court writer and thus knew her personally – placed her at almost 14 years old upon her marriage in January 1328, which would have meant that she was born in early 1314. His evidence has not always been trusted, as he placed the year of the marriage one year early and got the age of her groom wrong.[1] Philippa was one of nine or ten children that her parents had together, and the dates of birth of most of them are unknown. But recent historical research has given significant credence to the idea that Philippa was indeed born in 1314, the third daughter of Count William and Countess Jeanne.[2]

As the daughter of a powerful noble family, with the blood of monarchs running through her veins, Philippa would have had a very privileged upbringing. She would have grown up speaking French, the language of her mother and the surrounding regions, though she was also likely taught Dutch or Flemish too, and possibly even some English, considering England was one of the region's main trading partners. Though Valenciennes was a favoured home for her parents, as medieval rulers they were required to travel between their various territories to ensure they were being governed correctly and gather loyalty from and popularity with their subjects. Philippa and her siblings would have joined them at times, allowing them a chance to learn about all of the corners of their parents' lands as they grew up.

Philippa was part of a large family; not only did she have at least eight legitimate siblings, but her father was a notorious womaniser and Philippa is known to have had at least eight half-siblings as well. Unusually, Philippa enjoyed a very close relationship with her mother. Whilst many royal and noble parents in this period exercised some distance from their children, living in different households and travelling independently from them, Philippa's mother doted on her children. This loving family environment obviously made quite an impression on the young Philippa, and was to contrast quite sharply with the family of her future husband.

As a young noblewoman of great lineage, it was expected that Philippa would make a good match and so she needed to be taught well. She would have learnt from her mother how to successfully manage a household and how to exhibit feminine virtues expected of a consort. She would have been taught how to sew, dance, sing and perhaps play an instrument, and she was certainly taught how to read. Her parents' court was a cultured one, filled with poetry and music, and writing found a particular importance there, with the count and countess commissioning books and collecting personal libraries for their residences.[3]

Although there are many surviving images of Philippa, from her picture on her seal, to manuscript depictions, artwork in chapels and her tomb effigy, her exact appearance remains somewhat unclear. No concrete written description of her survives, and manuscript and seal imagery was often highly idealised to project the queen as a concept rather than as an individual. Her tomb monument is an excellent reference to how Philippa looked at the end of her life, but how she looked when she was younger, and smaller details such as the colours of her hair and eyes, is unknown.

A very famous description of one of the daughters of Hainault survives. In 1319, a marriage alliance was discussed between England and Hainault, and King Edward II of England sent an ambassador – Bishop Walter Stapeldon – to Hainault to engage in the negotiations. Stapeldon returned a thorough report to Edward, where he described the count's daughter who was proposed to marry Edward's son. Later in the century, an unknown person identified the girl as Philippa of Hainault by adding her name to the margins of Stapeldon's written report, but in all likelihood the description is actually of her oldest sister, Margaret, for she was the daughter who had been at the centre of discussions around this time.⁴ The girl was considered to be a pleasing match for the young prince, but negotiations ultimately came to nothing.

Philippa's family often travelled to the French court to visit their relatives and participate in important events, and her parents owned a house in Paris to stay in during these occasions.⁵ Possibly the first time Philippa travelled to Paris herself was in 1323 to attend the coronation of the new French queen, Marie of Luxembourg. Countess Jeanne's cousin, Charles IV, had become king in January the previous year and had married Marie that September. As Jeanne was a close relative of the new king, and William was a powerful neighbouring ruler, the couple would have been expected to attend Marie's coronation. They probably made it a family trip, bringing their numerous children with them to see the glamour of the French court and to make connections with the great and good.

The next year saw several important family weddings that Philippa almost certainly attended. In February 1324 her two older sisters, Margaret and Joanna, were married in a double wedding ceremony to the Holy Roman Emperor and the Duke of Jülich respectively. The girls were scarcely out of childhood, Margaret being 13 and Joanna 12, and both of their grooms were older: Margaret's new husband was 42 years old, and Joanna's was about 25. It seems that Countess Jeanne was not too happy at the age difference between Margaret and her husband, but the marriage was advantageous to Count William and his territories and so there was little she could do about it.⁶

Although Jeanne could not prevent the early marriages of her daughters, she made sure to act as a support for them. In spring 1326, Jeanne brought Joanna to stay with her in Hainault for three months because the young girl was suffering from homesickness. Three years later Jeanne travelled to her daughter's court and stayed with her for an extended period as 'through the absence of her parents [she was] very dejected'.⁷

Even at 10 years old, Philippa would have been aware of the implications of the marriages of her sisters. She would have known that the marriages were politically advantageous and would make her sisters very powerful and wealthy women, but she must too have been aware of the uncomfortable age gap of Margaret's marriage, and how much Joanna was suffering being parted from her family at a young age. This might well have made Philippa apprehensive at her own future match. What would her husband be like?

The year of 1325 brought the answer, although Philippa would not have been aware of it at the time. Towards the end of the year it became clear that Jeanne's father was dying, and as a devoted daughter she hurried to be with him. Jeanne left Valenciennes at the start of December and arrived in France a few days later, taking Philippa with her.[8] Jeanne arrived just in time, for her father died a week after she reached him. His body was taken to Paris for his funeral and burial just a few days before Christmas. Both Jeanne and Philippa attended, and they stayed in Paris to celebrate a more sombre Christmas with their relatives in the French royal family. There were two very important visitors to the French court at this time whose presence was to change the course of Philippa's life: Queen Isabella of England and her eldest son, Prince Edward.

Queen Isabella had travelled to the French court in March that year, ostensibly on a diplomatic mission to represent her husband, Edward II.[9] England and France were in dispute over territories in modern-day France and as Queen Isabella was the sister of King Charles of France as well as queen consort of England, she was seen as the perfect mediator. In the end, sending Isabella to France turned out to be a grave mistake of Edward's. Isabella had been increasingly isolated over the past few years by her husband's favourites, the two Despensers, a father–son duo who were hated in England for the influence they wielded over the king and the wealth and power they were lavished with as a result. Edward had turned against his wife and treated her poorly and this had culminated in 1324 with Edward confiscating all of Isabella's lands under the pretence of the safety of the realm, claiming that her territories were under threat from attack by France.[10]

Isabella viewed her ostracism as a gross insult to her position as queen and as a member of French royalty. A group of exiled nobles from England had taken refuge at the French court to escape the clutches of the Despensers and Edward's wrath. Now, Isabella had managed to escape England and was in the safety of her powerful brother's court. Importantly, she was welcomed by the exiled Englishmen who viewed her as suffering with them.[11]

In September, Edward II made the second grave mistake which played into the hands of his wife: he agreed to send his eldest son and heir, Prince Edward, to France to pay homage to the French king. Earlier in the year,

Isabella had arranged a treaty between England and France which would bring peace if King Edward agreed to pay homage to the French king for the French territories he controlled.[12] However, Edward knew that if he left England then the Despensers 'would not know where to live safely' because they were so hated in the realm.[13] A perfect solution seemed to be to send his son to represent him so that he could stay in the country and protect his favourites.

What Edward II did not consider was that when Prince Edward arrived in France he was now under the control of his mother. Prince Edward was the heir to the throne, and Isabella could now claim to act in his name. She declared that the Despensers had 'come between my husband and myself' and tried to break the bonds of their marriage, and as such she publicly stated: 'I declare that I will not return until this intruder is removed, but, discarding my marriage garment, shall put on the robes of widowhood and mourning until I am avenged.'[14]

Both Isabella and Edward were still at the French court when Philippa and Jeanne were in Paris at Christmas, and the four certainly met. The group were family, for Isabella was Jeanne's first cousin. By May 1326, Edward II was no closer to enticing them to return to him. In the meantime, King Charles of France had a new wife, and William and Jeanne again made the trip to the French capital to attend her coronation. They would have brought their children with them to witness such an important event, but beneath the surface there appears to have been another motivation – to allow their daughter Philippa another chance to meet with the handsome English prince.

In January, rumours had already been circulating of a deal struck between Queen Isabella and Countess Jeanne during the latter's stay in France. King Edward II had issued a public denial that his son was about to embark on a marriage in France, but his efforts were futile without possession of his son.[15] The coronation of the new French queen gave Isabella a chance to continue discussions with Philippa's parents about a possible combined future, and both sets of parents surely pointed out to their children the virtues of the other party.

That summer, shortly after the coronation, Prince Edward and Isabella left France for the court of Hainault.[16] Once there, political negotiations were undertaken swiftly and conclusively. Queen Isabella made a formal alliance with Count William, where it was agreed that Prince Edward would marry Philippa of Hainault. This would elevate William's daughter to Queen of England at some point in the future, and it would bring peace and prosperity between England and William's territories, and thus increased trade and wealth for William. In return, William would supply military support to the exiled queen as his daughter's dowry. His brother, John of Hainault, provided 700 troops and William himself hired around 100 ships filled with mercenaries.[17]

The marriage contract was sealed at the end of August, and Prince Edward swore on the Holy Gospels that he would marry Philippa within two years or else pay a £10,000 fine.[18] This period of time was necessary because there were numerous blocks to Edward and Philippa marrying there and then in Hainault. As second cousins, the couple required a dispensation from the pope because they were within forbidden degrees of relation. Time was pressing, and Isabella and Edward needed to make their way over to England and sort out the political problems in the country and, more importantly, within the royal family, rather than waste time organising a wedding. Finally, the marriage in itself was not actually legal, as Prince Edward required his father's permission and Edward II had expressly stated that he did not consent to the match. Despite these difficulties, 14-year-old Prince Edward had decided to support his mother over his father, and he recognised that the support of Count William was vital to this.

Although the marriage was politically motivated, it seems that the young prince and Philippa had an early attraction towards each other. Decades later, the chronicler Froissart was to write about the circumstances of their marriage. Froissart romanticises Edward and Philippa's meeting, saying that out of all of Count William's daughters Edward 'loved Philippa above all the others' because she was better company and had similar interests to him.[19] In his version, the politics of the match come second to the true love of the couple who had become enamoured upon their meeting.

Some have taken this story as evidence that an older Philippa was viewing her marriage with Edward 'through rose-coloured spectacles', for Froissart gathered much of his information at first hand from the queen and her court.[20] True, Philippa might have wished a more romantic story of her marriage to spread rather than the political reality. But this does not quite explain Froissart's version. Although Isabella and Jeanne had discussed marriage between their children as soon as they met in France in December, they might well have not initially told the youths of their plans and instead encouraged them to get to know each other, in the hopes that they would like what they saw.

The marriage depended entirely on Edward's co-operation, as Isabella had no authority to force it on him. It was therefore in Isabella's interests to make Philippa seem appealing to Edward and she might well have needed little help in this. Philippa had been raised well by her mother and so she would have acted in an engaging and attractive manner around Edward, knowing how to converse well. She was well educated and cultured, and if she was of similar appearance to her sister who had been described years previously, she was certainly considered attractive.

Philippa, too, would have needed little encouragement. Marriage would have already been on her mind, and Edward was a very appealing prospect. As a prince and future king he was of excellent status to marry, but he was also handsome and athletic, and he was a very similar age to her, unlike the much older spouses of her siblings. Whilst the marriage was political in nature for the parents, for Edward and Philippa it might indeed have been a love match from the start that had the convenience of fitting in with their parents' plans.

With the betrothal of Edward and Philippa, the path to war was swift. Isabella now had her relatives' forces and the support of Roger Mortimer, an influential baron of the Welsh Marches who had fallen foul of Edward II and the Despensers. Isabella, Prince Edward and their supporters landed in Suffolk towards the end of September 1326 with a small force of around 1,500 men.[21] Their aims were to reassert the royal power of the queen and prince, and to remove the hated Despensers from power. However, and perhaps to everyone's surprise, they quickly found themselves gathering supporters from across England. It was not only the exiled nobles who hated the Despensers, and Queen Isabella was a popular figure in the country.

Earls, bishops, towns and cities all threw their support behind Isabella, and even Edward II's two half-brothers, Thomas of Brotherton, Earl of Norfolk, and Edmund of Woodstock, Earl of Kent, and his cousin, Henry, Earl of Leicester, joined her. In October, Edward II was forced to flee London with his favourites, but he was ultimately unable to save them. The elder

Despenser was captured at the end of October and swiftly hanged, drawn and quartered, and in the wake of this Prince Edward was made Keeper of the Realm.[22] As Edward II was known to be on the run, making Prince Edward the country's custodian meant that Isabella and her supporters could control the government in his absence. Making this move right after the execution of one of the king's favourites was a strong statement of the power of the queen. In mid-November, Edward II was captured in Wales alongside the younger Despenser. Despenser was given a traitor's death, just like his father, and the king was lodged in a series of secure castles whilst Isabella's regime decided how to proceed.

Nominally, the aims of the invasion were complete. The Despensers were gone, and Isabella could take off her widow's clothing and return to her husband.[23] But Isabella and Prince Edward had seen how popular their revolt had been and had tasted power unrestrained by the whims of their husband and father. With everything that had happened, the pair realised that events had progressed too far for the family to ever go back to normal. Edward II was known for his vengeance, and he would not take kindly to such traitorous behaviour.

As such, it was decided that Prince Edward would continue to rule the realm on his father's behalf for the time being. At the end of November, it was noted in the official record that 'it pleased [Edward II] to send his great seal to his consort and son ... and that they should cause to be done under the great seal not only what was necessary for right and peace, but also what should please them'.[24] In reality, Edward II was anything but pleased. Isabella was now being given joint control of the country alongside her son, a unique situation in English history.

On 13 January 1327, England's parliament decided that Edward II, who had reigned for just shy of twenty years, deserved to be deposed. It was declared that he was a weak and incompetent king who had taken bad counsel, had abandoned his realm and was not fit to rule.[25] Instead, his 14-year-old son was to become king in his place. Plans were quickly put in place to secure this decision, and on 1 February Prince Edward was crowned King Edward III of England in Westminster Abbey.[26]

Throughout the dramatic events of late 1326, Philippa's family had been at the heart of the action. Much of the initial invasion force was made up of

Count William's and his brother's men, and John of Hainault played a conspicuous role in events. He now attended Edward's coronation and he would have been quick to remind the new king of his obligation to his niece.[27] Once Edward had taken time to organise his new government, the appropriate steps were made to ensure his marriage to Philippa could take place. At the end of summer, Pope John XXII finally issued a papal dispensation to allow the couple to marry.[28] Philippa would soon be a queen.

Not long after the granting of the dispensation, a shocking announcement was made at court: King Edward II had died at Berkeley Castle. The official story was that he had died of natural causes, but within a few years Roger Mortimer would be accused of orchestrating the deposed king's murder.[29] Soon the legend would spread that the king had been painfully killed by a red-hot poker being inserted into his anus, perhaps an allusion to his alleged homosexuality, although this story is dismissed today as apocryphal. After Edward II was removed from power, Mortimer and Queen Isabella embarked on a relationship together, and Mortimer found his seat at the centre of power as a result. He certainly would have been well placed to cause Edward's death, and with his newly budding romance with the queen he benefited from it too. Over the spring and summer, numerous plots to free the captured king had been foiled, and England's old rivals, the Scots, had used the instability to invade the north. Keeping the old king alive was becoming a liability to the new regime, and that was something Mortimer did not want.

In December, Edward III travelled to Gloucester Abbey for his father's funeral. Despite his deposition, the dead king was treated according to his status, with a wooden mannequin dressed in his coronation robes and adorned with crown, sceptre and rod placed on top of the coffin.[30] In the midst of organising the funeral, Edward had not forgotten his betrothed, and plans for his marriage to Philippa progressed. In October, Philippa was at her parents' home in Valenciennes surrounded by excitement. Some of the most important men in Europe – many of whom were related to Philippa – had arrived for the preparations of the young girl's wedding.

Edward now sent the Bishop of Coventry and Lichfield to Valenciennes to conclude the final parts of the marriage settlement with Count William. By the end of the month, the bishop had fulfilled his duty and the final terms were agreed upon. Whilst there, he also performed a marriage by proxy with

Philippa as another step towards her marriage with Edward.[31] The couple were now tied together. All that was left was to prepare Philippa for her departure to England and her new life as queen. More than ever, Philippa probably wished to rely on her mother, but amidst the elation of wedding preparation, tragedy struck – Philippa's sickly younger brother died, aged 2. The funeral was held in between organising Philippa's marriage, and Philippa's mother was dealing with the tragedy whilst heavily pregnant.[32] Between dealing with her pregnancy, the funeral of her child and the logistics of planning her daughter's wedding, Jeanne might have had little time to spend with her daughter.

The time was drawing near for Philippa to leave her home for new lands. With her marriage, her life would completely change. She would go from a 13-year-old girl to a queen of an important and powerful nation. She would move to a new country with different languages and cultures. She would have heavy responsibilities that put her in control of people's lives. On 28 November, Edward ordered two of his most reliable and loyal men, Bartholomew de Burghersh and William de Clinton, to bring Count William and Philippa to England safely.[33]

Though Philippa was to travel abroad, her father would accompany her to ease the transition – an uncommon occurrence among rulers at this time, and something that perhaps shows William's love for his daughter. The couple had a papal dispensation, had been married by proxy, and there was the treaty with a punishing fine made the year before. William could hardly have been worried about Edward reneging on his promises when the marriage was all but set in stone. The more likely reason is that he wanted to see his daughter off on her new life and confirm she was adequately cared for.

In the middle of December, Philippa bade farewell to her beloved mother, her siblings and her country. In the end, her father did not join her. Around the time that Philippa left for England, her mother gave birth to another son who died shortly afterwards. With a wife due to give birth any day, William obviously decided she needed his support more. After the death of two of their young children within two months of each other, the Hainault family and court spent Christmas in deep mourning, and many ladies were recorded as travelling to Valenciennes to comfort Jeanne in her grief.[34] Philippa had to grow up more quickly than she expected.

2

Becoming Queen

Philippa of Hainault landed at Dover near the end of 1327, escorted by her uncle John instead of her father, and she made her grand entrance into London just a few days before Christmas. She spent the festive season in the capital, preparing for the next leg of her journey and making her first impression on her new subjects. She was showered with 'most splendid' presents from the Londoners, including a variety of foods and items of gold and silver worth 300 marks (£200), a significant sum. Great feasts and celebrations were held over several days with 'all the ladies and all the barons of England'. Philippa stayed in London until 27 December, when the royal party made the 200-mile journey north to the city of York.[1]

York was not a usual location for a royal wedding, but in this case the choice seems to have come from extraneous circumstances. In November, the Archbishop of Canterbury had died, and his position had not yet been filled. It was thus decided that the Archbishop of York should perform the ceremony, and so it was thought fitting that he marry the couple in his own cathedral.[2] It took just shy of a month for the whole royal court to make its way there, with Philippa's retinue arriving on 23 January.[3]

On Sunday, 25 January 1328, Philippa of Hainault married King Edward III of England.[4] Edward's reign had officially begun on 25 January the year before, and it was also the anniversary of his parents' marriage, so the day was already auspicious in the court's calendar. Philippa and Edward were finally man and wife. As was the custom for royal marriages, celebrations lasted for several days, with most of the court there to feast, dance, joust and toast to the newlyweds. The couple would have had little time to themselves to get to know each other. Lavish and costly gifts circulated, and no expense was spared to make sure Edward and Philippa (and Queen Isabella) looked the part. Over £2,400 was borrowed from the Bardi, a group of Italian bankers who had been lending money to the English kings since at least 1290, to pay for gold and silver jewels purchased in Paris for the wedding.[5]

Philippa had her own gift to give her new husband: a beautiful manuscript that had been specially commissioned for the occasion.[6] Work had started in late 1326, just after the alliance had been made and Edward had pledged to marry Philippa. The book was a collection of texts and prayers which was carefully and elaborately decorated by a single artist, with Edward and his bride depicted within. The texts included advice for rulers, romances and pieces of history. This book was complemented with a second one that contained pieces of music thought to have been performed at their wedding, with a picture of Edward III holding a falcon on the cover.[7]

At the time of their wedding, Philippa of Hainault was almost 14 and King Edward III, at 15, was slightly older. Whilst the couple were considered old enough to be man and wife, royal convention tended to wait until the girl was at least 14 to allow sexual relations to begin and, partially for this reason, the couple were soon to be separated.[8] Not long after the wedding, Philippa was taken to London whilst Edward stayed in York to preside over a newly called parliament.[9] The reality of her situation now hit Philippa, and when her uncle John left her to return home, she wept.[10] Her family had left her in a foreign land, she was separated from her new husband, and she was alone, a young teenage girl.

Philippa did have some members of her homeland to keep her company, however. A household needed to be assembled to take care of the young queen, and several of her male retainers were native Hainaulters. Her new ladies and female attendants, though, were mostly English. As a young teenager, Philippa needed to quickly learn the customs, traditions and etiquettes of her new kingdom and the easiest way to do so was to have native women around her.[11] Queen Isabella, keen to keep a close eye on the new queen, might also have encouraged filling the girl's household with women she considered loyal, for several of Philippa's early attendants are known to have previously served Isabella.[12]

In her first few years in England, Philippa was generally served by two ladies and five damsels, attendants to the queen known today as ladies-in-waiting. Her ladies were the highest-status women who served her, acting as companions and confidantes, whilst damsels tended to be women of a slightly lower status, usually drawn from the baronial class. Philippa was granted permission by the pope to have her own confessor, and she was set up with her own treasurer.[13] These members of her household were to look after every aspect of her life. They were to ensure she had food to eat, wine to drink, clothes to wear and constant company. Philippa also took custody of Edward's 10-year-old sister Eleanor of Woodstock, who joined her household.[14] Philippa had been swiftly separated from her husband, but at least she was not entirely alone.

The separation of Edward and Philippa was likely a mix of Philippa's tender age and Queen Isabella's increasing desire to have control over her son and, thus, the country. But Edward was in fact being kept busy with political matters in the meantime. Queen Isabella and her lover Mortimer were deep in negotiations with the Scots, who had been causing trouble to their fledgling regime. In early 1327, Scottish forces had crossed the border and attacked English-controlled lands. Months later, Edward had led a retaliatory force – joined by Philippa's uncle John and some Hainault soldiers – into Scotland, but the campaign had been an utter failure and many English and Hainault soldiers were taken prisoner.[15] Now, in March 1328, peace was being organised.

As part of this peace, Isabella and Mortimer agreed that Edward III would give up his claims to sovereignty over Scotland, that English lordships in Scotland were to become Scottish, and that Edward's 7-year-old sister Joan was to marry the 4-year-old Prince David of Scotland.[16] These terms were punishing to the English, and very unpopular with both Parliament and the commoners of England, as well as with Edward himself. His first military campaign as king had been an embarrassing failure, and now his young sister was to pay the price. His grandfather, the legendary Edward I, had worked hard to obtain control of Scotland, later gaining the epithet 'Hammer of the Scots', and now that work was lost.

Further developments abroad threw up difficulties for Edward and the English throne. In February, King Charles IV of France – Isabella's brother – died, leaving a pregnant queen but no male heirs. France waited with bated breath to learn the sex of the newborn, who arrived in April as a baby girl. As a result, Charles's cousin was crowned Philip VI of France. Philip was the brother of Countess Jeanne, and thus Philippa's uncle. But the succession problems in France had highlighted Edward III's own claim to the kingdom, an uncomfortable reality for the French that was to become a key theme of Edward's reign.

France was governed under the theory of Salic law, which forbade a woman from ruling in her own right as queen regnant. However, it was not as clear whether a woman was allowed to transmit a claim or not. If so, then as Isabella was the daughter and sister of French kings, her sons had a stronger claim to the throne than Philip. At the moment, the English monarchy had little interest in pursuing this claim, instead having to focus on internal issues raised by the deposition of Edward II. In the meantime, though, a new French king meant that Edward III was now under obligation to pay homage for his French lands, as he had on behalf of his father when he was a prince.

Whilst Edward and his mother were busy putting the kingdom in order, and trying to build foreign alliances by finding a suitable bride for Edward's younger brother, the 11-year-old John of Eltham, Philippa was learning how to act as a model English queen. It had become English custom that a new queen would perform an act of intercession with her husband at her coronation, and she was expected to continue this role throughout her life.[7] Intercession was a vital duty of medieval queens, where a queen would literally intercede on behalf of a subject, usually asking for a pardon from a crime committed which could range from marrying without permission to murder. The frequency with which a queen might mediate with her husband varied with the individual woman, but she could be expected to do so several times a year. A coronation had started to be planned for not long after Philippa's wedding to Edward, but this had been postponed indefinitely due to Isabella's desire to keep control as the only anointed English queen.

Regardless, the young queen still needed to perform an act of intercession linked to her marriage to cement her role in the kingdom. In April 1328 Philippa obtained a pardon for a girl named Agnes de Penrith, who had been convicted of a robbery in York. Philippa had asked for the pardon 'in consideration of her tender age', as the girl was younger than 11 years old.[18] That this crime happened in York, where Philippa had been married a few months previously, could certainly link the events. It was also an easy pardon to grant, giving grace to a child, linking in with her duty as queen to protect the helpless.

As May arrived, attention was drawn to the fact that Philippa still had not received a dower. This was an annual income gathered from revenue from lands, fees and other grants, given by the crown to the queen to help her maintain a household and to pay for her clothes, jewels and servants. Edward promised that Philippa would be assigned a dower within a year, but this was quite a significant time frame when Philippa needed money to maintain herself now. In the days afterwards, Edward confirmed his promises to a variety of Hainault men 'made before he undertook the government' to give them annuities and lands, the implication being that they had helped his and Isabella's invasion force in one way or another.[19] Someone at court was clearly reminding the English government of their debt to the Count of Hainault and his men, and their obligation to care for Philippa.

Philippa's new position as queen had given her importance on an international scale, and she was now a person of interest for powerful men across Europe. Throughout August and September she received several letters from Pope John XXII regarding her marriage and her new responsibilities, not only as a wife but as a powerful queen. He '[pointed] out her duty to assist the king, her husband, in defending the rights and liberties of the church, protecting the poor, and exercising herself in good works', but also, importantly, 'to love her husband' – a somewhat poignant command, considering how Queen Isabella and King Edward II's relationship had progressed.[20] Philippa was probably indeed keen to get to know her new husband and fall in love with him, but their near-constant separation would have made this task difficult.

Philippa had been briefly reunited with her husband in July, when the couple stayed in Staffordshire together.[21] This meeting might have been designed to appease Edward, who was still furious at the Scottish peace; his sister Joan was married on 17 July at Berwick, and whilst Queen Isabella attended, Edward had refused to go.[22] The couple were together again in late November in London, when the mayor and aldermen of the city gifted them a variety of foodstuffs, including pigs, swans, herons, pike, eels and pheasants.[23]

Although Philippa had some opportunities to spend time with her new husband, there was growing unease at court. Queen Isabella's lover, Roger Mortimer, was growing in power and self-importance. In October, a parliament was called at Salisbury and Mortimer was elevated to Earl of March, a new title reflecting his power in the Welsh Marches.[24] Mortimer held a tournament in celebration of this honour which Edward was forced to attend, but the young king found a way to hint at his displeasure. Edward had tunics made for himself, twelve knights and fourteen squires for 'making a game which is called the game of the company of Craddok'. This 'Craddok' has been tied to a thirteenth-century French poem where a fairy sent a cloak to King Arthur's court which shrank if the wearer had been unfaithful.[25] This was a very overt move to make at a tournament celebrating his mother's lover.

Edward was not the only one displeased with the regency of Isabella and Mortimer. There were growing financial constraints on the regime as the couple had spent the large reserves of gold gathered by Edward II paying for war and peace against the Scots, repaying the Hainaulters for their support of the coup, and otherwise stabilising the regime (and aggrandising themselves). Now, they had to turn again to the Bardi, from whom the English crown borrowed a staggering £30,000 over the next two years.[26] The dire financial situation was impacting on the young king and queen.

Edward III was often made to travel across the country in the company of Isabella and Mortimer, under their control and their households, rather than hold his own independent household as a powerful king. This had not gone unnoticed, and in September the Bishop of Winchester had addressed a group of Londoners at Guildhall 'expressing the opinion that the king lacked good counsel and the means to support his own household'.[27] This was a view echoed by Henry, 3rd Earl of Lancaster, cousin of Edward II and some-one who had been vital in helping Isabella take control from her husband. At the end of 1328, Lancaster made his grievances known.

Lancaster complained that Edward was being badly advised, had no money to support himself, and that Philippa still had not been given a dower.[28] As the October parliament dispersed, both Lancaster and Mortimer retreated to gather troops ready for a rebellion. In the end, though, few of Lancaster's supporters were willing to rebel against Edward, and Mortimer and Lancaster came to terms. As no fighting had occurred, Lancaster escaped severe punishment by paying a fine, but a significant group of his supporters were forced into exile.[29]

The start of 1329 brought more positive outcomes for Edward and Philippa – perhaps spurred by Lancaster's rebellion – as they finally started living together permanently.[30] Now that Philippa was 14, it was deemed acceptable for her and Edward to begin a marital relationship, and it would help appease some of the complaints of the Commons. It would also help the crown's financial situation to have the young couple in the same place with the same servants. Philippa's presence would have been a great comfort to Edward. As much as he loved his mother, and had supported her coup, he was increasingly alienated from her because of Mortimer's behaviour, and her behaviour around him. Philippa was his wife and she would have been dependent on him as her main connection to a country she had only lived in for a year. Her loyalty and friendship would have been something Edward could rely on.

Further appeasements were made in April when Philippa was granted a small reprieve to her financial situation. Although not enough to cover her expenses, she was granted 1,000 marks a year 'until some better provision be made for her estate'.[31] Isabella's dower as consort had been worth around £4,000–£4,500 whereas this grant to Philippa was only around £666.[32] Clearly, this grant fell far short of what Philippa's parents would have expected for her by now. In contrast, Queen Isabella had granted herself an income of well over £13,300 upon the deposition of her husband in 1327, and she had since taken more land and money for herself.[33] Among the noble classes, Philippa was living in comparative poverty; even lowly knights were earning £400 a year.[34]

The following month, the royal couple were separated as Edward made his way to France to pay homage to King Philip for his French lands. Leaving his country as he had three years prior, he must have reflected on how much his life had changed since then. This time, he had Philippa to accompany him part of the way – she travelled with him through Kent, and before he left he gave his wife a gift of a gold crown worth 200 marks.[35] The gift was a reminder of his care for Philippa and of her position as queen, even if she had been placed in the shadows by his dominant mother.

The homage in France was a chance for Edward to meet other European rulers, for as well as the French king, the kings of Majorca, Navarre and Bohemia were all there.[36] Edward did not want to be away from his kingdom for long, perhaps worried about what Isabella and Mortimer would do in his absence, and he was back in England days later. With his return, Edward planned more gifts to bestow on Philippa. In July, he gave her a mirror in the shape of a basilisk, decorated with an image of an esquire holding a spear.[37] Images of basilisks were thought to bestow strength, perhaps reflecting Edward's request that his wife stay strong during this time of his mother's rule, waiting for the day they could rule on their own. Affection was clearly growing between the two.

In September, aged around 15, Philippa fell pregnant with her first child. It seems that she struggled in her first trimester. The royal court was itinerant, and the monarch and his consort would move between properties every few days, rarely staying in one place for more than a couple of weeks. However, the court stayed at Kenilworth Castle in Warwickshire between the end of October 1329 and early January 1330, a substantial length of time, and the only real explanation for this would be Philippa having a difficult pregnancy, likely a result of her youth.[38]

Now that Philippa was pregnant, her status as Edward's queen could no longer be ignored by Isabella. It was unthinkable that Philippa could give birth to Edward's child, the heir to the throne, without being a consecrated queen, so Isabella finally had to give in and allow Philippa to have her coronation. Plans began in earnest and the date was set for early February. A queen's coronation was one of the greatest events in the royal calendar, and a chance for the queen to show off the majesty and wealth of the monarchy.[39] It was essential for defining the queen's role in the kingdom and her duties to her husband and country. There was also a focus on the queen's expected role as mother, with an opening blessing that has been compared to a fertility charm.[40] This would have been especially poignant when Philippa was visibly pregnant at the time of her coronation.

Finally, the impoverished Philippa had her moment of glory. No expense was spared to make her look as wealthy as possible, and thus exude the power and stability of the monarchy. The day before her coronation, Philippa rode from the Tower of London to Westminster Palace, making offerings at St Paul's Cathedral and at Westminster Abbey along the way. She was wearing a green velvet dress made from 10 yards of cloth and a red and gold silk mantle made from a staggering 23 yards of material. The following day, 18 February 1330, Philippa arrived at Westminster Abbey wearing a new sumptuous green gown trimmed with miniver (a fairly expensive type of white squirrel fur reserved for the upper classes) with her hair flowing loose around her.[41] She entered the abbey under a canopy of purple cloth of gold embroidered with birds and animals made from red silk, which was carried by the barons of the Cinque Ports.[42]

The coronation of a queen differed from that of a king. Whilst the king swore an oath of obligation to his realm, the queen did not. She was blessed and reminded of her duties, particularly of her expected role as intercessor like the biblical queen Esther, who interceded with her Persian husband to save her people, the Jews, from extermination by one of his advisors.[43] During the ceremony, Philippa changed into a tunic and mantle made of red and grey samite, a heavy silk fabric, of a more simple design.[44] Philippa was then anointed with holy oil and given a ring and crown to remind her of her integrity, royalty and honour, and then she was given a silver-gilt sceptre, a symbol of her new royal power.[45]

After her anointing, Philippa changed into yet another outfit, this time in sumptuous purple cloth of gold with a long mantle lined with 481 bellies of miniver.[46] She wore this as she travelled from the abbey to Westminster Hall, accompanied by ladies-in-waiting dressed in luxurious clothing. They too would have changed throughout the day in order to reflect the majesty of the queen.[47] Finally, Philippa put on a hooded gown of red cloth of gold lined with miniver, in which she dined at her coronation feast.[48] As a crowned queen, with a potential male heir in her belly, Philippa's power could now surely only increase.

At last, measures were put in place to assign Philippa an appropriate dower to look after herself and her child. Just a few days before her coronation, Philippa had been granted a variety of lands, mostly in Wales and the Welsh Marches, 'in satisfaction of the dowry of £3,000 of land and rent granted to her at the time of her betrothal', and in April she was granted a few more manors and pieces of land to enlarge this.[49]

The royal family spent the weeks after the coronation travelling, arriving at the palace of Woodstock in Oxfordshire on 29 March. There were only a few more months to go until the arrival of Philippa's baby, and the court was anxious to make sure preparations were sufficient for its safe delivery. Philippa might again have been struggling with her pregnancy, as the court stayed at Woodstock for three months. Edward was clearly keen to stay close to Philippa, comfort her and ensure she was properly looked after, for he stayed by her side throughout.

As Philippa and Edward settled in at Woodstock to prepare for the birth of their first child, Philippa received some happy news from a yeoman of her sister Joanna, Countess of Jülich. Joanna had given birth to a child of her own.[50] Around the same time they would have received the news that Philippa's oldest sister Margaret had also given birth that month.[51] Whilst this would have cheered the royal couple, the wider political situation in England was reaching breaking point. Although Lancaster's small rebellion against Mortimer and Isabella the previous year had come to little, another man in the royal family had been plotting.

By the start of 1330, dangerous rumours spread that King Edward II's death had been faked. Some modern historians argue that these rumours were true, and there is enough evidence to lend plausibility to these claims, not least because of the status of the men who genuinely appeared convinced that the king lived.[52] In January, the Archbishop of York wrote a secret letter to the mayor of London informing him that Edward II was alive and well, and asking for money and clothing to give to the deposed king.[53]

The archbishop had probably received his information from Edmund of Woodstock, Earl of Kent and half-brother to Edward II. Since the previous year, Kent had seemed utterly certain that Edward II still lived, so much so that he travelled to see the pope and inform him of his knowledge and his plan: to rescue the old king from his secret imprisonment.[54] However, news of his plot soon reached the ears of Mortimer, who knew he could not let Kent proceed. Either the king was still alive and Mortimer did not want him freed, or he was indeed dead, but a successful rebellion by the king's uncle would be enough to see Mortimer removed from power and possibly even executed. In March, Mortimer made his move.

Mortimer had obtained a copy of a letter written by Kent to the keeper of Corfe Castle in Dorset, where it was thought Edward II was being held, detailing Kent's plans to free and restore Edward. This was enough evidence for him to have Kent arrested on charges of treason. Kent was hastily put on trial, found guilty, and ordered a traitor's end. His lands were confiscated and he was sentenced to death, being beheaded outside Winchester Castle on 19 March.[55]

At 17 years of age, Edward had been forced to assent to the execution of his uncle, something that weighed heavily upon him. It was Mortimer who had spearheaded the trial, Mortimer who had collected the evidence, and Mortimer who had been present at the execution. It was Isabella and Mortimer who had hastily ordered Kent's execution 'for else the King would forgive him'.[56] To rub even more salt into the wound, Mortimer tastelessly appropriated most of Kent's estates for his own son, and the rest for some of his retainers.[57]

This whole event had shaken the monarchy to the core. Rumours of Edward II's survival were swirling across the realm, Edward III's legitimacy and right to rule had been questioned, and the son of a king had been executed. It is no wonder that Edward retreated to Woodstock with Philippa to recover – and to plot his revenge. His household was filled with Mortimer's spies, but Edward had long figured out whom he could trust, and he now drew those men near.[58] His secrecy and paranoia are clear from a letter he sent to the pope around this time, hand delivered by one of his most trusted men, William Montagu, with a code to let the pope know when correspondence sent to him was truly from Edward: if the words *Pater Sancte* (Holy Father) appeared written in Edward's own hand.[59]

The other person Edward knew he could trust was Philippa, and the couple drew close at this time. Edward could confide anything in her, and the impending birth of his first child was a chance for him to start a new family. His own had fallen apart; his parents fighting and warring – with possible murder – an overbearing man involved with his mother, and now the execution of his uncle. His life with Philippa was a fresh start, where he could forge his own family who would not fight but would love and respect each other.

As the birth approached, Philippa went into confinement in specially pre-pared chambers at Woodstock Palace. Though Edward stayed at the palace to await the news, childbirth was strictly a female affair for queens at this time. She was sequestered away into private chambers and only women were allowed to enter to attend to her. The chambers were made as sumptu-ous and comfortable as possible to help her relax. New covers and canopies would be made for the bed and the walls and windows were covered in hang-ings to keep the rooms dark, although the queen could choose to have a window open so that she could have light.[60]

On 15 June 1330, Philippa and Edward's first child was born. To the jubilation of his parents, the baby was a boy, named Edward for his father, grandfather and great-grandfather. King Edward III now had a male heir of his own, and Philippa had completed a queen's greatest duty. Edward was so overjoyed that he gave the man who brought him the news an annual pen-sion of 40 marks for life.[61] A golden cradle had been made for the baby, and it was certainly fit for a prince. It was lined with scarlet (the name of an expen-sive woollen cloth which might have been red) and azure cloth and inside were two covers to keep the baby warm, both lined with fur and ermine as befitted his status – ermine was a white fur reserved for the royal family and upper nobility. Another, less ceremonial, bed was made for him which had a silk quilt decorated with pictures of beasts and mythical creatures.[62]

According to Christian tradition, a woman was expected to be ritually cleansed after giving birth and needed to wait forty days until she could be welcomed back into society.[63] For a queen, this meant that this time was spent away from the eyes of the court, resting and recuperating. At the end of it, a lavish ceremony would be held where the queen was at the centre. Her survival was celebrated, prayers and Masses would be said to give thanks to God, and it was an excuse for the court to eat, drink and be merry. The churching ceremony held for Philippa in July 1330 was especially important. It marked the first child of the king, and the birth of the prince who would one day become king – if he could survive the dangers of childhood.

As at her coronation, Philippa was swathed in wealth for her first churching. Two beds were specially made with red and green silk mattresses and hangings, although around this time Philippa's tailor had to repair one of her embroidered bedspreads as it had been chewed by dogs, a sweet reminder of domesticity at a time of great excess.[64] Excess it undoubtedly was, for it took 114 people working for 3,674 days across three months to make just three counterpanes for the ceremony.[65] For her churching ceremony, Philippa would have processed from her bedchamber to church to listen to Mass, where she would make an offering at the altar. Celebrations began immediately afterwards, with huge feasts and jousting.

For her churching, Philippa wore several outfits throughout the day. One dress was made of red velvet, another of red and gold woven cloth. The most outstanding dress, though, was one that Philippa had commissioned and which, it seems, she had her own say in designing, something the 16-year-old girl would have relished after nearly three years of control by her mother-in-law. It was made from purple velvet and trimmed with miniver, which highlighted her royal status. The dress was decorated with squirrels made from gold, a very unusual motif. It is not clear if the squirrels were intended to represent anything in particular. Perhaps Philippa was simply fond of the animals, which were often kept as pets. Another theory is that the reference was to a pet name given to her.[66]

As summer faded into autumn, the new father decided he needed to secure his family's future. Edward had '[begun] to grow in body and mind, despising the rule of the queen his mother, and hating the Earl of March, for the queen did everything in accordance with him'.[67] The constant sidelining of himself and his wife, the disrespect they were shown, and Edward's lack of autonomy had finally boiled over. Mortimer had been walking in front of the king, had gathered a larger retinue of men around him than the king, and his son 'through madness even called himself king'.[68] Mortimer was behaving in every way as if he wore the crown, not Edward, and his relationship with the queen and his ever-increasing wealth and status only confirmed this in his mind. More dangerously, around this time it seems that Queen Isabella might have fallen pregnant.[69] If Mortimer had a child with the queen, he might be encouraged to do something to Edward.

The time was near for Edward to act. He was approaching his eighteenth birthday and he now had an heir of his own to fight for. In October, Isabella and Mortimer travelled to Nottingham Castle, where they held an informal assembly on the 15th to discuss the defence of English-controlled Gascony in the face of rising tensions with France.[70] Edward arrived with his entourage not long afterwards, and he and his men started to discuss their moves against Mortimer.

The spies placed in Edward's household caught wind of Edward's plan and reported back to Mortimer. Mortimer ordered Edward and his men to appear before the gathering at Nottingham where they were interrogated 'in full session of the council' but all denied any knowledge of a plot. Mortimer was treading on dangerous ground – he hardly had the right to question the king. With no evidence, the men were let free back into the town, but they were kept out of the castle to protect Mortimer. Now Edward's trusted friend William Montagu came to him and said that 'it was better to eat the dog, than the dog eat them'.[71] If Edward did not act now, then Mortimer might make his move against Edward first.

Edward and Montagu spoke to the keeper of Nottingham Castle and requested his help in gaining entry. The keeper obliged, either by ensuring that a gate was kept open or by leading the king and a small band of his men through some secret tunnels under the castle that very night.[72] Around two dozen men climbed the stairs of the castle with Edward III, up towards the chamber where Isabella and Mortimer were holding a meeting.

Though the timing and nature of their plan was last-minute, the men had carefully planned how they would proceed. Mortimer was to be taken alive; Queen Isabella also needed to be protected. Edward had to be there to show that the coup had his support, but it was vital his person be protected from attack by Mortimer and his guards.[73] Edward's men rushed into the chamber whilst Edward stayed outside, and several of Mortimer's servants were killed in the ensuing scuffle. Mortimer was grabbed and dragged out of the chamber, and Isabella cried out to her son whom she knew was nearby: 'Good son, good son, have pity on noble Mortimer.'[74]

The young king had overthrown the man who had tyrannically controlled his life for the past four years. Now, he alone was in charge of his country, and his country rejoiced. A parliament was held in London the following month where Mortimer's fate was sealed. He was accused of causing the deaths of Edward II and the Earl of Kent, of disinheriting Edward from his right to the Scottish throne, of placing spies in Edward III's household and of stealing and depleting Edward II's treasure. The only answer was death: Mortimer was to 'be drawn and hanged as a traitor and an enemy of the king and of the realm'.[75]

As soon as Edward seized control, he made moves to raise up Philippa to her rightful status as the most powerful queen in England. Two days after Mortimer's capture, as Edward and the royal party processed towards London, they stopped at Castle Donington in Leicestershire, which had been the home of Edward's uncle, the Earl of Kent, before being taken by Mortimer's son. Here, Edward gifted the entire contents of the castle to Philippa.[76] The same month, Philippa purchased some expensive materials of green silk cloth painted and powdered with griffon heads and white silk cloth powdered with images of crowns.[77] Philippa was making a statement about her new wealth and status, and reminding everyone that she was now the queen who was in charge.

When Edward overthrew Mortimer, he placed his mother in honourable confinement and confiscated all of her wealth and lands. As soon as news reached the pope in Avignon of Edward's actions, he immediately wrote to England, anxious to be told that Queen Isabella was being looked after according to her status. On 7 November, the pope wrote a letter to Philippa asking her to 'insist with the king' to make sure that 'his goodwill towards her should be restored'. At the same time, he wrote letters to Edward chastising him for 'not showing signs of filial affection to his mother' and asking that 'should she have done anything to justify the king's behaviour to her' that he show mercy to her, in recognition of everything she had done and sacrificed for him.[78] Edward had subverted the natural order by acting against his mother, and the pope was keen to have the family reunited, especially after the previous breakdown in relations with Edward II and his subsequent murder. As Edward's wife, Philippa was expected to be a mediating influence on his temper and to intercede for her mother-in-law.

Now that Edward was in charge, he started to reorganise the realm according to his wishes. All of Kent's followers who had been involved in plotting to release Edward II were pardoned and restored to their previous positions, as were the Earl of Lancaster and his men for their own rebellion the previous year.[79] Although Isabella had been removed from power, and Philippa had risen in her place, there was still so much to sort out in the realm that Philippa had to take a back seat. Isabella was granted £3,000 a year for her expenses and was sent to stay at her manor of Berkhamsted and at Windsor Castle – comfortable palaces, but ones that were reasonably distant from the centre of courtly life.[80]

Philippa's financial situation, meanwhile, was still rocky. On 7 December, it was acknowledged that Edward owed Philippa's treasurer nearly £1,000 for expenses to maintain her household, and on the 21st the Bardi were assigned £400 in repayment for money given to Philippa for her household.[81] A few days before Christmas, Philippa was granted the use of the king's houses in 'la Roel' in London for her wardrobe.[82] This was a place where all of her clothes, jewels, furniture and other goods could be stored, ready for her use. Philippa used this opportunity to renovate the buildings, expanding outwards into other buildings in the vicinity.[83]

For Christmas 1330, the royal family gathered at Guildford in Surrey. Queen Isabella was allowed to join the king, queen and the baby prince, though it is debatable whether this was a sign of Edward's heart softening towards his mother or more about keeping up the pretence of harmony at court.[84] There is no further record of Isabella's pregnancy, so if it was more than rumour then the child did not survive, Isabella probably suffering a miscarriage.

Although tensions might have lain beneath the surface, the festivities must have been glorious for Edward and Philippa. It was the first Christmas that they could truly preside over. Not only could they lavish each other with wealth, but they had their child to share it all with. Philippa shared this generosity with her ladies who had been loyal companions to her over the years. One damsel, Idona Lestrange, was given a significant gift of 28 ells of sanguine cloth to a cost of over £11. The rest of the damsels were given gowns, corsets and furs as part of their winter livery, and the damsels of Princess Eleanor, who was still living in Philippa's household, were also given similar corsets.[85]

The future must now have looked bright. There was still a great deal of work to do to fix the countless problems caused by Isabella and Mortimer, but the young king and queen were exceedingly popular across the realm. Gone were murmurings of rebellion against Edward – they had all been based on hatred of Mortimer. The arrival of 1331 meant a hopeful future with a vigorous young king, and the fortunes of England were looking up. Philippa would have to learn quickly how to exercise her own power, so that she could be a pillar of strength beside her husband.

3

A Growing Family

With the arrival of the new year, Philippa of Hainault was finally able to build up her resources as queen. Her husband had given her a bumper Christmas gift of items confiscated from Mortimer. This included a fine cloth canopy powdered with black roses to hang above her bed or chair, and twenty-four rugs to decorate her chambers. She also commissioned a variety of clothing and jewellery, which she had hitherto been unable to do, such as two golden brooches encrusted with diamonds and pearls which she received at the start of February for Candlemas.[1]

More important, though, was finally securing her permanent dower income. Although she had been granted her dower the previous year in preparation for her coronation, it had been reported to Edward towards the end of 1330 that the lands in Wales that had been given a value of £3,000 were in fact only worth £150 a year because they had no livestock or other sources of revenue. As such, Philippa had been unable to pay 'the poor of the region' from whom she took food and clothes for her household at Christmas. Philippa also raised the fact that she was looking after guests such as Princess Eleanor and little Prince Edward at her own cost.[2] Edward ordered that appropriate lands be found to compensate her for the rest of her dower.

Over the next few months, Philippa attempted to sort her financial situation and properly maintain her ever-growing household. On 25 February, she was granted the income from the county of Chester, which had been confiscated from Mortimer, in order to pay for the support of Prince Edward and Eleanor. In early March, she was granted the right to dispose as she saw fit any lands given to her as part of her dower, a privilege few married women exercised.[3]

Philippa performed her duty of intercession by looking after some of the women affected by Edward's coup; at the end of February, she ensured that a woman named Agnes Maltravers was given money 'until other provisions be made for herself and her children' in compensation for her dower lands which had been confiscated by the king.[4] Agnes's husband, John, had been convicted in parliament alongside Roger Mortimer for his role in the trial and death of the Earl of Kent leading to the forfeit of all his lands.[5]

With the country settling down, and Edward slowly regaining control, the royal couple 'led a merry life of jousts and tournaments, and feasting the ladies'.[6] Philippa purchased more luxuries for her household, such as two sets of silverware for herself and her most important guests, one with the arms of England and Hainault and one with the arms of France and Hainault, reflecting both her new kingdom and her ancestry. Summer brought great jubilation in Philippa's household; in July 1331 one of her damsels, a woman named Elena de Maule, was married, and Philippa attended the wedding, bringing Edward's minstrels with her to celebrate.[7]

Philippa had her own reason to be excited: the prospect of a visit from her mother and her sister Joanna. Philippa had not seen her mother since she had left to marry Edward in the winter of 1327. The mother and daughter had kept up correspondence in Philippa's absence, and gifts were sent between them, but Philippa must have been overjoyed to show her mother her new kingdom and her new child. In early September, the king's butler was ordered to deliver 80 tuns of wine – an incredible 16,800 gallons or 76,000 litres – to Philippa's butler to prepare for the arrival of Countess Jeanne.[8]

The same month, Jeanne and Joanna, alongside Joanna's husband William, Count of Jülich, and an array of other nobles and servants, embarked on a ship provided by Edward and sailed to England.[9] Jeanne's journey might not have been made for entirely personal reasons. Another visitor to the English court at this time was Count Reginald of Guelders, an ally of Count William of Hainault. Now that Edward's reign was secure, he needed to start building up some international allies. His sister, Princess Eleanor, was 13 years old and a perfect age to find a husband. Marrying Eleanor to Reginald was an attractive prospect, especially as it would solidify Edward's allies in the Low Countries. Jeanne's presence would be important in facilitating marriage negotiations.[10]

At the end of September, great jousts were held at Cheapside in London.[11] Barriers were erected within which the jousting occurred, and a stand was built to allow the queen and noblewomen to watch the games. The first day was filled with great merriment, and after dinner the crowds returned to watch more jousts. But disaster struck when the upper staging where Philippa and Princess Eleanor were sitting collapsed; Philippa and Eleanor, alongside their ladies and knights, all fell to the ground. Many people were wounded, but thankfully no one was killed. The queen and princess escaped unharmed, although Philippa's crown broke.

The stand had collapsed because the carpenters who erected it had not done so properly, but 'through the prayers of the lady the queen' Edward pardoned them and 'had peace and love proclaimed everywhere'. Rather than be wrathful, Edward was simply relieved that his wife and sister were unharmed. Edward told Philippa to ride up and down the street on her horse to reassure the people that she was safe, and overnight the staging was repaired. The disaster did not affect the jousts, for they started again the next day, lasting for two more days.

Philippa was lucky to have escaped unharmed, because it was in August or September that she had fallen pregnant for the second time. She might not have been aware of her pregnancy at the time of the accident. By November, though, the signs were clear and the court prepared for the arrival of another royal child. At the end of the month, the sheriff of Wiltshire was ordered to survey the royal manor of Clarendon and repair the hall, chambers and other buildings as Edward wished Philippa to stay there until she gave birth.[12]

By early December, Philippa had been granted more lands to supplement her dower. She now commissioned men to survey these new castles, towns, manors, forests, parks and other pieces of land that she had been granted so that she could be made aware of their value and extent. This commission showed that she now controlled land across the country, with sixteen counties listed from Dorset to Derbyshire.[13] For Christmas, Philippa and Edward travelled to Wells in Somerset with their court and little Prince Edward. With a new baby on the horizon, the young family was growing. Philippa was only 17 years old, and Edward had just turned 19.

Over winter, Edward's negotiations for the marriage of his sister had taken some positive steps. In fact, so confident were the royal couple that Eleanor would soon be married, that in early October 1331 Philippa had commissioned an artist to illuminate two books of hours, at least one of which was to be given to Eleanor as a wedding gift. This beautiful book, known now as the Taymouth Hours, would have been an exquisite gift for the young princess.[14] Philippa had taken care of Eleanor for four years, and the two girls had grown close over this time. Philippa would have relished the opportunity to commission a special gift for her as she was about to embark on a new life in a foreign land.

The marriage between Eleanor and the Count of Guelders was formally agreed upon in March 1332. Reginald was keen to enhance his status by marrying the sister of the English king, and so he agreed to very favourable terms with Edward. Edward still needed to provide his sister with a dowry, however, set upon as £10,000. This sum was far higher than the crown could afford, as the treasury had not yet been refilled after its emptying by Isabella and Mortimer. Once more, Edward turned to the Bardi for help, but he also pressured the English Church to provide funds to pay for the wedding.[15] Eleanor's wedding was the first that Edward had been solely responsible for, and he was keen to show off the power of his new regime. His sister was supplied with a sumptuous wedding trousseau filled with expensive clothes and a beautiful carriage was commissioned to take her to Guelders, where she was married to the 37-year-old count.[16] Edward had now had his first success on an international stage.

Philippa was now heavily pregnant, and once again was attempting to balance her dire financial situation. In November the previous year, Edward had enquired on Philippa's behalf about her rights to Queen's gold.[17] This was a queen's prerogative dating back centuries that meant that whenever someone made a voluntary fine to the king, paying for things like a privilege or a pardon, they would pay an extra 10 per cent on top, which went to the queen.[18] When the crown was struggling to gather enough money to sufficiently endow Queen Philippa, ensuring she could collect Queen's gold was a way to get extra funding for her.

This does not seem to have been as easy a plan as first thought; in April, the sheriffs of twelve counties were ordered to delay a payment of £1,000 owed to Philippa under Queen's gold for several months, perhaps in response to a protest by the couple who owed the money.[19] Four years later, Edward repeated his request to his exchequer to assess which cases owed Queen's gold to his consort, and then in 1338 he issued a writ proclaiming that people had been 'scheming craftily to defraud our consort of her gold'.[20] It was obviously an unpopular device.

Although Philippa was still struggling with her finances, the majesty of the crown still needed to be projected. For Easter, Philippa had a new outfit made from green fabric which was lined with miniver and edged with ermine, a lavish piece that had cost £54 – enough money to buy nearly eighty horses.[21] Philippa's wardrobe was one of her most important aspects of queenship. The wealth and power of the king, and thus the English nation, was displayed visually on the queen's body. During Edward's minority, Philippa had been kept on a shoestring and thus betrayed the king's weak personal power. Now that Edward was king, he needed to show he was a strong leader and his wife played a powerful part in this. If the king could afford to bedeck his wife in jewels and fine fabrics, then he must have plenty of other wealth in reserve to look after his kingdom and finance war.

As such, the queen's wardrobe was expected to be constantly renewed. She might only have worn an outfit a handful of times, or even just once for particularly outstanding outfits. Within a few weeks she would have a closet full of new clothes, and her old ones would be passed to favoured ladies at court, or to religious institutions to turn into garments for their priests or cloths for their altars. The exquisite squirrel suit that Philippa had worn for the churching of Prince Edward had been donated to Ely Cathedral, where it was turned into three copes for its prior.[22]

Shoes and gloves were replaced with a particular frequency. Across the past year, Philippa had owned at least forty-eight pairs of shoes and twenty-four pairs of gloves, and the following year this increased to fifty-four pairs of shoes and fifty-six pairs of gloves, enough for one set a week.[23] Whilst this seems exceptionally lavish, and indeed has contributed to Philippa's reputation as a greedy spendthrift, her spending was very much in line with that of previous kings and queens. Despite her plentiful number of shoes, Philippa rarely spent more than 6*d* on a pair, and she certainly bought far fewer items of underwear than her father-in-law, Edward II, who in 1315 had bought 110 pairs of hose in just five months.[24]

As the Easter celebrations drew to a close, Philippa and the court started to prepare for the imminent arrival of her second child. Although the previous autumn Edward had stipulated that he wished Philippa to have the baby at Clarendon, on 30 April the royal household arrived at the palace of Woodstock, where it stayed for the next two months. This could well have reflected Philippa's wishes to return to the place of her first birth, where she was familiar with the chambers and had already successfully had one child. Being at Woodstock might have reassured her and made her feel more comfortable.

Quite when Philippa gave birth is unclear, as there are no surviving records that mention the baby's date of birth. Her second child was a little girl named Isabella in honour of her grandmother. Philippa had her churching for Isabella in mid-July, meaning Isabella would have been born at the end of May or in early June. Philippa had now safely given birth to her second child, and she and Edward doted on their new baby girl.

To prepare for her churching this time round, Philippa seems to have had much more say on the decoration of her chamber than with Prince Edward. At that time, she was still under the control of Isabella and Mortimer, and for a first child and male heir everything needed to be much more traditional. Philippa could now express herself more personally with her own taste in decoration, and she commissioned a side-hanging and bench cushion decorated with the arms of England and Hainault accompanied by sirens, birds, grotesques, animals and leaves.[25] Her bed covers were made of green silk and decorated with mermaids also bearing the arms of England and Hainault, and the canopy above her bed was embroidered with birds. Her clothes were also personalised, with a velvet robe embroidered with golden butterflies and another powdered with the letters 'E' and 'P', a sweet reminder of the royal couple's love for each other.[26]

The altar of the church where Philippa gave her offering and listened to Mass was decorated with a purple silk cloth embroidered in a similar vein to the decoration of her chamber, with birds, beasts, baboons and snakes. After the formal, religious celebration, the court returned to Woodstock Palace for feasting. So many people were present, and so many courses were served, that the feast cost nearly £300, ten times the usual daily cost of feeding the royal household.[27]

Though Edward had supported Philippa during her pregnancy and the birth of their second child, he had political concerns on the backburner. Ever since his humiliating defeat by the Scots, and the embarrassing peace treaty procured by his mother and Mortimer, Edward had vowed revenge. Scotland had been his first failure as king, and he felt that his sister had paid the price by being forced to marry the Scottish prince. Joan was now Queen of Scotland, her husband having ascended the throne in 1329, but all was not calm.

Many English lords had territories in Scotland as a result of previous campaigns and victories during the reigns of Edwards I and II, and they had been disinherited by Isabella's peace deal. They had lost valuable land and income as a result, and by 1332 these lords had attached themselves to a man named Edward Balliol, the son of King John Balliol of Scotland who had been forced to resign in 1296 after defeat in battle by Edward I. Although Joan's husband David had become king in 1329 upon the death of his father, Robert the Bruce, he was just 5 years old at the time, whereas Edward Balliol was a formidable man of 46 with a strong claim of his own. Now, three years later, Balliol was promising the disinherited English lords the restitution of their lands if they followed him.[28]

Edward could not give public support for Balliol due to the peace with Scotland and uncertainty of whether he could yet afford to finance a war. However, he had privately begun to help some of his lords join Balliol. Edward was also increasingly worried over the state of English-controlled Ireland, and the previous year he had planned a trip to the country to take place in 1332, even asking the pope for his advice. Whilst Philippa lay recovering from giving birth to Isabella, Edward was gathering a military force to leave for Ireland at the end of September.[29]

Before Edward could finalise his plans, Balliol and the English lords had already taken matters into their own hands. In early August, Balliol's forces had won a decisive victory against the forces of young King David, and many great and powerful Scottish earls, lords and knights were killed. This huge victory caused many remaining Scottish nobles to defect to Balliol, and on 24 September Edward Balliol was declared King of Scotland.[30] Now Edward delayed his trip to Ireland indefinitely. Scotland was his anathema, and Edward wanted to finish his business once and for all.

In September, Edward headed north into Scotland to support Balliol and his English lords, arriving in York in the middle of October. Before he left, Edward had travelled with Philippa to Canterbury to the shrine of Thomas Becket to ask for his saintly blessing on the expedition.[31] But by the time Edward had reached the northern parts of his kingdom, the tides of war had turned once more. Edward Balliol had been surprised in his sleep by supporters of King David. He had barely escaped with his life, whilst many of his men were slaughtered in their nightshirts.[32]

Balliol had fled to Carlisle, and he now made an offer to Edward III. If Edward supported his claim, he would recognise Edward's position as overlord of Scotland, giving homage and fealty to Edward for his throne. He also offered numerous Scottish territories for the English crown to hold in perpetuity and, conscious he had disinherited Edward's 11-year-old sister as queen, he even offered to marry her himself.[33] Due to her young age and that of her husband, Joan's marriage would not have yet been consummated, and it might have been possible to obtain an annulment from the pope.

Meanwhile, back in England, October saw Philippa experience the first parkbreaks of her reign. Royalty and the highest levels of nobility at this time were able to enclose their land into private parks where they could hunt and use its resources, but sectioning land off like this was very unpopular with other levels of society, and those who owned these parks would periodically find people attacking them. That Philippa suffered parkbreaks at this time does not necessarily mean that she was unpopular with her people, merely that her land was a political arena that could be used as a place of protest.

As Philippa was the wife of the king, attacking her parks could have been a way to symbolically attack him, or it might simply have been that her parks were not as well protected as others and so they were an easier target for poachers.[34] In this case, sixteen of Philippa's parks were attacked in Yorkshire, with her trees felled, her game hunted and her fish taken. At the same time, Philippa set up a commission to investigate 'alleged excesses of the bailiffs and ministers' in some of these areas, suggesting that these park-breaks could have been a localised protest at corrupt officials.[35]

With the change in circumstances of the Scottish campaign, and Balliol's appealing offer, Edward decided to call a parliament in York in December. Here, Edward asked his people how he should proceed, keen not to seem as tyrannous as the previous regimes. Parliament, however, did not want to give a clear answer to Edward, and so it was decided to close until the new year.[36] With Edward staying in the north over the Christmas period, Philippa travelled with Prince Edward and 6-month-old Isabella to join her husband for celebrations.

Despite the busy year, the couple had found time to commission presents for each other, given on New Year's Day as was tradition. Edward gifted Philippa a gold brooch garnished with an expensive sapphire, a beautiful piece of jewellery.[37] Philippa, however, had commissioned something much more personal. She gave Edward a ewer, a type of jug, which was decorated with images of popular heroes such as Julius Caesar, Charlemagne, King Arthur and Lancelot. The men depicted formed a selection of the Nine Worthies, a reference to a poem composed for Philippa's father back in 1310. The Nine Worthies were figures who were held up as ideal chivalric men, powerful military leaders who were aspirational men to live up to.[38] With Edward about to declare war as an independent king for the first time, intending to salvage his reputation and earn the respect and loyalty of his nobility, the ewer was certainly a poignant gift.

In January, parliament once again sat in York but its members were still ambivalent about committing to a Scottish war. Edward took matters into his own hands and decided to plough ahead, strong in his conviction that he would succeed. The court and government settled in York ready for a long campaign season, and Philippa soon set about resuming her queenly duties. On 6 February, she obtained a pardon for a woman for her actions against the Abbey of St Edmunds – she had been accused of robbery and trespass, and of burning down one of the abbey's houses. The following month,

Philippa had another woman pardoned for felony and trespass, and a few weeks later in early April a third woman was pardoned for stealing a surcoat and 3s in York. This last woman had been sentenced to death for her crime, but the execution had been deferred because she was pregnant. Now Philippa had it cleared altogether.[39]

This time also saw Philippa gather further benefits for herself, to help her manage her lands and household. She was granted permission to cut down and sell old oaks in her forests up to the value of £1,000 and the right to hold a market at the manor of 'Stokheth' in Nottingham every Monday as another way to raise funds. This right was extended to the town of 'Snayth' in Yorkshire, also held by Philippa, which was now allowed to hold a market every Thursday. Finally, Edward granted Philippa £2,000 from the treasury to pay for her debts to the Bardi, who had once again lent huge sums of money to pay for her household.[40] Although Philippa had, by now, been in receipt of her dower lands for quite some time, income had been slow to trickle in and she had already started her reign in debt because of the restraints placed on her by Isabella and because of how many years it took to give her a suitable dower. These debts were now so far behind that it was proving exceedingly difficult to catch up with them all.

By April 1333 Edward had sufficiently gathered his military resources for his excursion into Scotland. Leaving York with his men, Philippa travelled with him, staying close to her beloved husband. Towards the end of the month Balliol and his forces besieged Berwick, and a few weeks later Edward arrived with his own army to aid them. Despite the joint forces the siege was long, and so Edward was able to attend to other matters. On one occasion he took Philippa a few miles south to visit the Holy Island of Lindisfarne and its monastery.[41] Philippa returned to the nearby safety of Bamburgh Castle, whilst Edward advanced the siege.

Edward was close to winning the siege: the inhabitants of the town had sent twelve of their prominent sons to serve as hostages for Edward, on the promise that if the town was not relieved by the Scottish army within fifteen days, they would surrender. The Scots duly arrived and a small group of soldiers gained entry, but they refused to surrender and even taunted Edward by sending messengers to him announcing their intent to invade England, starting by attacking Bamburgh Castle. This direct threat to the safety of his wife and the disrespect shown to him by the Scots infuriated Edward to cruelty. He erected gallows outside the gates of the town and hanged the son of the town's commander. He then sent a message that he would hang two more boys every day because they had broken their promise to him.[42] The Scots would learn that he was not the young, useless boy they had defeated six years prior.

In the end, Edward III and Edward Balliol succeeded in the siege of Berwick, destroying the Scots in open battle at Halidon Hill despite being outnumbered two to one.[43] Edward and Philippa returned to London victorious and jubilant, leaving Edward Balliol as King of Scotland. Balliol kept his promise to Edward and performed homage to him, as well as granting him the captured town of Berwick and five counties to hold for himself.[44]

The royal couple's return was well timed, for Philippa was by now heavily pregnant with her third child. Whilst Edward undertook a small pilgrimage across England, Philippa was preparing for the birth. She was aided in this by another visit from her dear mother who stayed in England for several weeks in late September and early October.[45] This time, Philippa might not have made her way to Woodstock for the birth, instead retiring to the luxurious royal apartments in the Tower of London.[46]

As with Princess Isabella, it is not clear when exactly this child was born. Philippa's churching seems to have taken place in early February 1334, which suggests that she gave birth sometime in December or early January.[47] Unlike for Philippa's first two children, Edward and his court did not spend months with Philippa as she prepared to give birth, and this could mean that the 19-year-old Philippa had finally had an easier pregnancy, or that Edward was not as worried for his wife this time round. By early 1334 the couple welcomed into the world a baby girl, named Joan after her maternal grandmother.

Once more, Philippa purchased a plethora of beautiful and expensive fabrics to adorn herself and her chambers for her churching. The ceremony itself was held at Philippa's favoured manor of Woodstock and, as with her last churching, the coats of arms of England and Hainault were prominent on her bed covers. Philippa wore a gown of purple scarlet with miniver and green velvet, but this time her young children were included in the celebrations. Prince Edward, who was now 3 and a half years old, was given a tunic and a cloak of green velvet bordered with large pearls to wear, whilst

Princess Isabella, who was almost 2, was given a large cradle decorated with mythical creatures and the coat of arms of her parents. As was traditional, a large joust concluded the celebrations.[48]

Another baby meant more expenses for Philippa to incur, for her children stayed with her. In March, Edward granted her further income to care for their three children out of lands that belonged to their son, who had been made Earl of Chester.[49] Philippa did not only take money and grants for herself, though, and this year she made sure that several of her servants were rewarded for their service. One of her female servants was granted tenements in London, whilst one of her favoured damsels, Joan de Carew, was given the manor of 'Erleslane' in Hereford valued at over £21 a year, and one of her male servants was given 41 acres of land and pasture on the Isle of Wight during the minority of its heiress.[50]

In summer, Philippa suffered further parkbreaks in thirteen of her Yorkshire parks and two of her parks in Nottingham. Again, her trees were felled, her ponds fished, and her game – including 120 young sparrowhawks – stolen. Her servants, too, were assaulted. This second affront to her lands was not to be tolerated, and a commission was ordered to investigate the crimes committed.[51]

The rest of the year went by with few further disturbances. Philippa had reached her twentieth year with three children and a doting husband. The couple had now been married for six years, and their love had only gone from strength to strength.

Philippa and Edward spent much of the winter up in Roxburgh in Scotland, one of the territories given to Edward by Balliol, arriving there on 22 November and staying right up until 3 February.[52] This remarkably long sojourn was only similarly matched by the court's long stay with a pregnant Philippa during her first two pregnancies, though this does not appear to be the reason this time. Edward had been required to again march north with armed forces to support Balliol, as was his duty as his overlord, but few soldiers had met him at Roxburgh and the gathering was further hampered by particularly cold weather. As February arrived, the army dispersed and Edward and Philippa moved south to York.[53] On the way home, Philippa was granted further parcels of money to use 'towards the support of the heavy charges she has to meet daily' to maintain her household.[54]

Edward re-equipped himself with provisions from a parliament at York across May and June, then headed back into Scotland during the summer of 1335, joined by Philippa's brother-in-law the Count of Jülich.[55] Philippa turned her attention back to her vast landed estate, ordering another commission in July for more parkbreaks in Yorkshire. A few days later, she also organised a commission 'to survey the wastes in the forest and chace' across many counties that she owned in order to improve them and thus 'make leases of these for life or in fee' in order to make better money from them.[56] As the campaign progressed, Edward kept his wife informed of his activities, writing letters to her about his movements and how the war was going.[57] Philippa soon headed north to be reunited with Edward, and the couple spent Christmas with each other and their court at Newcastle.[58]

With the arrival of 1336, the Scottish war was still raging on. But Edward now had time to turn his head to the international stage. He had several children and a brother who were all unmarried, so he began to make negotiations with European royalty to forge new, powerful alliances. Traditionally, Philippa would have had little say in Edward's choice of partners for her children, though her vast family network certainly influenced Edward's options and knowing their closeness Edward might well have taken Philippa's opinions into account on a personal level.

Philippa was indeed able to assist her husband in ruling the kingdom. On 2 July, whilst Edward was in Scotland, Philippa held 'the hall of the king' at Northampton, gathering bishops, barons, lords and knights from across the kingdom 'to consider the issue of Scotland'. Only the king's most important ministers could call a council, and that well over fifty powerful men attended showed that Philippa was respected as a part of Edward's government. It is not clear whether Philippa contributed to the council, but what is important is that she had the authority to call it at all.[59] Edward was relying on his wife to help him manage his vast realm.

In early August, Benedict XII wrote to Philippa regarding vows she had made which she 'cannot conveniently observe, those of pilgrimage to the Holy Land, Rome, and Santiago'. When Philippa had made them is unclear, but the pope now granted permission that her personal confessor could commute these vows, meaning that Philippa could substitute the vows for equivalent good actions. The reason why Philippa could not 'conveniently observe' them is not mentioned, and whilst it could simply be that it was not currently practical for the queen of England to leave for the furthest reaches of Christendom, a further grant by the pope on the same day may reveal some other clues. He allowed Philippa, 'on the advice of her physician', to eat meat on traditional days of fasting and abstinence.[60]

That Philippa had been granted permission to eat meat when others could not suggests that she was struggling with her health. This might have been an ongoing problem, but it could have been related to the fact that Philippa was once more pregnant, and as with some of her previous pregnancies this could have been a difficult one for her. The royal household spent the rest of the year in the north, settling at Hatfield in Yorkshire for Christmas. Philippa gave birth sometime towards the end of December or early January to a second boy, named William after Philippa's father. However, the boy seems to have been born very sickly and lived no more than a few weeks.[61]

For the first time, Philippa and Edward had lost a child. Their personal life had been strong and successful up to this point, with three healthy children and a deep love between them. Edward was unable to stay with his wife and comfort her, for across January he travelled between Kent, Hertfordshire and London, popping back to see Philippa in Yorkshire for a few days at a time intermittently. He visited Canterbury on 18 January, perhaps to pray and make offerings at the church and shrines there for his boy.[62]

The tragedy of the death of their child followed the death of Edward's only brother a few months previously. John of Eltham had died aged 20 whilst on campaign with Edward in Scotland. Edward was so devastated by John's fate that a year after the funeral Edward's household accounts recorded that he was having nightmares about his brother's death.[63] He also ordered 900 Masses to be said for John's soul to aid his way to heaven.[64] Edward had to travel to London without his wife at the start of January to attend his brother's funeral, and with the ill health of his newborn son, the sorrow would have been amplified.[65] Philippa was not there to support him, and instead was struggling by herself across the country.

The little Prince William was buried 30 miles from his birth, in York Cathedral, on 10 February 1337, almost exactly nine years after his parents married there.[66] Edward was still in London at the time, having spent several days with Philippa in Hatfield at the end of January and the start of

February. Why he did not attend the funeral of his son is not known, but he returned to Yorkshire between 14 and 18 February to support Philippa at her churching ceremony. Records of this churching are scant, and it is likely that with the tragedy of William's death, the ceremony was pared back in respect.[67] The royal couple had little to celebrate.

The year 1337 was not finished dealing tragedy to Philippa's family. In June, Philippa received word from Hainault that her father had died in Valenciennes.[68] Philippa suffered a strong blow with the death of her father, made all the more poignant by the recent death of the son who was named after him. Two years later, she commissioned a minstrel and poet named Jean de le Mote to compose a huge elegy dedicated to Count William, entitled *Li Regret Guillaume* ('The Regret of William').[69] Philippa was apart from Edward when she heard the news of her father's death, but Edward showed his sympathy for his wife by paying for Masses to be said for William's soul.[70]

Despite the tragedies that had plagued her family, Philippa continued to act as a model queen. Across the summer she had successfully obtained pardons for several criminals convicted of murder and larceny, including a girl who had been convicted of stealing sheep and was, at the time, too young to be punished.[71] She had also granted gifts to several of her servants for good service to her and Edward, such as a manor in Dorset to a William Fitz Waryn, an annual payment of £12 to an Isabella de la Hilde, and the confirmation of the estate of several churches to a Master Robert de Chikewell.[72] This year also saw another marriage of one of her ladies, Sybil de Patteshull, to one of Edward's knights of the chamber, Sir Roger Beauchamp. The royal couple attended the nuptials, and Edward provided cloths for the wedding.[73]

With everything going on this year, matters inevitably turned again to money and war. Philippa's financial situation was becoming more and more dire, and on 10 October several promises were recorded on the Patent Rolls to repay money owed by her to certain merchants. She had borrowed £4,850 from John de Portenare, and she owed the society of the Bardi another staggering £4,535. She had also borrowed £450 from another Italian banking group, the Peruzzi.[74] These were extraordinary sums of money, totalling over £9,800, twice Philippa's annual income from her dower provided by the English crown. A century later, only seventy families in all of England earned between £300 and £2,500 a year, showing just how significant a sum this debt amounted to.[75]

The arrival of 1338 promised a better future for the royal family. After the successes of his Scottish campaigns, Edward had decided to turn his attention to France. Ever since the death of his uncle, the last of Queen Isabella's brothers, the English crown had entertained the idea that Edward was the rightful heir to the French throne. Up until now, Edward had no need or opportunity to push this claim: from fighting the regency of his mother and Mortimer to taking revenge on the Scots, he had no time to turn his head elsewhere. Now, though, he was 25 years old and he had won his spurs fighting the Scots. He was a feared military leader, with plenty of men and support in the form of Philippa's many relatives. Plans were made, and in the summer of 1338 Edward set sail for France with an army, leaving his 8-year-old son Prince Edward as regent, supported by the Archbishop of Canterbury, in his absence.[76]

Edward arrived at Antwerp in the independent duchy of Brabant in July with nearly 3,500 soldiers and archers. Queen Philippa and their daughters, Isabella and Joan, had joined Edward on his voyage, an unusual situation as the royal family usually stayed in the safety of England when the king travelled abroad for war – even more so as Philippa was about four months pregnant with another child.[77] The couple's first night in Antwerp was marked by disaster when their house caught fire, with the royal family and their servants barely escaping in their night clothes.[78]

Once more, Edward called upon the significant Continental connections of his wife, travelling to Germany to meet with the Holy Roman Emperor, who had married Philippa's sister Margaret. The Emperor recognised Edward's claim to the French throne and agreed to support Edward against the French king for seven years.[79] Whilst there, Edward also had time to meet his sister-in-law Margaret, who sent him home with 'beautiful gifts for the love of her sister'.[80]

In November 1338, Philippa gave birth to the couple's third son, a boy named Lionel (meaning 'little lion' or 'son of the lion') after his father's jousting alter-ego.[81] Philippa had given birth at the Abbey of St Michael in Antwerp, and Edward expressed his gratitude to the monks for caring for his 'dearest' wife and newborn son, who was also baptised at the abbey, by granting them the advowson (the right to appoint a member of the Church) of the church of Thyngden in Northampton.[82] Philippa and Edward spent Christmas with their two daughters and new son at Antwerp where the Emperor showed his appreciation for the family and new alliance by sending a piper to entertain them on Christmas Day, and on 6 January 1339 Philippa had her churching.[83] The year was beginning on a high note.

Edward spent a lot of time in his first year in Antwerp ingratiating himself with the locals and building up alliances with the great families to whom he was connected. As well as Philippa's brother-in-law, the Emperor, his own brother-in-law, the Duke of Guelders, was proving to be of great help to him; Edward allegedly found that he was the only person there that he could trust.[84] Edward also worked hard to build a strong reputation with the common men of the Low Countries. This was particularly important for gathering his allies in the region, as the 1330s had been marked by hostility between England and Flanders.[85] His work paid off when the Duke of Brabant, in whose land he had been staying, agreed to join his side, and the Flemish finally agreed to make an alliance with the English.[86]

Whilst Edward's long stay in Antwerp was necessary to build a power base from which to launch his campaign against the French, it soon began to grate on his English subjects. The French had made some pre-emptive attacks on the English, using their fleet to raid, burn and plunder Portsmouth, Guernsey, Southampton, Plymouth, Swanage, Portsea, the Isle of Wight and the Channel Islands throughout the autumn of 1338. Whilst Edward and his court were jousting with gaiety in January in celebration of the birth of a healthy son, his people across the Channel were suffering.[87]

With war on the horizon, it was vital that the crown kept on top of its finances. From their arrival on the Continent until November 1339, Philippa was given £9,660 from Edward's wardrobe to pay for her household expenses and the wages of her soldiers, vital to ensure the royal family was protected and safe whilst Edward was out fighting, but also as a useful resource for Edward to draw upon himself.[88] Edward also made sure to pay off vast sections of their debt to the Italian merchants whose loans he had so relied upon since his accession, repaying a staggering £74,000 between July 1338 and January 1340.[89]

With the advent of a new year, there was much activity at the relocated royal court. The now 25-year-old Philippa was heavily pregnant with her sixth child, showing the continued strength of the king and queen's relationship. In January, the royal family made plans to move to Ghent in Flanders to solidify their new alliance. Philippa, Edward and their children thus took up residence in the town's Abbey of St Bavo.[90] Shortly afterwards the family gathered in the marketplace, surrounded by their soldiers and the important men of the town, where Edward was publicly recognised as King of France as well as of England.[91] From this time onwards, Edward used the title of King of France. He was determined to assert his rights.

After this public display of propaganda, Edward was forced to leave his family behind and return to England. Two years abroad with a standing army had drained the royal coffers, and the English parliament had many grievances they wished to air before they would give Edward any more funds. Leaving Philippa, who was due to give birth any day, with their children, Edward set sail for his homeland.

At the start of March 1340, Queen Philippa gave birth at the abbey to a healthy baby boy, named John. She immediately sent three of her ladies to England to bring the joyous news to Edward, whose jubilation was reflected in the generous gift of £200 he granted to the women for coming to him.[92]

In June, Philippa was granted a further increase to her income of 2,000 marks (around £1,300) a year because she had 'been put to such heavy charges in her stay beyond the seas' and 'that the rents assigned for her chamber are not sufficient to meet them'.[93] Philippa had been maintaining soldiers to aid her husband, had been caring for two to four children, and had been upholding her personal majesty to project a strong monarchy in order to attract allies. All of that was very difficult to do on her current income.

Edward's return to England had been vital for the stability of his kingdom and for the obtaining of war funds, but his absence from the Continent had been disastrous to his war effort. In April, two of his earls – including his close friend Montagu who had been so instrumental to his 1330 coup – had been captured by the French, whilst across April and May the French ravaged Hainault.[94] Edward desperately needed to return to get things back in order, but a huge French fleet was patrolling the Channel, blocking his way. In June, Edward met the fleet with his own at the Battle of Sluys. Hundreds of ships were involved, but the outcome was a resounding success for the English who lost just a handful of vessels, whereas the French lost almost their entire fleet.

Edward had been injured in the fighting, suffering a severe leg wound, and it took two weeks for him to be sufficiently healed to make his way to his family in Ghent.[95] Philippa had been unable to wait for his return, and she made her way towards her husband, anxious to know that he was well.[96] Edward's fate could have so easily been different, and Philippa would have been well aware of the danger her husband was placing himself in by declaring war with France. The jeopardy of Sluys and the birth of a new baby boy had highlighted to the royal couple how vulnerable their family was in the Low Countries, so close to the fighting. As much as the family had tried to stay together up to now, it was decided it was in the best interests of their children if Isabella, Joan, Lionel and baby John were sent back to the safety of England.

Over the summer, Philippa and Edward organised a joint household for their children in England.[97] A noblewoman named Isabella de la Mote was appointed chief mistress of the four children (Prince Edward, as heir and regent, was to remain with his own independent household) and a group of men were appointed to run the household under Isabella, acting as treasurers, clerks and chaplains. More women were appointed to serve as attendants to the young children, including wet nurses for young Lionel and John. At the end of July, Philippa bade farewell to her dear children, whom she had rarely been apart from, and entrusted them to her closest friends and servants. The children arrived at the luxurious royal apartments in the Tower of London on 5 August 1340.

This elaborate and unprecedented household situation had been created with the intent of running for at least two years, as Edward and Philippa envisioned being away for an extended period whilst Edward waged his war. In the end, Edward suffered military defeat in his failure to besiege the town of Tournai, and with growing financial concerns and unhappiness in England the couple returned home that winter. Philippa was reunited with her children for Christmas and she was likely thankful for the return for another reason: she was already pregnant again. With her last two children being born abroad in foreign religious institutions, Philippa would have enjoyed the prospect of giving birth in a comfortable English palace.

At the end of January 1341, Philippa travelled to the palace of Langley in Hertfordshire where she stayed until mid-March. She had obviously decided she enjoyed the comforts of the palace, for she returned there for the birth of her next child. Another boy was born to the couple in late May or the start of June and named Edmund. It seems the little boy was born prematurely as Edward had left Philippa for the siege of Tournai in mid-July and not returned until the end of September; Philippa cannot have been pregnant before he left, and so the child should have been born at the start of July at the earliest.[98] Philippa's churching was held at Langley in late June or early July, and the little prince was healthy despite his early arrival.

Thirteen years into their marriage, Philippa and Edward now had six living children, although they had lost little Prince William. With four boys and two girls, the royal family was strong, and Edward would have plenty of diplomatic opportunities in organising marriages for them all. Edward was nearing his thirtieth birthday, whilst Philippa was about 27 years old. Through Philippa, Edward had built the loving family he had always dreamed of. His 11-year-old son had no hint of the drama of Edward's own childhood, and would not need to see his parents spout hatred at each other. Philippa had become a powerful and wealthy queen, fulfilling the hopes of her parents, and although she was still struggling with her household finances she was acting as a model queen on all other accounts, being a loving mother, generous to her servants, and regularly interceding on behalf of her less fortunate subjects. It was clear this decade was going to be difficult with Edward's desire to claim the French throne for his own, but the family would be able to weather the coming storm.

4

Love and War

As Queen Philippa prepared for the arrival of Prince Edmund in the spring of 1341, she had clearly decided that she wanted the rest of her children back with her more permanently. At the end of April, around a month before Philippa gave birth, her children's independent household was dissolved and the four children returned to their mother's care. In May, Edward organised for money to be assigned to pay the debts that his children's household had gathered – Philippa was not alone in the great costs of maintaining the monarchy.[1] Now that the children were back in her custody, Philippa required more money to pay for their expenses. In June, Edward granted her £1,000 a year to pay for their care.[2]

Part of Philippa's eagerness to have her children with her might have been spurred by a serious illness that Princess Joan contracted in April. What Joan was afflicted with is not recorded, but it caused enough concern that Edward sent his own personal physician to care for his daughter.[3] Thankfully for the royal couple, Joan recovered well.

At 7 years old, Joan was now to become diplomatically useful, for this year Edward sealed a marriage treaty betrothing her to the Duke of Austria. Despite this, she stayed in England; Edward argued that with the war with France raging, it was too dangerous for his young daughter to travel.[4] This could be the voice of Philippa talking, for she would have been mindful of the suffering of her sister Joanna who was sent away for marriage at a young age, and she would have wanted to avoid this for her own child.

With her return to England, Philippa decided to turn her attention to making a more permanent mark as queen. This year, she launched an extensive two-year building programme at her manor of Ludgershall in Wiltshire. She customised it to her own tastes, ordering glazing with her coat of arms and painting the timbers of the chapel in blue. She had the chapel rebuilt, the roof of the great tower repaired, and a new chamber block constructed.[5]

More importantly for Philippa's legacy, she took over patronage of a new college at Oxford University, the older of England's two universities. Her clerk, Robert Eglesfield, founded the Queen's College, named in her honour, in the hope of gaining her help in establishing a foothold for the college.[6] Eglesfield was well primed to get Philippa's assistance and he might have been inspired by his knowledge of her interest in literature and education. In fact, he might have had Philippa's active encouragement to found the college, as a note in the papal registers for the following year states that 'Queen's Hall' had been founded by Philippa herself.[7]

Either way, Philippa's patronage was vital in the college obtaining sufficient endowments to ensure its survival. The pope confirmed the foundation of the college and granted a licence for the construction of a chapel and cemetery to 'celebrate divine offices, receive oblations, and minister the sacraments'. He also granted the appropriation of two churches in Salisbury and Carlisle to the college, giving it an income and a place to assign members of the church that it would train.[8] With Philippa's influence, the college would easily obtain honours and funding to help it gain a foothold within the sphere of higher education. With the founding of Queen's College, Philippa hoped that her queenship would bestow a legacy on the future clergy and learned men of the country.

The queen also inadvertently left a legacy of a different kind, for it was around this time that Philippa established the presence of rosemary in England. Although the herb had been known to the English for centuries, it was a plant native to southern Europe and had never been grown in England. Today known for flavouring food, in medieval Europe rosemary was a popular ingredient in medicine. At some point between 1338 and 1342, Countess

Jeanne ordered the composition of two copies of a book on the medicinal use of rosemary which was called *The Little Book of the Virtues of Rosemary* to be written in French. One copy she kept for her own library, but the second copy she sent to her daughter Philippa, alongside cuttings of the plant.[9]

Philippa ordered her gardeners to plant the cuttings, most likely first at the privy garden in Westminster, but then across other royal palaces, including some of Philippa's favourite residences. Once Philippa's gardeners had perfected the art of growing the herb in England, it began to spread more widely in society: one contemporary noted that he had received at least one cutting of the plant from Philippa's herber.[10] Later in the fourteenth century the English began to write their own pieces about rosemary, all of which trace its introduction to this 'little book' given to Philippa by her mother.[11]

As the winter of 1341 arrived, Edward was once again on the path to war on two fronts. In September, Edward had shown his favour to John de Montfort, one of two claimants to the duchy of Brittany, by granting him the earldom of Richmond.[12] Edward announced that he was going to finance a military campaign to help John seize his territory, but in reality this was a chance to restart hostilities with the French, who naturally chose to support the other candidate, Joan of Penthièvre. But to the north of England, the Scots were once again causing problems.

Although Edward had helped Edward Balliol take the Scottish throne, by the end of the 1330s Balliol had lost much of his territory. In June 1341, King David returned from his exile in France to reclaim his throne, and he quickly grew his power base among Scottish nobles who opposed the regime of Balliol and the English. David led some raids into northern England, provoking Edward, and worrying the English enough that it was decided that Edward needed to spend the winter focused on Scotland instead of Brittany.[13]

In November, Edward bade farewell to Philippa and made his way up to Newcastle. Philippa had fallen pregnant again not long after the birth of Edmund, and the departure of her husband for war must have caused some anxiety. In the end, Edward's army was met with little action and he spent the Christmas season entertained by jousts and feasts in some of his Scottish castles before returning to England in January.[14]

Once again, the circumstances surrounding the birth of Philippa's next child – her eighth, a girl named Blanche – are shrouded in mystery.[15] The princess was known as Blanche of the Tower, indicating that Philippa gave birth to her at the Tower of London, and historians have placed her birth in March or June. Edward's household accounts place him at the Tower at various times between March and August, giving little indication of definite points for him being there when Philippa gave birth or returning for her churching there.[16] If Blanche was born in March, she might have been born slightly prematurely, as Edmund had been, as Edward and Philippa would not have recommenced their marital relations until after Philippa's churching in late June or early July the previous summer.[17]

There were other reasons to celebrate this year, and Edward organised numerous elaborate tournaments to mark these occasions. In the summer, Philippa and Edward's 3-year-old son Lionel was married to a remarkably rich heiress, Elizabeth de Burgh. Elizabeth was just 10 years old herself, but she had been orphaned at 11 months old. She was to inherit the earldom of Ulster, and by marrying their son to her, Edward and Philippa were securing a vast inheritance in Ireland for their son. The little boy was provided with a lavish red bed embroidered with knots and leaves and powdered with roses to use for the celebrations.[18]

Philippa's brother, Count William, visited her family in England across spring and summer, a visit that must have been greatly appreciated by the family-orientated Philippa. William participated in a joust held by Edward at Eltham in May as well as another tournament in August. The dangers of these chivalric games were highlighted at the Eltham tournament, though, when William was injured, though luckily not seriously so.[19]

Summer was not all given to tournaments and jousts. With the Scottish campaign abandoned, Edward turned his attention back to the question of Brittany. Edward's contender for the duchy, John de Montfort, had been captured by the French and it would have seemed that hope was lost were it not for Montfort's wife, the formidable Joanna of Flanders. Joanna declared that her infant son was the heir to his father's faction and she mustered an army in support of her husband and son. She valiantly defended the town of Hennebont from siege, wearing armour and inspiring the defenders, until relief arrived in the form of an English fleet sent by Edward.[20]

By October, Edward was ready to set sail to Brittany with more troops, and he landed on the 26th of the month. With the arrival of the English, the tides of war changed, and Montfort's faction began to take over more and more territory. Edward made sure to write to his beloved wife whilst he was apart from her, their affection evident in his addressing her as his 'sweetheart' in the letters.[21]

Whilst Edward was abroad, tragedy struck when the infant Princess Blanche died in January 1343. With the king absent, his eldest son, the 12-year-old Prince Edward, was left to support Philippa and make arrangements for her funeral. In a letter dated 30 January, Prince Edward wrote of the funeral of 'Lady Blanche, our very dear sister' which was held within the next few weeks at Westminster Abbey.[22] Philippa had now lost two children; being a queen did not spare her from the high rates of infant mortality in the Middle Ages. Once again, Philippa had had to bear the pain of losing a child without her husband by her side.

Whilst Philippa was mourning the loss of her baby, Edward was agreeing to a temporary truce with King Philip VI of France, to last until September that year.[23] At the end of February, Edward prepared to return home to his family, but a terrible storm was raging across the Atlantic which made it impossible for his ships to cross the Channel. After three days, he finally landed at Dorset with Joanna of Flanders and her children, who had been invited to stay in England. Edward rushed to London to meet Philippa, and once they were reunited, the couple went on pilgrimage with their family through southern England during Lent, arriving at Philippa's manor of Havering-atte-Bower for Easter.[24]

Philippa was occupied with personal business and in July she was again working to ensure her new college was sufficiently endowed, with Edward granting the institution 'at the request of queen Philippa' the advowson of a church in Oxfordshire.[25] This year, Philippa also made an intriguing gift to Gloucester Abbey, where Edward II was buried, sending a golden heart and urn to be placed at his tomb.[26] The gift might have been part of an attempt by the royal couple to make amends with their past, reflecting a promise Edward made whilst deep in the throes of the tempest in the Channel. Edward had prayed to the Virgin Mary to keep him safe during the storm, and during his Lenten pilgrimage he had made offerings at shrines dedicated to her. But he had also visited his father's tomb in Gloucester, suggesting he might also have prayed to Edward II to keep him safe.[27] Philippa's gift, therefore, could have been a thank you to her deceased father-in-law for the protection of her husband.

Edward spent the rest of the year in a state of relative peace and calm, and without the demands of war and funding soldiers he could begin to clear some of his mounting debts and restore his monetary reputation. Across the autumn Edward bestowed further sources of income on Philippa, granting her a variety of lands during the minority of their heirs, as well as a one-off payment of all the money that had been due to the previous Earl of Richmond when he died.[28] Edward had also been working to reclaim precious royal regalia that had been pawned in 1340, when the couple were residing in the Low Countries. The previous year, he had arranged payment of over £2,000 to a John Portenare to return two of Philippa's crowns, and another £800 to a Francis Drisattorne for another of her crowns. He was also working to see the return of his own great crown of England, which he finally got in 1344.[29]

After Edward had made prayers to his father for his safety, this seems to have spurred something of a reconciliation with his mother. Queen Isabella had never quite been restored her position at court after her downfall in 1330, but in 1344 Edward made more concerted efforts to include his mother in activities. On one occasion, he ordered mulberry-coloured Turkish cloth and taffeta for Isabella, Philippa and four countesses to wear as they joined him on a hunt.[30] Philippa herself seems to have held little ill will against Queen Isabella for her part in suppressing Philippa's queenship in her early years in the country, and in the coming years she would often visit her mother-in-law.

Indeed, Edward's whole family took a starring role in 1344. In late January Edward hosted a magnificent tournament at Windsor Castle, inviting all of the noblemen and ladies of the realm. At the centre of the celebrations were Queen Philippa and Queen Isabella, Prince Edward and the rest of the royal children. At the celebrations there 'was no lack of dancing between the lords and the ladies', and jousts lasted for three days.[31] The reconciliation with Edward's mother was further shown by several visits to Isabella across spring, and towards the end of the year Edward decided his family would spend his thirty-second birthday with Isabella at her home of Castle Rising in Norfolk.[32]

The Windsor tournament was a key point in Edward's reign. Edward was now a well-established, powerful king who had won numerous military battles. He had an ever-growing family – Philippa had recently fallen pregnant again, though the couple were probably not yet aware of it – and a significant number of powerful allies across Europe. Edward wanted to make a huge statement of his authority and his place in English history, and this tournament would be his staging ground.

On the last day of the tournament, Edward appeared in his greatest regal attire accompanied by his equally resplendent mother and wife, and then made a proclamation to all of the greatest lords and ladies of the land who were there assembled: he was going to establish a Round Table just like King Arthur had done centuries before. As the nobles departed, Edward ordered workmen to begin constructing a tower to hold the meetings of the Round Table, which, according to one chronicler, was an impressive 200 feet wide.[33]

After the tournament, Edward was busy again making plans for the marriages of his children. Princess Joan, who had been betrothed a few years previously to the Duke of Austria, was instead offered to Pedro, son and heir of the King of Castile. Expanding his power base into northern Spain was a way for Edward to build more allies around France. Edward also requested a papal dispensation to allow his eldest children, Princess Isabella and Prince Edward, to marry the son and daughter of the Duke of Brabant, but these plans quickly fell apart.[34] Autumn brought more joy to Edward, as a month before his birthday Philippa blessed him with yet another child, a daughter named Mary. The little girl was healthy, and Edward and Philippa spent another blissful Christmas with their family.

The next year proved quiet for Philippa. She attended to her usual queenly duties, obtaining more pieces of land and income for her Oxford college in April. In September, she obtained a pardon for a woman who had been sentenced to death for trespass and theft within a church in Yorkshire, whose sentence had been delayed because she was pregnant.[35] This pardon was similar to one Philippa had made in the county a decade previously, perhaps showing Philippa's concern for the plight of pregnant women. Philippa was also able to use her position as queen to help those close to her. She persuaded Pope Clement VI to grant her godson, Philip de Beauchamp, a benefice in the church.[36] Philip was the child of her lady Sybil, whose marriage Philippa and Edward had attended back in 1337, and was named in her honour. The boy was now 5 years old and had been designated a career in the church. Later in life, Philippa financed his education at Oxford University, amply fulfilling her duties as godmother.[37]

September 1345 was to bring more death to the royal family. On the 22nd of the month Henry, Earl of Lancaster, died.[38] As Edward's great-uncle, Lancaster had been instrumental in supporting the king in his early reign, aiding Isabella in her invasion and fighting for Edward's rights under the stringent regency. Though Lancaster's death was a blow to Edward, for Philippa it provided another opportunity to stabilise her finances; just a few days after his death, Edward granted Philippa 1,000 marks a year that had originally been a gift to the earl 'in consideration of the great charges which his consort, queen Philippa has borne about the sustenance of their children'.[39]

Philippa had seven living children, six of whom spent most of their time living in her household, and this unusual situation certainly put pressure on her wardrobe and exchequer, which had to find a way to provide for this brood of children, all of whom required lavish clothes and servants of their own. A second death just a few days after Lancaster was to prove to have a far larger impact on the royal couple, though. On 26 September 1345, Philippa's brother Count William died in battle, leaving no legitimate children behind.

The death of William threw up great problems for his territories, as his sisters were now his closest heirs. This posed no problem in Hainault, which had a history of female succession, but William had also been count of Holland and Zeeland, where the matter was not as clear cut. Theoretically, the German Emperor – husband of Philippa's oldest sister Margaret – could claim reversion of the lands as overlord of the territories. Edward himself was keen to push Philippa's rights to the region, arguing it should be split between the sisters instead of all going to Margaret, and a month later Edward gave power to Philippa's uncle, John of Hainault, and several other men to maintain Philippa's rights in the territories, collecting income, receiving vassalage and appointing officials.[40]

As uncle to the recently deceased count, and brother to the previous count, John had his own claim to rule the contested territories, but he was seemingly overlooked in the succession due to the power of the husbands of three of the four sisters. John would struggle to assert his rights when the King of England, the Count of Jülich and the Emperor all wanted a slice of their wives' inheritance. As much as Edward believed Philippa should have an equal portion of her natal lands, others did not necessarily agree with him, and the consensus moved towards Margaret inheriting all four as the eldest sister.

With the arrival of 1346, Philippa of Hainault was once more pregnant. The baby marked her tenth known pregnancy, a significant toll on the body of the queen who was only just turning 32. As the royal family were attending the funeral of the Earl of Lancaster towards the end of January, the Holy Roman Emperor granted his wife sole sovereignty of the territories of her brother. Margaret travelled to her homelands and received homage from her various vassals, solidifying her position as countess in her own right. Edward was displeased at this underhand move by the Emperor, and towards the end of April he repeated his request to some of his men to keep possession of Philippa's inheritance abroad.[41]

On 12 July, Edward III and his 16-year-old son, Prince Edward, landed in France, having left Philippa and the other children in England.[42] Philippa gave birth to a baby girl named Margaret the following week at Windsor Castle, and being apart from her husband and son must have made the experience difficult, particularly knowing the danger they were sailing towards. The previous year, hostilities with the French had again ramped up and the problem of Brittany had been compounded by the death of Montfort, the claimant whom England had been backing. Edward once more had to take an army to the Continent to pursue his claims to the French throne and to protect his interests in Brittany, and the prince was seen as old enough to accompany his father on campaign. After all, Edward III had first seen battle in Scotland when he was just 14.

It was not long before Prince Edward was to be thrown in at the deep end. On 26 August 1346 in northern France, the Battle of Crécy was fought between the English and French armies. Edward III led his troops into battle, but he delegated men to his son, who was made a commander. Prince Edward was keen to prove his worth to his glorious father and to his countrymen, of whom he one day would be king himself, and he charged into battle on the front line. The prince came across many of the greatest men in western Europe: the kings of France, Bohemia and Mallorca, and his uncle and great-uncle, the deposed Holy Roman Emperor and John of Hainault, who had both defected to the French.[43] The battle lasted for hours, but eventually the English came out victorious. Both Edwards had survived the battle unscathed.

Many important French noblemen were killed during the battle, including one of Philippa's uncles and numerous cousins. Though her husband and son were safe, the wars with the French that Edward had waged for the past decade still hit Philippa's family. Not long after the battle Philippa had her churching back in England, with £500 set aside for the celebrations by Prince Lionel (or, rather, his advisors, given that the boy was 7 years old), who had been made Guardian of England.[44]

With Philippa officially welcomed back into society, and with her baby girl seemingly healthy, she was keen to join her husband and son in France. After the victory at Crécy, Edward's forces had moved on to Calais to besiege the valuable port. If Edward could win Calais, then it would be another important accomplishment. Although Philippa had only just given birth to Princess Margaret, it was not at all safe to bring the newborn into a war zone. Philippa had to leave her behind, alongside all her remaining children, but it seems she wanted the comfort of having at least one child with her, for she brought her oldest daughter Princess Isabella with her on the journey. Queen Philippa arrived at Calais with her substantial retinue towards the end of September.[45]

With the absence of both the king and the queen, and with the realm nominally ruled by a child regent, the Scottish came to the aid of the French. The disaster of Crécy had been a devastating blow to the cause of the French king, and he needed all the help he could get. Scotland was under the control of Edward's brother-in-law, King David II, and he was ready to finally make an impression. The French king had cared for him in exile and it was time to repay his debt. In October, he crossed into England with an army and started ravaging the countryside. On 17 October 1346, David's forces were met by an army led by the Archbishop of York at the Battle of Neville's Cross, not far from Durham. The archbishop successfully repelled the invaders, but the greatest victory came in David's capture.[46] This was an overwhelming triumph for Edward.

Intriguingly, the chronicler Froissart gives an account of the battle with Queen Philippa present, even though she was not in the country at the time. In his retelling, the 'good lady, the Queen of England' left Newcastle and met the assembled troops, dividing them into four battalions and assigning commanders. She then gave the army a speech rousing them to protect Edward's honour, and the honour of England, then returned to Newcastle to wait out the battle. With the success of the English, Philippa returned on horseback to the site of the battle and took custody of the captured Scottish king.[47]

Froissart had personally spent time with many people involved in the battle and so would have known Philippa was not there. Chroniclers were known to embellish stories for entertainment, but Froissart must have had a purpose in giving Philippa such a starring role in one of the most important battles of Edward's reign. The story first appeared in another account written before Froissart composed his version.[48] Perhaps in repeating it, Froissart wanted to show how important Philippa was in maintaining Edward's government when he was abroad, and how he relied on her for many of his successes. That it was thought plausible for readers that Philippa could have rallied the troops for battle in this way says something important about how her contemporaries perceived her. Edward had trusted his wife on many occasions to look after affairs in England whilst he was away warring. She had held great councils on his behalf to discuss the war effort, so it was not such a leap that she was thought capable of leading armies. After all, her formidable mother-in-law had done so.

Whilst Philippa did not lead troops against the Scottish in October 1346, she was still busy helping Edward's cause on the Continent. That month, Philippa's sister Margaret agreed to meet with her to discuss her rights to their family territories. Edward, wary of the safety of his queen when he was in the middle of besieging the French, did not want to let Philippa travel, but she was keen to assert her rights, particularly when her husband desired them so much. Edward finally agreed to let Philippa travel to Ypres in Flanders for the conference, for it was an easy distance for him to come to her aid should she need it. To protect Philippa he assigned the Earl of Warwick, 200 archers and a large contingent of knights to escort her there.[49]

Though Edward had met Margaret in Germany eight years previously, there is no evidence that Philippa had seen her sister since she had left

Hainault for her marriage in 1324. This was possibly the first time the sisters had been together in over two decades, though they had exchanged letters and gifts during this time. The two women spent several days debating their rights and on 17 October – the same day the battle at Neville's Cross was fought – the two women bade farewell, having signed a charter defining how they were to proceed. Philippa agreed to halt any hostile action against Margaret whilst she prepared documents to support her claims to the inheritance. In return, Margaret would recognise Philippa's claims in the meantime.[50]

Philippa, Edward, Prince Edward and Princess Isabella spent Christmas outside the walls of Calais. Philippa and her daughter had been accompanied overseas by a large group of her ladies and damsels, and so the festive season was spent jovially for the relocated English court.[51] What could have been a lonely Christmas abroad for the king's soldiers was made happier by the presence of so many noble ladies, and the subsequent feasting and celebration in their honour. Edward knew that the siege of Calais would take many months, and he had erected so many tents for his men and his court that it was as if they 'were in a city raised in the fields'.[52]

It was not all joviality in the camp outside Calais, though, and the winter was long and cold, with the soldiers suffering from dysentery and other diseases. With the arrival of another year, Edward needed to build up his allies once more. He had lost the support of his brother-in-law, the former Emperor, over their clashes on the Hainault inheritance, and the death of Philippa's brother, the previous count, had subsequently lost Edward the support of Hainault, Holland and Zeeland. John of Hainault had also defected to the French, and in May the Duke of Guelders did likewise.[53] The previous Duke of Guelders, who had married Edward's sister, had died in 1343, but Eleanor's son who had become the new duke did not have the same loyalty to his uncle. Edward's supporters were dropping like flies, and he desperately needed to secure new ones.

Edward needed to consolidate his position in the Low Countries. He turned to the Flemish to consider a marriage with his daughter Isabella, and with the death of their count at Crécy, the Flemish mercantile class were keen to make amends with the English king. After his recent military victories and the capture of the Scottish king, Edward and England seemed like a good choice over France. The Flemish pressurised their new teenage count,

Louis II, into accepting the proposal, even though he had made it clear he wanted to stay loyal to the French.[54]

As spring arrived, Edward III, Philippa and Princess Isabella left Calais to meet with Count Louis at the monastery of Bergues in Flanders, leaving Prince Edward to manage the siege. In early March, a formal marriage agreement was drawn up between the parties, and the marriage set for the first week of April. Edward and Philippa hurried to gather a suitable wedding trousseau for their daughter, 'making preparations for rich presents of cloths and jewels to distribute', with Philippa in particular 'anxious to acquit herself on the occasion with honour and generosity'. But disaster struck the week before the wedding when the young count escaped his guard whilst out hawking. He fled to the French court where he submitted to the King of France and professed his loyalty.[55] King Philip was delighted, and quickly rewarded the count by marrying him to the daughter of the Duke of Brabant.

How the young Princess Isabella felt about being jilted is unclear, but the count's escape was certainly a humiliation for Edward. Despite the support of the people of Flanders, their leader was so eager to avoid an alliance with Edward that he had fled his own county. Edward was desperate for allies, and this escapade was not a good signal to other potential alliances. Philippa would have been there to comfort her family and help keep appearances together, and the royal family swiftly returned to Calais to see how the siege was faring.

In happier news for Philippa, in April her second-eldest daughter Joan arrived at the encampment outside Calais.[56] Philippa had been separated from her daughter for seven months, and so the reunion would have brought her pleasure. She must, though, have felt yearning for her other children, particularly Princess Margaret whom she had left at around 2 months old, and who was now reaching 9 months. Philippa was missing crucial early milestones, and knowing the maternal instincts of the queen this must have weighed upon her.

Eleven months after the siege of Calais began, the city finally surrendered. Nearly a year of being cut off from outside contact had weighed heavily on its citizens, who had been starving to death and suffering, relieved only temporarily when a fleet of ships had sneaked supplies in by sea in April.[57] The inhabitants had begged the French king to come to their aid, but King Philip was unwilling or unable to take Edward on in battle again. In June, the citizens of Calais sent Philip a desperate letter, intercepted by Edward, saying that they had been forced to eat dogs, horses and rats, and were even contemplating eating their own dead.[58] His help should come now or never.

The call for help was never answered. For holding out against the English king for so long, no quarter was expected. The humiliated and starving leaders of the city walked out of its gates, with the mayor and six prominent men of the city, known as burghers, wearing nooses around their necks to symbolise their knowledge that their lives were now in Edward's hands. They gave him the keys of the city, and all of the remaining citizens left their homes and belongings behind, knowing the English king was now to take all they owned.

According to the most famous chronicle stories, Edward was determined to have the men executed as punishment for resisting him for so long. His gathered knights and lords begged for the men's lives, but Edward would have none of it. Finally, his dear wife Philippa, who was exceedingly heavy with child, fell to her knees in front of him and 'wept so badly' that those around her could not take it. She pleaded for him to spare their lives, for 'since I have crossed the sea in great danger, as you know, I have asked you for nothing'. Unable to bear the sight of his wife in such a state, Edward's heart softened. He exclaimed, 'Lady, I wish you were anywhere else, for you pray to me so tenderly that I dare not deny you!' Edward then released the men into Philippa's custody, sparing their lives, and she gathered new clothing for them.[59]

This story is one of the most famous of Philippa's life. But once more the event might have been elaborated or even fabricated by the chroniclers. Indeed, only two contemporary writers, le Bel and Froissart, recount the story in this way (and Froissart seems to have copied the story closely from le Bel). Other chroniclers, such as Henry Knighton and Geoffrey Baker, wrote that the king was 'moved by compassion' of his own accord after seeing the sorry sight of the men, and accepted their pleas for mercy.[60]

Without official records, it is difficult to verify what exactly happened at the surrender of Calais. It certainly seems well agreed that the burghers of the town did come out with nooses around their necks, and Edward did forgive them. But whether this was at the intervention of Philippa or out of his own mercy is less clear. Philippa would certainly have been very well placed to intercede for the men. It was expected of her as queen to help the needy and temper the king's wrath, and the whole event could easily have been staged by Edward, as public acts of intercession by queens often were.

As a strong, military king who had been thwarted by the citizens of Calais for almost a year, it was expected that he should show no mercy, to send a message to others who might act against him. But, for a Christian king and as a matter of practicality, it was good to show acts of compassion. It was much easier if this compassion was caused by love for his wife, rather than from weakness of character. Behind the scenes, Edward and Philippa could have orchestrated the whole event to give Edward a way out of punishing the people of Calais who had already lost their homes and many of their fellow citizens.

So, the events of the surrender of Calais could very well have found Philippa at its heart, but one thing for certain is that Philippa was not heavily pregnant as she was portrayed. No official records survive showing that Philippa gave birth at this time, and the dates do not line up with Philippa's movements.[61] Philippa being portrayed as heavily pregnant during her intercession was in fact a literary trope. Giving birth to children and interceding for the public were two of the most important queenly duties, and indeed both were mentioned explicitly during her coronation.[62] To portray both happening at the same time held powerful symbolism for medieval writers, and it crops up across the period relating to different female rulers. For example, one French chronicle tells the story of Joan of Navarre, Duchess of Brittany, who interceded with her husband whilst heavily pregnant and with her infant children in her arms less than fifty years later.[63]

With the fall of Calais, England rejoiced. Edward and Philippa certainly personally celebrated, for she swiftly fell pregnant. Finally, over a year after they had left, the royal family returned to England in mid-October.[64] Edward returned home as a legend. For years, many had doubted his abilities and his aims, including his own people. But in the space of a year, he had won a glorious victory at Crécy, conquered Calais (which was to now stay in English hands for over two centuries) and captured the King of Scotland. Far from questioning him, people across Europe now hailed the English as the noblest warriors known.[65]

Christmas was spent at Guildford in Surrey, and the celebrations were suitably lavish. Edward commissioned elaborate masks and headpieces for performers who wore tunics painted with stars and peacock eyes to entertain the court.[66] Expensive gifts were exchanged on New Year's Day, such as two gold brooches encrusted with rubies, emeralds, diamonds and pearls which Prince Edward gave to his sisters Isabella and Joan.[67] King Edward's own personal spending also increased at this time. Edward now needed to look every bit the powerful king of his reputation in Europe, and in the medieval period that meant dressing yourself in the finest, most expensive materials available. Across the next sixteen months Edward's wardrobe purchased over 20,600 skins of pured miniver to be used almost solely for his own clothes.[68] Pured miniver was the most expensive type of miniver as it had the grey removed to leave a pure white fur.

As the court settled into 1348, the fortunes of the English were once more looking bright. Edward continued his campaign to solidify the glory of the English crown, and he turned his mind once more to Arthurian chivalric ideals. Though he had announced the creation of a great Round Table two years previously, the French campaign had stopped the plans in its tracks; the money was needed for war, not frivolity. The tower that had been started was never finished, and its foundations sat at Windsor Castle taunting the newly returned king. Edward had been passionate about his idea to found a knightly order, so now he came at it at a fresh angle and founded the famous Order of the Garter.

The exact date for the creation of the order has been hotly debated, but at the Christmas celebrations in Guildford in 1347 vestments embroidered with a garter and the motto *honi soit qui mal y pense* ('shame on him who thinks evil of it') were delivered to Edward and some of his nobles to wear. As Edward hosted more tournaments in early 1348, the garter and motto appeared several more times, including at the Eltham tournament of May 1348 where Edward wore a robe decorated with twelve embroidered garters.[69] The Order of the Garter was formed to honour Edward's most loyal, chivalrous knights, and represented the greatest of the English nobility. Every year on St George's Day (23 April) the knights would gather at Windsor Castle, which Edward had previously envisioned being home to his knightly order, to hear Mass then feast and celebrate.

As Edward prepared for his tournament at Eltham in May, Philippa was preparing for the imminent arrival of her eleventh child. At 34 years old, Philippa was now an expert in childbirth, but in the medieval period the arrival of each child was still a dangerous business. Even the most experienced of mothers could succumb to childbed diseases or complicated births. Once more, though, the queen was safely delivered of a child, her sixth son. The boy was named William after his late brother and grandfather; it was not unusual for parents to reuse the name of a deceased child.

Records of the royal household and tailors illuminate with great detail the sumptuous churching ceremony Philippa held at Windsor after William's birth. She had a bed with three curtains, whose quilt and other decorations were created with twenty-one ells of scarlet cloth and three cloths of gold. On top of the bed, a bed cover was made with a staggering 1,798 bellies of miniver.[70] For the celebrations, Philippa wore a dark blue gown with a tunic decorated with golden birds inside circles of pearls. The new prince was given a bed of green taffeta embroidered with red roses, and Edward hosted another great joust to celebrate his birth, attended by his other children and the captive King of Scotland.[71]

Once Philippa had recovered from childbirth, her mind immediately turned to her daughter Joan. The time had come for the 14-year-old princess to make her way to Castile for her marriage, and she left for her new future around June. Philippa and Edward had prepared an impressive trousseau for their daughter, who was their first girl to be married, including a stunning cloth of gold dress to wear for her wedding ceremony.[72] Joan set sail, heading for France first, and she was accompanied by 130 archers and the Bishop of Carlisle. But when the illustrious procession arrived at Bordeaux, they were met with a scene of desolation.

The Black Death had been creeping through Europe since December the previous year, and though its devastation was great, its passage towards England was slow. In May, Edward and his court had been able to celebrate the birth of his son with great abandon whilst just across the Channel in Paris the disease was ravaging the city.[73] Why Edward chose to send his daughter overseas when he must have heard reports of the great plague by the time it came for her to set sail is unknown. Perhaps he did not take the reports too seriously, and this would be a fatal undoing.

Princess Joan's party, despite the warnings of local people, took up residence in one of her father's castles in Bordeaux. Inevitably, it was not long before the group was struck by the Black Death, and Joan was to become England's first royal victim. On 1 July 1348, the teenage girl died.[74] It seems it might have taken quite a few weeks for the news to reach Philippa and Edward back in England. It was not until 15 September that Edward composed a letter to the King of Castile informing him of Joan's death. The letter is deeply poignant, and the father's despair is clear. He mourns with 'intense bitterness of heart' the destructiveness of death, which had 'lamentably taken from both of us our dearest daughter, whom we loved sincerely above all others'.[75]

The summer was not finished dealing tragedy. At the end of August, the 3-month-old Prince William passed away. It has often been thought that the little boy also died of plague; the truth of this is uncertain, though the Black Death had indeed arrived in England at some point that month.[76] Having lost their second child in two months, Philippa and Edward were overwhelmed with grief. They spared no expense for the little boy's funeral, which took place on 5 September 1348 at Westminster Abbey. A chariot covered in black cloth brought the body to his place of burial. The coffin was placed in state within the church, surrounded by black cloth and silk hangings stamped with gold; 170 torches blazed around the coffin, and 50 poor people were paid to mourn for the prince.[77]

Prince William was buried beside his sister Blanche, who had been laid to rest five years earlier, but Philippa and Edward had no such closure for their daughter Joan, whose body had been left behind in Bordeaux. Edward seems to have dealt with his grief by deciding to face the deadly disease head-on, for at the end of October he organised a trip to Calais, ostensibly to attempt to progress peace negotiations with France, taking his son and heir Prince Edward with him. The journey was seen as incredibly dangerous, for France was feeling the worst ravages of the Black Death at this time, but Edward and his entourage returned home safely in mid-November.[78] How Philippa felt about her husband's reckless journey with their son, having just lost two children, is not recorded.

Over the winter, England felt the full devastation of the Black Death. The plague spread across the country, starting in Dorset but quickly swallowing up each new town in turn until 'all of England was violently invaded, that hardly a tenth of men or women survived' and 'cemeteries were not sufficient' to bury the dead.[79] The terror the Black Death conjured up is impossible to imagine. Across Europe, entire villages were abandoned, monasteries lay vacant as all the monks had died, and whole families vanished. Philippa and Edward were not alone in the loss of their daughter, but in comparison to most in England they came out fairly unscathed; no other member of their immediate family died even though as many as two thirds of Europe might have perished.

The following year, the royal family did what they could to keep themselves safe, but ultimately they had to continue to make progresses across the country and host celebrations to keep up morale. Edward transported his significant collection of holy relics to Kings Langley in Hertfordshire, where his court was based, to protect those gathered from the plague.[80] In October 1349, Philippa's wardrobe purchased a case to hold the basins used for washing her feet, a reminder that at this time people did, in fact, wash regularly – the queen most often of all.[81]

Edward chose this year to found a new religious college at Westminster Palace in the recently completed St Stephen's chapel. He dedicated the college (a religious community, rather than a school) to his patron, the Virgin Mary, to whom he had shown great dedication throughout his life.[82] The interior of the chapel was filled with the glory of Edward's family with Philippa. The walls were meticulously painted with stunning frescoes showing Edward and Philippa flanked by eight of their children: the boys behind their father, and the girls behind their mother. This portraiture was quite an innovation, as previous dynastic depictions had focused on glorifying oneself through one's ancestors or relatives, rather than one's children. The boys were depicted wearing armour, and the girls in sumptuous, fashionable clothes.[83] Edward and Philippa were making a powerful statement with their choice of artwork.

As the 1340s came to a close, the royal family would have had much to reflect on. They had started the decade in foreign lands, waging Edward's dynastic war for the French throne. Philippa had given birth to six more children, though she had lost two of them as infants as well as her teenage daughter. The years had been filled with highs and lows, seeing the greatest and most glorious of Edward's victories yet, but also the death of many other members of their extended family and the loss of many valuable allies. The complicated web of intermarriage that dominated western Europe meant that Philippa had ended up with family on both sides of the war with France, and this must have taken an emotional toll, no matter how loyally she stuck by her husband's side. The decade had ended in a deep, collective tragedy with the utter desolation of the Black Death. But Philippa and Edward were fighters, and they were determined to exert their rights and demonstrate their wealth and glory on a global stage. Together, the couple could take on the world.

5

The End of an Era

Edward III was a great king, and he wanted everybody to be sure of this fact. When he had come to the throne as a teenage boy, he and his young wife had been restricted in their freedom and income. Over two decades later, Edward was conquering France and had control of the Scottish king. With the recent establishment of the Order of the Garter, Edward needed to make sure his kingdom was as glamorous as his person, which was increasingly draped in luxurious furs and silks dyed in a rainbow of colours. As Windsor Castle was to be the home of the order, it needed to be one of the most impressive residences in the kingdom. Across the next twenty-seven years, Edward was to spend over £50,000 upgrading the castle, constructing new royal apartments, building the chapel of St George, and otherwise improving and extending the fortification. This was the most money Edward spent on any one building during his reign.[1]

Philippa undertook some building work of her own in 1350, though nothing on the scale of the king's. At the start of May, a man named Walter Wyght was ordered to bring carpenters, workmen and timber to her park at Brigstock in Northamptonshire for some building work. On the same day, the warden of the forest of Rockingham was to make sure the enclosure of her park at Brigstock was completed by allowing Wyght to construct dykes, deer leaps and lodges in the park and make any other necessary repairs. In October, Philippa ordered carpenters, stonemasons and plasterers to repair houses and buildings within her castle of Devizes in Wiltshire.[2] Philippa, too, was making sure royal appearances were up to scratch.

In late February, King Alfonso XI of Castile died of plague, which was still raging across Europe, making Prince Pedro king just shy of his sixteenth birthday.[3] If Princess Joan had not died on her way to marry the boy, she would now have become queen. As it was, the would-be alliance turned to hostility. A member of a cadet branch of the Castilian royal family, Don Carlos de la Cerda, made an alliance with the French, who were desperate to disrupt Edward any way they could. In the first half of 1350, la Cerda plundered numerous English ships, stealing their cargo and killing the men on board. Whilst a truce brokered between England and France in June meant that King Philip had to cut his ties with the Castilian pirates, la Cerda decided his escapades were too profitable to give up, and he parked his fleet firmly in the Channel.[4]

Edward could not stand this insult to his kingship and the theft and slaughter of his people, and so in August he launched an English fleet to disperse the Castilians. Edward by no means had the upper hand in this battle, for the Castilian ships were far greater in size than the English and were equipped with missiles to attack smaller ships with. Philippa accompanied Edward to the coast, where she was lodged in an abbey overlooking the sea from which she could observe the battle. Edward had also brought along two of his sons, Prince Edward and Prince John. John was only 10 years old, and even by medieval standards was not considered old enough to fight, but he joined Prince Edward on his ship because Edward 'was very fond of him'.[5]

Philippa watched as the Battle of Winchelsea unfolded on 29 August. The battle was hard fought, and both Edward and the princes' ships were badly damaged. Edward had to move on to a captured Castilian ship during the battle as his own was sinking rapidly, whilst the princes were rescued by the Earl of Lancaster just before their own ship sank.[6] From her position on the land Philippa would not have known the full extent of what was going on, even though the weather was clear enough to see the battle. If she could see the royal ships sinking, she would have had no knowledge of whether her husband and sons were on board or not. Thankfully for the queen, who 'had suffered great anxiety' that day, the king and princes all survived unharmed. The battle was a great victory for the English, who captured over a dozen Castilian ships whilst losing few of their own. English casualties had been heavy, however, and Edward rewarded eighty survivors by knighting them.[7]

The following year was a quiet one for Philippa and Edward. Even though at 37 years old she was still fertile, it was almost three years since Philippa had last had a child. This might have been an active choice on her behalf. She had given birth to eleven children in eighteen years, meaning she had spent the past two decades in an almost constant state of pregnancy or recovery from giving birth. Many of her pregnancies had signs of having caused her difficulty, including a couple of potential premature births, and the grant by the pope years earlier to eat meat for her health certainly suggests that it had all taken a toll on her body. As much as the king and queen still adored each other – and were almost constantly in each other's company – their physical intimacy might have taken a back seat to Philippa's wishes to stop having children.

Rather than caring for more children, Philippa focused on properly managing her resources and vast landed estate. In May, men were hired to work a lead mine in the region of her castle of High Peak in Derbyshire to use for her various building works. In August, she ordered carpenters, stonemasons, plumbers, tilers and plasterers to bring a variety of resources to Banstead Manor in Surrey for works she was carrying out there. The following month, the clerk of her wardrobe was asked to bring timber from her parks and stone from her quarries to Kent for preparation, ready to be stored in her Great Wardrobe in London for when it was needed.[8]

Towards the end of 1351 or early 1352, Philippa received a visit from members of her family. Her nephew, William of Bavaria, and his mother, Philippa's sister Margaret, came to England to stay at the court. In early 1352 William married Matilda of Lancaster, the daughter of Edward's cousin the Duke of Lancaster. Philippa had a chance to meet with her sister once more, this time under happy circumstances rather than fighting for their inheritance.[9]

Just as Philippa's sister was preparing to leave England in March, sad news arrived in England: Countess Jeanne of Hainault had died.[10] Philippa would have felt the loss of her mother keenly. Jeanne had played an important role throughout her life, and the pair were closer than many other women in Philippa's position. It was not common for a daughter of Philippa's status to see her mother so many times after she had left for marriage. The closeness between Philippa and her own children was a mirror of her own relationship with Jeanne, and her death would have left a hole in her life.

Towards the end of February 1352, Philippa launched a huge investigation across all of her landed holdings. A group of men were assigned to investigate parkbreaks across at least 110 of her properties throughout England for a plethora of related offences: stealing royal goods and items from shipwrecks, hunting deer, rabbits, pheasants and partridges, destroying her crops and felling her trees, and assaulting her ministers. However, there was perhaps a more important offence that needed investigating, for 'a great number of her ministers and others, by conspiracy had between them, have concealed and withdrawn rents, escheats, wards, marriages and other profits pertaining to her ... and still take the profits to their own use'.[11]

Philippa's own men had been stealing from her, exploiting her land to their benefit, and by oppressing local people they had encouraged retaliation on her lands. This not only hurt Philippa financially, but led to the ruin of vast swathes of land and damaged the royal reputation in local communities. This could not stand, and at the head of the investigation Philippa and Edward appointed Sir John Molyns, a man they trusted well. Molyns would make sure the injustices were rooted out, but it seems he did too thorough a job: in the next parliament, called in September 1353, the Commons dealt with many petitions complaining about the 'extremely heavy fines and amercements' that Molyns had assigned during his investigation.[12]

Aside from Molyns's investigation, 1353 passed with little incident. Life felt like it was taking on a slower pace, and Edward was amenable to envoys of the new pope, Innocent VI, suing for permanent peace between England and France. Edward seems to have suffered with ill health during the summer, for on 31 July he paid his apothecary over £16 for medicines for his use. Whatever Edward was afflicted with, it was probably not very severe, for he continued to move between various palaces throughout the summer.[13]

Philippa spent Christmas with her family at Eltham Palace, where Prince Edward participated in a festive jousting competition.[14] Her eldest son was now 23 years old, and he was a handsome, athletic man like his father. He was shaping up to be a noble prince, having already become an experienced military man; Philippa had reason to be proud in how successfully she and Edward had raised him. Other monarchs had struggled to control their wilful sons who were eager to exercise the reins of kingship before their time, but Philippa and Edward had cultivated a loving, harmonious family. There were no hints of discord among them.

As the summer of 1354 arrived, Philippa had to deal with a shocking realisation: she had fallen pregnant again. She had not given birth for six years, and this year she celebrated her fortieth birthday. Perhaps she had reason to believe she was no longer fertile, and so she and Edward had resumed marital relations, and if this were the case then she now stood to be corrected. She must have approached the birth of her twelfth child with trepidation. She had struggled in the past and she was now a lot older. Her body had taken the effects of all of her previous births, and she might have been fearful for her health and her life.

In early January the following year, Queen Philippa gave birth to her final child, a little boy named Thomas. Mother and baby both came out of the experience healthy, at great relief to the royal family. Just over a month later, at the end of February on the first Sunday of Lent, Philippa's churching was held at the palace of Woodstock, where she had given birth. Edward held a huge feast and tournament to celebrate the surprise of his latest child, and the baby was baptised by the Bishop of Durham.[15]

Summer brought Philippa the joyful news of the birth of her first legitimate grandchild. There is a single record in 1349 that references an illegitimate child of Prince Edward, but nothing else is known of this supposed child.[16] This time, the happy father was her second surviving son, Prince Lionel, who had not yet turned 17 years old but had already been married for fourteen years. The child was a girl, and she was named Philippa in honour of her grandmother the queen. Philippa must have been overjoyed to see the birth of a little grandchild, though it did serve to highlight the unexpected birth of her own child earlier that year. Philippa acted as godmother to the little girl, who was baptised at Eltham Palace.[17]

Philippa had celebrated the birth of this child in the midst of war preparations, for at the start of July Edward III had put plans into place to restart the war with France, and he decided to take all four of his grown sons with him.

The infant Prince Thomas was appointed Guardian of the Realm, though he was barely 6 months old, as his siblings went off to war.[18] The youngest was Prince Edmund, who was turning 14 this year. At the end of October, Philippa said goodbye to her husband and sons, and she once more had to wait behind for news of their health and survival. In the end, Edward was only abroad for two weeks, and Philippa was reunited with her husband for Christmas, which the couple spent at Newcastle.[19]

When King Edward had returned to England, Prince Edward had remained behind in France, moving to the south of the country. Prince Edward spent the next months fortifying Gascony with his army, and encouraging local nobles to provide their own men and supplies. Throughout 1356 he attacked French territories with a number of chevauchées – short raids where towns were plundered and burnt. On 19 September the prince met the French king, John II, in battle just outside the city of Poitiers.

The resulting battle was one of the most famous of Edward's reign, and the most famous of Prince Edward's lifetime. Though heavily outnumbered by the French, the leadership of the English prince saw an unprecedented victory for the English. Most crucially of all, King John and one of his sons were captured at the battle. English chronicles describe the battle with glee, dedicating pages and pages to the tide of battle and the changes of fortune experienced by the English, bragging of not only the elite prisoners taken, but the sheer number of them; one chronicle claimed 2,000 men-at-arms were captured.[20]

In May 1357, Prince Edward returned to England to be reunited with Philippa and the rest of his family, whom he had not seen in over eighteen months. The prince hastened to the capital with the French king and his son, alongside a plethora of the most powerful French nobles. London was jubilant, and its citizens lined the street dressed in their best clothes to be part of the glory.[21] Philippa watched on proudly as her son fulfilled the greatest hopes of his father. England now had two foreign kings captive within its fortresses, and Edward's domination of his area of Europe seemed complete. With the arrival of the French king in England, the Scots finally decided to come to terms and in October a peace treaty was signed. A ransom was agreed for King David, and he was allowed to temporarily return to Scotland to raise the funds to secure his permanent release.[22]

Throughout the year, a number of royal servants were rewarded for their long service to Philippa and her family, and no member of the household was too insignificant to be remembered. A collection of smaller rewards were dished out, from 2*d* a day given to a John de Wykyneston, an annuity of 10 marks (around £6 13*s*) to Peter de Wyght, and £6 a year to Maud de Pudyngton. Favours for having served the queen could be far more significant, as Richard de Lancastre found out when he was pardoned for murder due to his good service to Edward and Philippa.[23]

The grants relating to Philippa found within the Patent Rolls this year could suggest that Philippa's health had taken a turn. Numerous grants that she made giving land and other favours to her servants and subjects include terms for if the grantee was to 'survive the queen' – the grants were making provisions for after Philippa's death.[24] Philippa had turned 43 this year, and whilst this was a significant age for her time, it was not unreasonable to expect a woman of her status to live for several more decades. Her mother-in-law, Queen Isabella, had likely just entered her sixty-second year after all. To include provisions for 'if the queen [shall] die' does make it seem as though it was expected she could do so soon.

There are no explicit mentions of Philippa's ill health, so it is not clear what might have been wrong with her this year to prompt the inclusion of these terms, though it has been suggested she might have suffered from gynaecological problems after the birth of her last child.[25] After this point, her life certainly did start to slow down, and she did not make any grand travels to the furthest extents of her husband's kingdom as she had in her youth. It might be that the effects of giving birth to so many children had taken a toll on her body that she was now feeling as she entered middle age.

As autumn arrived, Edward had begun a schedule of tournaments and celebration. With three kings at the English court it had become a hub of international activity, as foreign nobles came to visit their captive monarchs and revel in the luxury of Edward's monarchy. The Scottish king had spent a decade in English hands, and now Edward also controlled the French king. The season of pageantry he and Philippa embarked on was not only to celebrate their victories, but to cement their power and wealth in the minds of all who attended, and the captive kings were to play a great part in this.

The first tournament was one held at Smithfield in London, with knights from England, Scotland and France all participating in front of their kings. The Christmas court was held at Marlborough in Wiltshire, and the royal family moved on to Bristol for the Feast of the Epiphany in early January where Edward organised the first tournament in England to take place at night.[26] But it was at the Garter feast of 1358 that Edward's extravagance truly reached its peak.

Edward sent heralds across the kingdom to proclaim that any knight from anywhere in the world would be welcome to attend a tournament held during the celebrations. The people of Europe duly answered, and as well as the captive French king and his nobles, Edward's sister Queen Joan of Scotland came down to attend accompanied by a plethora of Scottish ladies, as did a myriad of Continental nobles.[27] The resulting celebrations were some of the greatest England was to see during Edward's lengthy reign, and Philippa was at the centre of the festivities: Edward had ordered the keeper of his wardrobe to grant her a staggering £500 to make outfits for her to wear during the revelries.[28]

Edward and his wife saw much of Queen Isabella through the first half of 1358, all hints of earlier rifts seemingly mended. Edward, Philippa and Prince Edward had visited Isabella in her London home in October the previous year, and Edward made his own visits to his mother in March, April, May and July this year.[29] These regular visits certainly suggest affection, rather than trips borne out of duty, though Isabella's royal blood was certainly useful to provide diplomatic links with the captured French king. Philippa seemingly had her own personal relationship with her mother-in-law, for the two women dined together in London on 11 May this year.[30]

The healing of the rifts between mother and son were welcome, for Isabella of France died in August 1358. This great queen had been one of the most influential figures of the fourteenth century. Her queenship had seen much, and she had made English history by overthrowing her husband and ruling for herself for several years. Her lengthy widowhood led to an unusual situation where for thirty years there had been both a queen consort and a queen dowager in England, and though Philippa had been a dazzling queen in her own right, her mother-in-law's shadow was ever present. Despite this, there is no evidence that Philippa ever held resentment against Isabella for her role in Edward's reign. Philippa stood by her husband's side at the end of November when the queen was buried at her request at the Greyfriars church in London, the resting place of Isabella's aunt Margaret, who had married Edward III's grandfather.[31]

At the end of the year, Lionel's 3-year-old daughter Philippa was married to 6-year-old Edmund Mortimer, the great-grandson of the disgraced Roger Mortimer whom Edward had executed decades earlier.[32] Edward was not a vindictive man; he had forgiven Mortimer's family for the father's crimes many years ago, and both he and Philippa attended the nuptials. With the marriage of their granddaughter, it became even more apparent that only one of Philippa and Edward's many children was in fact married. This had not been from lack of trying on their parents' behalf, and most of their children had already been betrothed many times, but none of the planned marriages had come to fruition in the ever-changing politics of the four-teenth century. Plans now swung into place to rectify this, and over summer the couple organised the betrothals of their son John and their daugh-ter Margaret. John married Blanche of Lancaster, his third cousin and the daughter of the Duke of Lancaster. Margaret, meanwhile, was to wed John Hastings, the 2nd Earl of Pembroke.[33]

Though the end of 1358 had been bustling with wedding plans, it was also marred by tragedy. Not only was the funeral of Queen Isabella a source of mourning, but Philippa suffered a horrendous accident at this time. Philippa and Edward loved going out riding and hunting, and had done so together on countless occasions. But this summer, whilst hunting with Edward around Marlborough, Philippa's 'shoulder was torn apart from the joint'.[34] This accident was severe enough to be recorded in a local chronicle, and it certainly sounds like an incredibly painful injury. It would have taken weeks, if not months, for Philippa to recover, and it seems that she was never able to hunt again after this incident.[35]

Philippa spent the first part of 1359 recovering from her injuries and pre-paring for the grand wedding of Prince John. In summer, Edward's two-year truce with France expired and he demanded a settlement be found that was, of course, greatly favourable to him. He did, after all, have their king in his possession. The French, though, were not amenable to Edward's great demands and so in the autumn he gathered an army and crossed the Channel to force them to submit.[36] His four elder sons joined him once more, and as Prince John's new wife was already pregnant, Edward suggested the 17-year-old girl stay in Philippa's household so she could be well cared for.[37]

Blanche gave birth to her child in March the following year whilst her husband was still abroad. Philippa would have carefully arranged the circumstances of the birth to make sure her daughter-in-law was well looked after, and that her next grandchild was born safely. The child was a little girl, who – as with Lionel's first daughter – was named Philippa in the queen's honour.

Over the winter of 1359–60, Edward experienced disappointment in France. The campaign he had launched had not been as successful as he hoped, and so by spring he was ready to negotiate with the French once more. This led to a formal agreement, the Treaty of Brétigny, which appeared to finally solve the question of the war. Edward agreed to renounce his claims to the French throne and to the sovereignty of Brittany, but in return he received sovereignty of Aquitaine and extra territories in France. Importantly, the ransom of King John of France was set at a staggering 3 million gold florins, or £500,000.[38]

News of the peace was dispatched to England, where Philippa sent one of her messengers to King John to inform him of the treaty. A few days later, Philippa and King John dined together at Westminster Palace in celebration.[39] John was to be allowed to return to France after an initial ransom payment, and in return a number of his most powerful nobles would be sent as hostages to England as surety for the rest. Edward landed back in England in the middle of May, and a few days after his return the royal household experienced a huge change.

On 26 May 1360, the households of King Edward and Queen Philippa formally merged into one. The royal household in the medieval period was a fluid entity, with servants moving between serving the king, the queen and their children as need dictated. When the king and queen lived together, the two households integrated, but the queen's household was often merely a sub-entity of the king's: both of Edward I's wives had been dependent on his own household, and even Queen Isabella's household had often merged with her husband's. In Philippa's time her household had formed a semblance of independence, allowing the queen to pay for her own clothes, food and servants from her own income, even though she often accompanied Edward on his travels.[40]

Time and again, though, it had been shown that Philippa's income was not set up to fully fund her. Throughout her reign, Edward had constantly increased her landed estate and grants from the exchequer to help her deal with ever-growing costs. Just the previous year, he had granted her dozens more pieces of income 'beyond the lands already assigned to her in dower which are insufficient for the necessary expenses of her household and chamber'.[41] The largest of these grants was a huge addition to her income at £2,000 a year.

Despite all of these increases to her income, Philippa had ever been in debt. Upon the merger of their households, Edward assigned over £5,800 to pay off her creditors. The exact organisation of this new, joint household is unclear, but Philippa was to pay £10 a day into Edward's wardrobe to pay the expenses of her servants, who would come to work within the joint household. The new, shared household numbered in the region of 400 servants to serve both king and queen, showing the astounding costs of maintaining royalty at this time.[42]

It has long been assumed that the households were merged as a way to curb Philippa's excessive spending. Indeed, the new arrangement was likely part of a wider attempt at financial reform in the English government at this time. But this cannot be the full story. Looking at previous queens, Philippa's household's complete independence was in fact an unusual situation, and so returning to a joint household was returning to an old standard of managing the expenses of the queen.

Though Philippa had constantly been given more and more money over the years, the context of these grants is important. Philippa had given birth to twelve children, and though not all had lived, most of them spent many of their formative years in her company and care. In the past two centuries, only Edward's grandmother Eleanor of Castile had rivalled her in the number of her children, and many of them had died as infants, lessening the pressure on her personal expenditure. Philippa needed to have her income constantly supplemented to account for paying for the miniature households of her own children. But beyond that, Edward had spent his entire reign spending with abandon as part of his grand propaganda scheme. If he were to be the greatest king since Arthur, who created knightly orders and conquered Scotland and France, he needed the expenditure to match – and so did Philippa.

The great individual expenses of Philippa always came as part of ceremony, particularly for her churchings. The astounding £500 spent on her clothes for the Windsor tournament of 1358 had been part of Edward's statement to western Europe of his glory. Though Philippa most likely did have a great taste for luxurious clothes and fabulous jewels, she was a powerful queen who had a need for this. And though she was often in debt, this more likely reflects the failure of the English government to provide adequate income for her to live up to Edward's dreams.

Though Philippa's household was in nearly £6,000 of debt, the household of Queen Eleanor of Provence in the previous century had at times hit a deficit of £22,000.[43] Philippa's income, in reality, was not enough to sustain a great queen, and it is no wonder she constantly ran into debt. Her original dower, and that of the previous two queens, was around £4,000–£4,500 a year, but Philippa's eldest son had lands worth nearly £10,000 and Queen Isabella had died with over £12,700 in assets.[44] If the queen dowager had died with that much money, then Philippa's income should have far exceeded that, but it did not.

The final consideration of the merger is Philippa's poor health. For the last few years there had been hints that she might not have been very well, and her riding accident only compounded her health problems. During the 1360s, Philippa steadily became more and more ill. Philippa and Edward had spent a significant part of their lives travelling together and staying in the same properties, and so it might now have been decided that it was simply practical for the two households to unite formally. After all, Edward was about to have two kings' ransoms enter the English coffers. If he wanted to grant Philippa a larger income to support herself, he could have done so easily.

Christmas 1360 was spent by the royal family in bliss. Philippa and Edward were joined by Edward's sister Queen Joan of Scotland, as well as their three daughters – Isabella, Mary and Margaret – and certainly their eldest son Edward, if not their other sons. The royal family were dressed in the finest new clothes and furs for the festivities.[45] But the next year was to be marred with death. The end of 1360 had already seen the deaths of two of Edward's cousins, and now March 1361 claimed the life of the Duke of Lancaster, Edward's second cousin and father-in-law of Prince John.[46] The whole royal family attended his funeral in Leicester, but little were they to know that the year was to claim more of those dear to them.

In happier news, another of the royal children was married this year when Princess Mary was betrothed to John de Montfort. John was the child of Joanna of Flanders and the senior John de Montfort, whose claim to the duchy of Brittany Edward had championed so many years ago. John had been brought up at the English court after the death of his parents, and he was now a dashing 22-year-old man. Mary was five years younger than him and with the marriage Edward was tidying up the enterprise he had started so many years before. The next year, Edward was to pass suzerainty of Brittany to John, making him Duke of Brittany, and the marriage of his daughter to him was both a goodwill gesture and a way to ensure John's loyalty in future.[47] The wedding took place in the summer, and Mary wore a robe made from cloth of gold and furred with ermine.[48]

Another of Philippa's children was busy this year helping Edward with his political ambitions, for in September Prince Lionel was made Lieutenant of Ireland. Ever since Lionel was a toddler, Edward had designated Ireland for him by marrying him to a great Irish heiress, and now that he was in his early twenties he was considered capable of tackling the difficult kingdom. Ireland had long been a thorn in the side of English kings and now the country was in turmoil, with the Irish Great Council begging for help from England. Lionel was to be sent to wrangle the country into submission and he spent significant periods across the next five years there – at the time, this was the longest period that any member of the English royal family had spent in the country.[49]

But just as Lionel left to prove himself to his parents, death returned to the royal household. In September Princess Mary died suddenly, having never set foot in her new home of Brittany, and just weeks later Princess Margaret also died. The two princesses were the youngest two daughters of Philippa and Edward, and they were just 16 and 14 respectively. Both had survived the dangers of childhood, and had bright futures ahead with their new husbands. What caused the deaths of the two girls is not known, but the year had seen a return of the 'great pestilence'. As both died so close to each other it is possible they had followed the way of their sister Joan and also died of the plague.[50]

The loss of the two princesses left the court reeling. Just months before, the household had been buzzing with energy preparing for Mary's wedding, and now they were mournfully organising her funeral. Philippa and Edward's grief must have been severe. Philippa had given birth to five daughters in total, but now only their eldest, Princess Isabella, remained. The two girls were buried together at Abingdon Abbey in Berkshire, and the royal family was left to mourn.

Whilst in the midst of death, Philippa and Edward had some happiness to cling to, when in October their eldest son Prince Edward finally married, aged 31. Prince Edward had chosen his own bride, and rather than marrying a foreign princess, as was expected of the heir to the throne, he chose an extremely unconventional bride, a woman named Joan of Kent. Joan was two years older than the prince, and had already been married – controversially she had in fact been engaged in a bigamous marriage as a young woman. When she was around 13 years old, she had secretly married a knight who subsequently left on military campaign. Her parents, oblivious of the clandestine vows, married her to another nobleman, and the first marriage was not revealed until eight years later when her husband returned to claim her.

Joan had also already had children with her previous husband, and she was first cousin to King Edward III, making the married couple very closely related. Despite all the reasons that the marriage was a bad idea on paper, Joan had been brought up in Philippa's household alongside Prince Edward and the pair had retained their friendship throughout their lives. Now they were in love, and neither Philippa nor Edward stood in their way. They must simply have been happy that their son was happy. Having faced so much death, that must have been all they wanted right now.

With the arrival of spring in 1362, hope was again in the air. This was the year that King Edward would turn 50. The Garter feast was celebrated, as was now tradition, in April at Windsor Castle. Work had been ongoing at

Edward's glorious knightly centre for many years now, and this year Philippa too put her glamorous mark on the buildings. Whilst mirrors were not uncommon among the upper echelons of European society, they were small, often hand-held. So Philippa now ordered the creation of one of the most unique rooms of her time: a chamber of mirrors.

Boards were purchased to slot the mirrors into, and the finished effect would have been extraordinary. No one in England and very few beyond would have seen a room like it, and visitors would have been awestruck at the wealth and luxury of the English monarchy. Between the mirrors, the walls were lit with stained glass windows, and the combination of the glass and mirrors would have bounced light and colour across the chamber. Next door was a dancing room for the court to gather and celebrate, and both rooms would have been filled with the greatest lords and ladies of western Europe during its day.[51]

The chamber has unkindly been called a vanity project of Philippa's, saying that it shows she enjoyed 'reflecting on her appearance', and whilst this could have been the case, the uniqueness of this room in her chambers cannot all be put down to personal narcissism. At this time, the French king and many of his most important and powerful nobles were captive in England, and they made regular appearances at Edward's Windsor tournaments. Foreign knights were usually invited to take part in jousting and feasting at the castle, and this room was not a private room for Philippa's use alone. The room was an important part of Edward's propaganda. If he was to be one of the greatest kings of his time, powerful enough to be the first king of both England and France, he needed to show this visually to everyone around him. For his wife to have a chamber of mirrors and light that all of the most important people of their time would pass through on their way to dance was a striking message indeed.

As summer arrived, Prince Edward and his wife Joan were bestowed Aquitaine in order to rule Edward's newly enlarged territory there on his behalf.[52] Though Prince Edward was preparing to leave his mother behind for an extended period of time, there was a new arrival at court this year who was to have a profound impact on our understanding of Edward's reign and of Philippa in particular. At this time, a young man named Jean Froissart left the court at Philippa's home of Valenciennes and travelled to England.

Froissart was about 24 years old and to prove his worth he brought along a book he had written.[53]

The content of Froissart's first book has been lost along with the volume itself, but he obviously impressed Queen Philippa, for she took him into her household as a clerk of her chamber. Within the next few years, Froissart would become a literary staple in Philippa and Edward's court, writing 'handsome ditties and madrigals of love', but perhaps more importantly for us, gathering information from anyone he could talk to at court, including Philippa herself.[54] Later in life, Froissart would use this information to compose his chronicle of Edward's reign, a key source for historians. As Philippa was his patron, Froissart endeavoured to include her throughout his chronicle, giving a rare insight into her life; most chroniclers tended to ignore women, even queens.

Before the year ended, there was one more set of sorrow and joy for the royal family. In September, Edward's sister Joan – who was still residing at the English court – died. Joan was the last of Edward's siblings, and with both his parents dead too, Edward was the last remaining member of his family. Joan was buried at Greyfriars church near to her mother.[55] But Edward had his family with Philippa, and in November, as he celebrated his fiftieth birthday with them, he gave Lionel, John and Edmund suitable places among the peerage: Lionel was made Duke of Clarence, John was made Duke of Lancaster and Edmund was made Earl of Cambridge.[56]

With the advent of 1363, King Edward III of England and Queen Philippa of Hainault celebrated their thirty-fifth wedding anniversary. Their marriage had been one of the strongest England's royal family had seen, and even as they approached middle (or old) age their love had not wavered. The couple were constantly in one another's company, enjoying their time together as they travelled from one glamorous palace to the next. But Philippa was starting to get sicker. So many years of childbirth, a severe riding accident and natural ageing were taking their toll on her body.

Though provisions for Philippa's death had begun appearing in grants several years previously, from 1363 onwards such phrasing increases in frequency. From this time, her mobility began to be impaired, and the royal couple generally confined their movements to within the reach of the Thames, allowing them to travel more comfortably by barge.[57] It was around this time, too, that Philippa became aware of disturbances in her own household. Rumour had it she was no longer the only woman in Edward's affections.

About two years previously, Philippa had taken on a new damsel in her household called Alice Perrers. Alice was a member of London's mercantile class, and a somewhat unusual choice for Philippa's ladies. But Edward's household had always been open to those who worked hard to better themselves, and Philippa extended this grace to her own home. This was now to backfire on her, as the much younger woman caught the eye of the king. Alice was about 20 years old, had a body unmarked by childbearing, and was an attractive, intelligent woman. As much as Edward adored Philippa, and always would, Philippa's failing health has usually been linked to Edward looking to Alice for physical comforts that Philippa could not give him, and the timing certainly lines up well for this to be the case.

Though it has been said that it was 'doubtful' that Edward had been entirely faithful to Philippa throughout his marriage, there is no real reason to believe otherwise.[58] True, it was very common for high-status men at this time to have mistresses or one-off illicit liaisons with other women, but there were still plenty of examples of men faithful to their wives throughout their lives. At no previous point in his reign was Edward ever accused of having been with another woman, and so there is no concrete evidence to lead us to think he had not been faithful up to now. The only hint at indiscretion had been a slanderous story spread by the French that Edward had raped the Countess of Salisbury back in 1342 after he had fallen in love with her beauty. This story was false, with almost none of the details lining up with fact, and was simply intended to besmirch Edward's reputation years after the alleged incident.[59]

It has also been suggested by multiple historians that Edward's blossoming romance with Alice Perrers had Philippa's acceptance and even her blessing.[60] This seems unlikely. Whilst Philippa could feasibly have begrudgingly accepted Edward having a short affair here or there, accepting he was a man of his time, his new relationship with Alice struck at the heart of Philippa's home. Her own lady-in-waiting, who served her daily as a companion, was sleeping with her husband, and this was no short-term affair. Edward was to stay with Alice until Philippa's death and beyond. As Philippa grew sicker and sicker and began to contemplate her own death, it must have stung to know that her once-devoted husband now had another woman to fill his time with.

Though Philippa was struggling in her personal life, she continued to fulfil her queenly duties where she could. Over summer and into autumn she obtained pardons for two people indicted for murder, and another sentenced to death for stealing spoons and cloth worth 10s.[61] She also again ordered investigations into misdemeanours on her land with the help of her council; one to find those who had carried away a whale and fish in her lands in Ipswich, and others into parkbreaks in Yorkshire and Huntingdonshire.[62]

In April 1364, King John of France died in London. Though he had been free to return to his kingdom a few years before, he had voluntarily returned to England to restore his honour after his son Louis, who had been left as one of the hostages against payment of the ransom, escaped English custody the previous summer. His actions dismayed his French subjects, but he was greeted in England with jubilation and welcomed back by Philippa and Edward, who had lodged him at the Savoy Palace.

With John's death, Edward had his body honourably conveyed to Paris so that the king could have a suitable royal burial in his homeland. His body might well have been accompanied by Philippa's loyal lady, Marie de St Pol, the Countess of Pembroke. Marie had been a lifelong friend of Philippa's, ever since her arrival in England so many decades ago, and now she was entrusted with a most important task by Philippa. It was around this time – perhaps spurred by the death of John – that Philippa seriously turned her mind to providing an adequate tomb for the time of her own departure.

Marie was given a payment of just over £66 'for the making of the queen's tomb at Paris, on the order of the said queen', as she had identified the perfect sculptor for Philippa's tomb. A gentleman known as Jean de Liège had been working for the French royal family for a few years by this time, carving various tombs and monuments, and his skills were evidently greatly appreciated by them. Philippa had a great appreciation for French fashion and art due to her heritage and upbringing, and so a sculptor used by her French relatives would be the perfect person to design her own tomb monument.[63]

The tomb that Liège would ultimately create was an innovation in English royal burials. Philippa's figure was carefully carved out of stone, seemingly at her own instruction, to depict her as close to life as possible. Previous effigies of English queens had been highly symbolic, much like their representations in manuscript pictures. They showed an ideal youthful queen with free-flowing hair, but little personal identifying characteristics. In contrast, Philippa is shown as she was at the end of her life; middle-aged and plump, with a swollen belly and folds under her chin. As Philippa was alive and able to dictate how she wanted her effigy to look, this design clearly reflected her wishes to be portrayed as she was, and not as a concept.[64]

As much as Philippa has been portrayed as being obsessed with her own image, the choice of her tomb effigy instead paints a picture of a wise queen who knew who she was and was proud of it. Though historians have taken glee in describing how the effigy shows a larger woman squeezing into too-tight clothes, contemporaries might have viewed it differently. A larger woman was sometimes preferred among the aristocracy as it showed someone wealthy enough to eat well, and Philippa's clothing on her tomb reflected the latest high fashion from Paris.[65]

Showing her weight also reflects the many children whom Philippa had blessed her husband with, and how she had fulfilled her queenly duty as asked of her at her coronation decades earlier. Philippa did not intend her tomb monument to simply be a personal expression of herself, for its place in Westminster Abbey was symbolically significant for future generations. Philippa wanted to make a statement with her tomb, continuing her task even in death to promote Edward's kingship. Around her tomb was space for images of thirty-two weepers that represented her vast familial ties across Europe. Her siblings and their spouses, and her surviving children and their partners were represented on the tomb in order to 'emphasise a powerfully European dynasty' that her union with Edward had made.[66]

Though Edward had taken a mistress, his love for Philippa was still as strong as ever. They were almost constantly in each other's company during 1364, and Edward continued to give Philippa gifts to show his affection. This year he commissioned two robes for her embroidered with her English mottoes *ich wyndemuth* ('I twine myself [around you]') and *myn biddeneye* ('my bidding').[67] Philippa turned 50 this year, and she was able to celebrate with the remaining members of her family around her.

As the new year arrived, Philippa and Edward received some happy news from their son in Aquitaine: Joan of Kent had given birth to a healthy baby boy. Following tradition, Prince Edward's first legitimate son was named Edward after the line of men before him, and he now had an heir of his own. Edward could rest sure knowing that the succession was well and truly secure and he celebrated in typical fashion by hosting a grand ten-day feast and tournament.[68]

Spring 1365 saw more joy for the royal family when Princess Isabella, the eldest and only remaining princess, finally married at the unusual age of 33. Edward seized this opportunity to lavish extreme wealth on his daughter – not only through the happiness of a proud father, but because it was politically expedient to do so. Isabella was marrying a French nobleman, Enguerrand, Lord of Coucy, who had been held as a prisoner in England for the past five years. By having his daughter marry an important noble like Coucy, Edward was signalling to other French nobles that he was still an attractive alternative to the French monarchy. As such, he needed to make the wedding drip with wealth to emphasise the power of the English crown.

Edward set about ordering expensive gifts for the couple, commissioning a gold crown encrusted with sapphires and diamonds at the cost of 1,000 marks (around £666) for his daughter, and another crown intended for the groom at a huge sum of £733 6s 8d. Philippa was not to be outdone by her husband, and she gave Isabella gifts worth over £1,270.[69] In total, at least £4,505 2s 4d was paid to goldsmiths to create gifts for the couple – the equivalent of well over £2 million today.[70]

Whilst Edward and Philippa had been buoyed by the happy news their family brought them, the following year saw health scares for the couple. In spring, Philippa experienced a severe illness and had to be carefully nursed to health by her ladies. Just as she was recovering, Edward too fell sick and required his apothecary to make him a variety of medicines. The couple spent the rest of the summer at Windsor Castle and in the New Forest recovering together.[71]

Perhaps prompted by her health scare, within a few weeks of her recovery Philippa had decided that now that her own tomb was under construction, she needed to create a suitable monument to her daughters Mary and Margaret, who had died five years earlier. Whilst Edward organised payments for the work, he specified that Philippa was in control of the project.[72] Philippa was keen to properly commemorate her children and spared no expense. At least £100 was paid to construct the monuments, which sadly do not survive today, but would have beautifully portrayed her two beloved daughters.[73]

In January 1367, Joan of Kent was delivered of a second baby boy who was given the name Richard. This was Prince Edward's second legitimate son, and ultimately this little boy would become his heir – his son Edward died as a child. The news of yet another grandchild would have raised Philippa and Edward's spirits, and it was an excuse to extend the Christmas celebrations at court. The year was auspicious for the birth of English kings, for just a few months later Prince John's wife gave birth to a healthy son who was called Henry. This boy would eventually depose his cousin Richard to become king himself. For now, though, the royal family simply celebrated in the miracle of life – Princess Isabella also gave birth to her second daughter at Eltham Palace that spring, naming the girl Philippa.

At the start of the year Prince John and Prince Edward were in Spain to aid King Pedro, Princess Joan's intended, in his fight for the throne against his half-brother. The English helped Pedro win a great victory, but the campaign was an untold disaster for the future of the English crown. Whilst in Spain, Prince Edward contracted a serious disease that would debilitate him for the rest of his life, and ultimately lead to his untimely death before his father's. Never would this great prince become King of England, and instead the succession was thrown into turmoil, eventually pitting cousin against cousin. Moreover, the campaign had cost an eye-watering £405,000 and Pedro had murdered many of the prisoners-of-war, meaning the princes could not recoup their costs through ransoms.[74]

Though Philippa's health was worsening, she continued to remember those around her. In August she arranged a payment of £20 a year from the exchequer to her illegitimate sister, Elizabeth de Holand, who had come to England at some point during Philippa's reign and become a nun at Stratford-le-Bow. About a week later one of the ushers of her chamber was granted 100s a year as a reward for good service, whilst earlier in the year she had given two more of her male retainers gifts of land, property and other income.[75]

In October 1368, Philippa of Hainault and Edward III experienced the seventh death of one of their children when 30-year-old Prince Lionel died suddenly in Italy. Lionel's wife had died in 1363, and in April 1368 he had left England to undertake a second marriage to Violante Visconti, daughter of the Lord of Milan and Pavia. The marriage was designed to give Lionel access to a wealthy heiress and new Continental ambitions outside of Ireland. But just months after the wedding, Lionel was dead. Chroniclers firmly believed that he had been poisoned, but as Lionel had written his will a few weeks before his death it seems that he had in fact contracted a serious illness of some sort.[76]

A month previously, in another blow to the royal family, Prince John's wife Blanche had died. But in the world of monarchy one was not always allowed proper time to grieve, and in December Philippa sent one of her household knights with a letter to Count Louis II of Flanders proposing a marriage alliance between their families. Though years before Louis had rejected the hand of Princess Isabella, Philippa now suggested that Prince John marry the count's only child and heir, Margaret, in a move that would have eventually seen John rule Flanders as count through the right of his wife. This would finally give Edward the alliance with Flanders he had long strived to achieve, and it would give John a bright future independent of the English crown. In the end, the count declined the marriage as he had already betrothed his daughter to the Duke of Burgundy.[77] Though Philippa had been sick for many years by now and already completed her tomb ready for her impending stay within it, she was still to the end doing what she could for her family and for Edward's policies.

Christmas that year was spent with Edward and Philippa's remaining children, apart from Prince Edward, who was still in Aquitaine with his wife and two boys. Several of their grandchildren were also present, and Philippa must have relished this time together. But as soon as the festivities were over, Prince Edmund left England to join his brother in Aquitaine. Philippa would not see either of them again – she had already been parted from her eldest son for around six years.

On 15 August 1369, Queen Philippa of Hainault died at Windsor Castle. 'As long as she lived, the kingdom of England had grace, prosperity, honour and all good fortune,' mourned Jean Froissart. She had 'done so much good in her lifetime and comforted so many knights and so many ladies and damsels, and so generously gave to all her people'.[78] Froissart recounts a mournful deathbed scene. With the end near, Edward came to Philippa in her bed, where she took her hand out from under her blanket and placed it on his own. She reminisced over the wonderful reign they had had together, and asked him to grant her three dying wishes. She asked that Edward would pay her outstanding debts, and that he would maintain her donations to churches in England and beyond. 'Thirdly, my lord, I beg that you will choose no other burial than next to me, in the cloister of Westminster, when God makes his will of you.'[79]

With the death of Philippa, Edward had lost his consort of over forty years. The couple had been pledged to each other when they were mere teenagers so that his mother could overthrow his father, but their love developed into one of the greatest romances of the fourteenth century. Their adoration for each other, their closeness and desire to be together always, was remembered by chroniclers for aeons to come. Eight years later, the opening speech of Edward's parliament asked those present to 'consider, lords, if ever any Christian king or other lord in the world had so noble and gracious a lady for his wife'.[80] Philippa had been Edward's loyal companion. Her dedication to him had never wavered, though he waged war on her relatives and had an affair with her lady-in-waiting. Philippa had been the ideal English queen, and the entire nation was in mourning with her husband.

It took many months to organise Philippa's funeral. In the first few days of January 1370, the great queen was laid to rest at her tomb in Westminster Abbey. Edward had decided the exequies were to last six days to properly honour his wife. On 3 January her embalmed body was moved from Windsor Castle where it had lain for six months, and slowly made its way to the capital. The procession was filled with members of the royal household dressed in black cloth, mourning as they went. On 8 January her coffin was led through the streets of London to St Paul's Cathedral, allowing the capital to see their queen one more time.

Thousands of people thronged the streets to pay their respects to Philippa. The event was one of the greatest of their lifetime, with every noble from across the realm who could make it in attendance. The following day, Philippa's funeral was held in Westminster Abbey where her coffin was placed on a stand surrounded by blazing torches. The hearse that carried her there stayed in place in the abbey for a whole month after her death, when Edward finally allowed its removal. Alms were distributed to the poor, and at last the queen was at rest.[81]

Edward outlived Philippa by eight years, and the queen was granted her dying wish when Edward was interred in a tomb adjacent to hers. Philippa had lived to be 55 years old, had given birth to twelve children and survived the hazards of warfare and plague that had ravaged the world around her. She had been an ideal queen, interceding on behalf of her poor subjects, rewarding her servants generously and patronising religious and educational institutions. Her household had been a refuge for children and women who came under her protection when their own lives were in tumult. She formed a rare bond with many members of her extended family, keeping in touch with her parents and siblings, cousins, aunts and uncles. She bestowed presents on her children's spouses and her godchildren, making her beloved by anyone who met her.

It was not sheer flattery that led so many chroniclers and writers to eulogise her after her death. She had truly been seen as one of England's greatest queens, and her absence was to leave a hole in the country. Her death paved the way for Edward's mistress, Alice Perrers, to make her own mark on the country, and her presence was feared and hated. She was nothing compared to Philippa. But Philippa was always remembered on her own merits, for her mercy, charity and humility, even if later also for her excessive wealth and perceived greed. Philippa of Hainault was a medieval queen not to be forgotten.

6

Making a Mistress

Just after the New Year celebrations of 1376–77, a mother watched on proudly as her 12-year-old son married a young noble girl. The union promised great things for her family. The 9-year-old girl was a great northern heiress whose lands and lineage would be a great boon. Her son was no ordinary boy, however: he was the illegitimate son of King Edward III, a powerful, enigmatic man who had been ruling England for fifty years. With royal blood in his veins and a wealthy wife with significant landed estates, this young boy was fulfilling the highest hopes of his mother, a woman who could never have dreamed of such prominence in her life. But before the family could celebrate their next New Year together, all of these promises were shattered.

Alice Perrers is perhaps one of the greatest enigmas of the fourteenth century. She appeared suddenly at the court of Edward III in the early 1360s, and within a decade she had become one of the richest and most powerful people in the entire kingdom. Despite this, nothing about her origins has been known for the nearly 700 years that have passed since her meteoric rise. The only writer to make a guess at the time as to who Alice's family were was the chronicler of St Albans Abbey, Thomas Walsingham. Walsingham claimed that Alice was of base birth, being the daughter of a thatcher from

Henneye.[1] The identification of this town has been difficult to pin down, with suggestions that it could be West and East Hanney in Berkshire, or Great and Little Henny in Essex. But his statement has never really been considered as fact; throughout his chronicle, Walsingham was unfailingly critical of Alice, insulting her at every opportunity. He was disapproving of Alice's status as a mistress, and she was also involved in disputes with St Albans Abbey during her lifetime. To deride Alice as the daughter of a thatcher was a way to besmirch her name, giving her a low station in society and highlighting her unworthiness.

Another theory, which held great weight with many historians for a long time, was that Alice might have been the daughter of Sir Richard Perrers from Hertfordshire.[2] Being the daughter of a knight would account for Alice joining the court as a damsel to Queen Philippa. But if Alice was from a landed family in the same county as Walsingham then he would have written so in his chronicle. It would make no sense for him to attribute her to an unnamed person from an obscure town.

Then, in the early to mid-2000s, a ground-breaking discovery was made during a cataloguing project at the National Archives. Three hitherto-unnoticed petitions were found that gave two important clues about Alice's real identity.[3] Finally the origins of this mysterious woman began to unravel, and subsequent research began to piece together Alice's early life before her dramatic arrival at court.[4]

Alice seems to have been born in London to a family of goldsmiths as Alice Salisbury, and surviving evidence suggests that she was born in the 1340s. Traditionally, Alice was thought to have been quite young when her affair with the king started – even a young teenager. But one of the petitions revealed that Alice had been married before she had come to court, explaining why she had subsequently taken the name Alice Perrers. Alice had her first child around 1364, for which she would likely have been at least around 15 years old. But if she were this young at the birth of her first child, she would have been just 11 years old in 1360 when we now know that she was married. Although members of the nobility did often marry as young children, for members of the lower classes this practice was much less regular. It would be more common for Alice to have been in her late teens when she married and thus in her early twenties when she gave birth around 1364. Alice was therefore most likely born in the first half of the 1340s.

Being born into a network of London goldsmiths would have given Alice a privileged upbringing. During the fourteenth century the mercantile classes of London experienced a rise in wealth and fortunes; trade was booming, and craftspeople in the capital benefited from it. In fact, they were doing so well for themselves that in 1363 Edward III's parliament passed England's first sumptuary legislation. This regulated what food people could eat and what clothing they could wear, according to their status. Clothing was the most immediate visual sign of a person's class, as historically only members of the nobility could afford the most luxurious of cloth. Now, however, the new riches of London merchants meant that 'craftsmen wear the apparel of gentlemen … and poor clerks wear clothes like those of the king and other lords'.[5]

Alice was born right as this boom was happening, and so she would have had a much better upbringing than those of the decades or centuries before. She was most likely educated to some extent, something which was usually reserved for girls of the nobility. She could have learnt at home – perhaps observing her family members at their work – or she might even have attended a school, as some were running in London at this time that admitted girls.[6] Although it is unclear if Alice could write, the evidence certainly points to her being able to read as she owned several religious books in the late 1370s.[7] It is of course possible to simply own books as a status symbol without being able to read, but the fact that the books were in English suggests that Alice had at least been taught to read English at some point in her life.

Whilst Alice was a child, French was still very much the language of the court. Parliament was only opened in English for the first time in 1362, and so a large part of the government functioned chiefly using the French language.[8] The significant amount of international trade that passed through the city and the fact that England owned vast territories in France meant that it would have been useful for Alice's family to know how to speak it in their everyday lives. Alice might therefore have been taught to speak and possibly read it alongside English.

Being a member of a mercantile family at a time when London traders were experiencing an upturn in fortune and wealth meant Alice likely had a comfortable house to live in. Her family might still have only had one bedroom to share among all the family members, but she probably lived in a multi-storey house with a hall, kitchen, parlour and simple furniture. If her family were fairly successful, they would have had some soft furnishings to decorate the house with, such as woollen hangings.[9] Alice therefore would have had quite a pleasant upbringing, and her family business had found a future husband for her too.

At some point during 1342/3, a boy named Janyn Perrers joined the Salisbury family as an apprentice goldsmith.[10] Training under Alice's uncle, he would have learnt his craft alongside Alice's brother, John, who was also an apprentice. Quite where Janyn came from is unclear. His name is unusual, and initially it was thought he could have come from Italy, as Walsingham claimed that Alice had been the mistress of a man of Lombardy.[11] There is little further evidence that Janyn was Italian, though he might have been French or had French ancestry; Janyn was known to have had several French workers in his service in 1359, when he was issued a writ of protection to travel and trade in England by the crown.[12]

Half a century earlier, in the royal accounts of 1303, there is mention of a goldsmith named John le Perrier, and the surname Perrers comes from this 'Perrier', meaning a stone polisher or someone who dealt in precious gems and jewellery.[13] Therefore, it is possible that Janyn came from an established family of goldsmiths and jewellers based in London who originated in France, and after he finished his apprenticeship with the Salisburys he went on to hire fellow French workers.

Janyn Perrers would have spent several years working with the Salisburys to qualify as a goldsmith. Alice was probably born just prior to Janyn starting his apprenticeship, meaning he would have been around thirteen years older than her. He obviously continued his friendship with Alice's family through life, and as Alice grew up this connection led to the natural suggestion of their marriage. For Alice to marry another established goldsmith – one who had obviously been judged to have been of good character through his time working with her family – would have been a good marriage. She would have been able to help Janyn in his work, having learnt numeracy and other useful skills from her family's own business. Janyn was in fact doing particularly well in his business and the marriage could even have improved Alice's fortunes.

The 1359 writ that gave Janyn and his workers protection in England was issued by Edward III himself. In the writ, Edward refers to 'our beloved Janyn Perrer, our jeweller'. This significant line shows that Janyn had been providing jewels, as either a trader or a craftsperson, to the king. Janyn was clearly succeeding in his business, and if this was to continue then Alice could expect to live quite a comfortable life indeed. It was probably around this time that Alice and Janyn were married. Alice would have been aged between 16 and 18 at the end of the 1350s, and Janyn was around 30 years old. He was established in his business, and now that he was secure financially he could look to settle down and have a family. She certainly seems to have been a good choice of wife. Judging by her later career, she was almost certainly attractive, she was quite educated, was particularly intelligent and astute, and had quite a charming personality.

Whenever the couple got married, they must have been together by June 1360. At this time, Janyn and Alice purchased 3 yards of scarlet cloth and 3 yards of red cloth from tailor John Kendale in order to make a cloak for Janyn. At the same time, they bought 3 yards of black cloth to make into two pairs of black hose, and 3 more yards of mixed cloth which Janyn gave to a man named William Bridport. This purchase totalled £4 15s 8d, and was to be paid to Kendale by Christmas.[14] That Alice and Janyn were able to afford to buy cloth of this quality and cost certainly shows that they were doing well for themselves. A family could send their son to university for two years for as much money.[15] Janyn did not, in fact, pay Kendale his money by Christmas 1360, and it is not quite clear why.

If Alice was happy and settled in her new married life, then things were to shortly change. Sometime between May 1361 and May 1362, Janyn Perrers died. No record survives of what caused his death at the still rather youthful age of 31 years old. But during this year, Janyn left a bequest of 60s to the alms fund of St Dunstan, the patron saint of the Goldsmiths' Company, and by December 1362 Alice was acting as a single woman.[16] At the cusp of her twenties, Alice Salisbury – now Alice Perrers – was a young widow. It seems the couple had not yet had children together, and Alice was made executrix of Janyn's will. This will and his inquisition post mortem (an investigation into what assets a person owned upon their death) have not survived, although a later petition of John Kendale shows that Alice had to take responsibility for Janyn's debt in her capacity as executrix. Janyn might have had a piece of property to leave to Alice as a home, and she could even have been left part of his jewellery business. Alice would have had some money to sustain her, but her position was now quite uncertain. Fortunately, this was soon to change, as she swiftly managed to find her way into the sphere of the royal household.

It has long been a mystery as to when exactly Alice became a damsel to Queen Philippa. In 1366 she was described as having given long service to the queen and in 1364 she was said to be undertaking business on the king's behalf.[17] Many people from all levels of society served the queen in a variety of ways, and at least 180 women have been identified who served in her household throughout her reign.[18] There was a hierarchy of serving women: between two and six ladies who held the highest status of her servants, followed by between five and fourteen damsels. At various times Philippa also had a group of under-damsels and female night-watchers. Whilst the highest level of her handmaidens were from baronial families, most were from the landed gentry. Alice would have been an unusual choice given her social status, but she was not the only damsel with connections to mercantile families. By the time Alice joined Philippa's household, there were around thirty-one female attendants who would serve the queen every day. Alice was in an exclusive club.[19]

How Alice managed to get this esteemed place serving the queen is more mysterious. One theory is that she approached the royal family after the death of her husband, who was clearly known to the king.[20] Perhaps she was attempting to claim a debt owed to Janyn from the crown for some outstanding payments for jewellery, or she hoped that Janyn's connection to the king might be enough for a small favour. It is most likely that Alice joined the royal household at some point in 1362 after the death of her husband. This was to change her life.

In 1362, Philippa's servants were still adjusting to the merger of the king and queen's households of two years earlier. More than £5,800 was to be paid to Philippa's creditors between 1360 and 1363, and interestingly most of these creditors were tailors, embroiderers, jewellers and goldsmiths. This does lend credence to the idea that Janyn had been owed a debt by the crown and thus provided the link for Alice to join Philippa's service.[21] By the time

Alice joined Philippa's service, most of Philippa's servants were living under the same roof as the king. From this time onwards, Alice and Edward became more than well acquainted.

If Alice did become one of Philippa's damsels at this time, then it was quite a tumultuous year for her. Having just buried her husband, she would now find herself at the centre of courtly life. Her previous life as a fairly wealthy member of a London goldsmith family would have paled in comparison with the daily excess of the court. Her position saw her receive gifts of clothes from Philippa, which were likely to have been of a higher quality than she was used to, and she would have often eaten at the court and enjoyed the luxury of the palaces that Philippa stayed at. Her job required her to attend to the queen almost constantly. It would certainly have kept her busy. Being one of the lower-status women in the group around the queen might have made her feel insecure about her lowly birth, but it could well have made her – and her family – very proud to have been shown such favour.

Now that Alice had joined the court, she started to take charge of her affairs as a single woman. A week before Christmas, Alice gained her first independent landed interest. On 18 December, a knight named John de Mereworth granted Alice and another man, John de Hanneye, the manor of Westpekham in Kent.[22] In return, they would 'grant the same to him'. This was a very important deal for Alice. This is the first record of Alice making a land deal, meaning it could well be the first property she owned. Even if Janyn had left her their marital home, it was the first piece of land Alice gained an interest in by herself as a *femme sole*. That Alice was able to make such a deal with a knight supports the idea that Alice was part of the queen's household by this point. Alice would have legitimacy as the queen's damsel, and she might well have met Mereworth at court.

Perhaps more importantly, this deal is an example of 'enfeoffment-to-use' which later became very important to Alice. Under this system, someone who owned land or property (the feoffor) could grant it to another person (the feoffee) under particular instruction. The feoffee would thereby technically own the land and could draw benefits from it, but the feoffor still had an interest in the land. This system could be used for a variety of reasons. For example, if the feoffor died, the land which they had granted in this way would not come under charge of inheritance tax. The feoffee(s) could then give the income from the land to the feoffor's widow as a way to maintain her, or they could grant the land back to the heir. Moreover, the land was exempt from confiscation if the feoffor committed treason, as it was no longer technically theirs.

Enfeoffment-to-use therefore had some very important applications, but it was risky. The grantor had to trust those to whom they were giving their land, as they could steal the land for themselves because the feoffor had signed away their legal rights. That Alice was chosen to engage in this scheme shows that she must have been trusted by John de Mereworth as someone who would stay loyal to his interests. It is certainly interesting that Alice, as a recently widowed young woman, was making a land deal of this sort.

Alice now had her own landed interest in Kent, and although the nature of her deal with Mereworth is unclear, Alice was probably able to use the manor of Westpekham to live in, or at least to draw a partial income from. Having her own income and home would have given Alice a degree of independence, something she desired throughout her life. Whether Alice knew John de Hanneye, her co-feoffee, prior to this point or met him for the first time as a friend of Mereworth, he was to continue to work with her under this scheme in future.

Alice's first two years serving Queen Philippa would have been a time of great excitement for her. The glamour of the court was intoxicating. Under Philippa and Edward's patronage, the court was filled with musicians, poets and writers. Just prior to Alice's arrival, Jean Froissart had joined the court from Hainault. He wrote 'pretty ditties and treatises of love' for Philippa, and her ladies would have been around to enjoy readings of these verses.[23] Music was a constant feature at court, with trumpeters, drummers, harpists, lutenists, organists and more entertaining the king and queen and their followers. Tournaments and feasts were also a common occurrence, with Edward attending an average of ten or eleven tournaments or games in a year.[24] Though Philippa's health was deteriorating as Alice joined her service, she continued to attend many exciting courtly gatherings, bringing her ladies with her.

Alice would have also had a chance to become acquainted with members of Philippa and Edward's large family. Philippa's youngest child, Thomas of

Woodstock, was only 7 years old when Alice joined the household, and so Alice would certainly have spent time with the young boy. Philippa's older sons, meanwhile, were of an age where they were taking an active part in running the government and Alice's contact with these men would have been somewhat intermittent. In 1363, Prince Edward and his wife left England for Aquitaine and were gone for the rest of the decade, whilst Prince Lionel had been made Lieutenant of Ireland and so was busy wrangling control of the territory.

Alice would have been better acquainted with Prince John of Gaunt who spent more time in England with his wife, Blanche, with whom he was busy building a family of his own. Blanche and John were regular visitors to the court, and Blanche had previously stayed in Philippa's household when King Edward and Prince John were away fighting in France.[25] Edward and Philippa often cared for children of the nobility, and they also acted as a refuge for noblewomen, meaning there was a constant buzz of activity around the queen. Philippa's Continental connections and Edward's alliance-building meant that there were usually foreign dignitaries staying at court, not to mention the plethora of French nobles who were kept there as hostages. Alice would have met many of the greatest nobles of the time.

In late summer 1363, Alice would have accompanied the royal household in a grand progress through the Midlands. Edward and Philippa took all of their household and servants, alongside some captive French princes and nobles, to various royal hunting grounds in Northamptonshire, Leicestershire and Nottinghamshire. As well as enjoying the hunting grounds, they would have to make official appearances at local priories and towns. As one of Philippa's damsels, Alice would have played her part in displaying the majesty of the English monarchy by making sure the queen was well cared for and always looking her best. It would not have been all hard work for Alice, and she certainly would have enjoyed the formal feast at Nottingham Castle on 8 September which finished the tour.[26]

As 1364 arrived, the court started to quieten down somewhat. Apart from the annual Garter feast at Windsor in spring, Edward seems to have not held any major tournaments of his own this year. This was, at least in part, due to concerns for the health of Queen Philippa. There was an increasing need for medicine at court, with apothecaries being commissioned more frequently for a variety of medicines.[27] Alice would have been kept busy looking after the queen and tending to her when she was sick. It seems that the king was starting to rely on Alice more, too.

The first official record that ties Alice to Edward is found on 9 December 1364. An intriguing entry in the Memoranda Rolls of the City of London records that a man called Richard Lyons was ordered to 'keep the peace with Alice de Perers, and not to interfere with her going where she wished on the King's business and on her own'.[28] Alice was a young widow, and the king certainly had little need for a woman to be undertaking business on his behalf – he had plenty of male servants and courtiers to do so for him. What kind of business could Alice be undertaking? It also suggests that Alice and Richard Lyons were having a dispute that Alice asked Edward to intervene in. Lyons was a London merchant who was possibly of Flemish birth, but whatever his dealings with Alice and their potential disagreements were in 1364, the two were to become close allies within the next decade.[29]

The entry clearly indicates a close tie between Edward and Alice, and is suggestive that the couple had begun their relationship by this time. In fact, this entry could very well hint at something even bigger: that Alice was pregnant. Alice was to have three children with Edward, although their dates of birth have never been established as no records survive indicating their ages at various points in their lives. It has generally been considered by historians that all three children were born within the lifetime of the queen, leading to the need for discretion. It has also been generally agreed that Alice's son was her oldest child. He was serving abroad in the military in 1381–82 and he could not have been younger than 17 years old to be doing so. This would tentatively place his birth in 1364/65 at the latest.[30]

Of course, Alice's son could have been born several years earlier. Alice was a widow by 1361/62, and assuming that her relationship with the king did not begin until after her husband's death, this could place her son's birth anywhere between 1361 and 1365. When considering this record in the City of London's rolls, the idea that Alice was pregnant in December 1364 – or even had recently given birth – seems very plausible. It would certainly explain why Edward wanted Alice to be allowed to travel around unmolested, beyond her position as his mistress. If Alice was indeed pregnant, then it is possible her relationship with the king had been going on for a while, from the beginning of the year if not earlier. Edward's concern for Alice's wellbeing in this order does suggest that their relationship was established, rather than Alice having fallen pregnant from a short-term fling. With the court settling down and Edward travelling less from the start of 1364, then the timing would line up well for his eyes to start to drift to one of the ladies at court during this year.

The following year there was once again much activity in the royal household. Philippa's health had continued to deteriorate, and it seemed that she did not have many years left. In happier news, this year also finally saw the marriage of the king and queen's eldest daughter, Princess Isabella. Although records of the wedding do not survive, it is clear it would have been one of the biggest events of the year at court. Alice certainly would have liked to be in the thick of these elaborate celebrations, but it is unclear whether she would have been able to attend as she might have been tending to her new-born child.

Alice's first child was her only son. The little boy was given the name of John de Southeray and, like so many things in Alice's life, this name has been a source of debate. During this period, most people took their names from their trade (if from the lower classes), the place they were born or their family titles (if members of the nobility). The princes and princesses of the royal family followed this trend – Isabella, who was getting married, was known as Isabella of Woodstock for her birth at the palace of Woodstock in Oxfordshire. As such, that John was known as 'de Southeray' suggests that he was born somewhere with this place name. It has often been proposed that the surname was perhaps diminutive from 'Surrey', and this certainly is the most likely place for his birth as his name was sometimes spelled that way.[31]

Alice and her family had many connections to the county. In later years, one of Alice's daughters married a Surrey lawyer, and Edward III was often in Surrey; one of his favourite manors, Sheen, was there, and in the 1360s and 1370s Edward spent much time at his residences in the county. Alice herself had landed interests in Surrey later in life, owning a garden, dovecote, meadow and tenement in Bermondsey.[32] Alice would have wanted to give birth in a place she was comfortable in, that was tied to Edward, and that was not too far from London. Although her family were based in London, she needed to give birth in secret so as not to arouse the suspicions of the court, and so staying in London would have been too dangerous. With its proximity to the capital, perhaps some of Alice's family had property in Surrey that she was able to retreat to in order to give birth.

Alice and Edward probably decided not to name their son Edward as that would have drawn a little too much attention to their illicit relationship and it might have been considered to have been in bad taste. It was not unusual in this period for parents to name their firstborn children after themselves or, failing that, a grandparent. As Alice had a brother called John Salisbury, that might also have been her father's name; if this were the case, then the baby boy might have been given his name from his maternal grandfather.

In late November, Alice started to dip her toe into the world of property and business deals. It had been three years since her first property transaction with John de Mereworth, and she had since become much more established at court. She also now had a baby to think about. On 18 November she lent a man called Anthony de Lucy 1,000 marks (just over £666) which was to be paid back to her the following Easter.[33] Quite how Alice had so much money – the same amount as the exceedingly expensive crown given to Princess Isabella upon her marriage – to lend to Lucy is not quite clear. Perhaps she had received some favours due to her position in the royal household and she had made some wise investments with them, or perhaps Edward had given her some money following the birth of John de Southeray. She might also still have had an interest in Janyn Perrers's old business or any properties left to her by him. The following day Alice used this loan to get a deal out of Lucy. Alice submitted a cancellation of the bond, meaning Lucy did not need to repay the 1,000 marks. In return, Lucy agreed to give Alice a life estate in the manor of 'Roddeston' (Radstone, Northamptonshire) which would come to him upon his father's death.[34]

Lucy's father, the second Baron de Lucy, died sixteen days later, so Alice was swiftly to enjoy the benefits of this deal. This was a wise investment. Money was useful, certainly, but Alice was clearly aware that the wealth of the nobility at court was gained through their landed interests. Alice was still young, around 25 years old, and could expect to enjoy this estate for decades to come – certainly repaying her initial investment over time. Moreover, whilst acting as a damsel to the queen, Alice would be spending a lot of time at court and thus be enjoying privileges which came alongside that which could include food, clothes and accommodation. If Alice had saved 1,000 marks, she did not necessarily need that money at that moment in time and so shrewdly recognised the benefits of investing.

In the spring of 1366 the court received a shock with a sudden downturn in the health of Queen Philippa; she needed intense attendance by her ladies and damsels. So great was their care that on 13 May Edward rewarded them with a gift of £66 13s 4d to be split between them.[35] Alice was almost certainly among these ladies caring for the queen. One wonders what Alice's feelings were towards her rival for the king's affections, a woman around thirty years her senior who was seriously ill and beloved by courtiers and the country alike. Alice and Edward were still seeing each other two years after their relationship had begun, and perhaps Alice was someone for Edward to turn to whilst he was concerned for the life of his queen.

On 20 October Alice received a grant for life 'for long service to Queen Philippa' of two tuns of Gascon wine yearly in London.[36] The measurement of a tun could vary between regions, but in England at this time it generally measured about 955 litres.[37] Alice was being gifted nearly 2,000 litres of wine a year. Drinking wine was a symbol of status, as the lower classes could only afford ale or limited amounts of wine. At this time in England, Gascon wine cost around 6d per gallon, making the value of this gift around £10 10s a year.[38] In the fourteenth and fifteenth centuries, £10 was a significant amount for most people in society, and it was considered the minimum annual income required to support a gentleman.[39]

Wine drinking was very common among the middle and upper classes. In parts of Europe where wine was produced, the average person drank between 100 and 300 litres per year. Courts of dukes and duchesses and kings and queens, of course, had a much higher volume of consumption, with the household of Duchess Isabel of Burgundy drinking 2 litres of wine per person per day in the first half of the fifteenth century, totalling over 700 litres a year per person.[40] Even at the highest ends, then, the amount of wine given to Alice was more than enough to sustain her, with plenty extra for her own household of servants, if indeed she had any, and to entertain guests or even to sell on.

It was not necessarily unusual for royal servants to receive gifts of wine. Some other loyal servants of Edward and Philippa's had received similar grants, including four of Philippa's damsels.[41] However, gifts of money (usually in the form of annuities), or of places in religious institutions to retire, or small grants of land, were far more common ways to reward servants. Just a few weeks earlier, a Thomas Levesone had been awarded 'for long service to the king and Queen Philippa' a 60s (£3) annuity at the exchequer. A month earlier, Philippa Chaucer, wife of poet Geoffrey Chaucer, received an annuity of 10 marks (around £6 12s).[42] In this context, then, Alice's grant does stand out for its value and format, showing her as a particularly favoured member of the household.

It has previously been suggested that this grant could have been a gift upon the birth of Edward and Alice's son, John. John had in fact been born a few years earlier, but it could well have been a gift upon the birth of one of their daughters. If John was born in the first half of the 1360s, then it is likely his sisters were born within a few years of him. In this context, then, the birth of Alice's eldest daughter, Joan, in 1366 makes complete sense.

This favour to Alice, and the possible birth of her first daughter, marked a new era for her relationship with Edward. The couple had been together for several years and now had two children, marking it out as a relationship more serious than a casual fling. With this, the affair was also harder to ignore within the royal household. It has been suggested that after 1366 Alice was removed from Philippa's household as the queen could no longer tolerate her presence. Philippa might indeed have originally thought their relationship was nothing serious, but now that Alice had become pregnant with a second child of Edward's she had to accept the reality that her once-faithful husband had found space for another woman in his affections. Whilst she could do little to stop the relationship, she might indeed have requested the removal of Alice as she did not want to have the indignity of having Alice serving her on a day-to-day basis.

Also to consider is Philippa's declining health during the 1360s. Commonly given as a reason for Edward to take a mistress after so many years of apparent faithfulness to his dear wife, it might have given impetus for Edward to comply with her wishes and send Alice away. Although Philippa had been ill for several years, it was becoming apparent that she did not have long to live. It is understandable that Philippa would not want to spend her last days with her husband's mistress.

In reality, the evidence is conflicting. The idea that Alice was removed from the royal household is based on the assertion that Alice did not appear on the 1366 and 1369 livery lists for Philippa's ladies. In fact, the source quoted in support of this argument only shows that Alice was not given robes for the court's Christmas celebrations in 1368.[43] Although this is still unusual, there are many reasons why Alice might have been absent from court during this festivity. Women often came and went from court as they got married, had children and had to tend to their own estates. If we look instead at the list of the members of the royal household who were given robes to attend Philippa's funeral in 1369, Alice was named alongside all of Philippa's damsels, which suggests that she had in fact continued to serve in Philippa's household.[44]

But if Alice no longer served the queen, it is clear that her relationship with Edward continued. Despite his desire to not hurt his wife, Alice had taken a firm hold of his affections. Although Edward had been careful not to draw attention to their relationship by granting her lavish presents, he decided to help provide for her in other ways. On 14 May 1367 Alice was granted the lawn of Morton and the covert of 'Mortonscogh' in Inglewood Forest, Cumbria, to hold for life. This had been held by one of Edward's knights, Robert Tilliol, who had died the previous month.[45] At the same time, she was granted the wardship of Tilliol's 10-year-old heir along with the right to sell his marriage. For the right of wardship, Alice had had to pay 'a certain sum paid in hand'.[46] She might have obtained a discount from Edward, which could be why the amount is not disclosed. Two months later, Edward added the wardship of Tilliol's lands in Scotland.[47]

The landed aspect of the grants meant Alice was starting to build a small but significant portfolio of properties, whilst the money she would be able to make from the wardship and marriage of the heir would have bolstered her finances. Alice had gained four manors and a castle in England, as well as lands in Scotland. This favour from Edward was small enough that it could have gone unnoticed at court, but was very important to Alice. Tilliol had been a knight, and these landed holdings meant that Alice was now coming in line with lesser members of the nobility. These properties gave her not only status but also a much-needed income. Alice could lease them out for people to live in or to work the land, she could collect local dues associated with the manors and castles, and she could sell produce that came from the holdings such as crops, animals or timber. As a single woman, Alice had few lines of revenue open to her, but she now had resources to support herself independently of the court. Many of her contemporaries would have been more than happy with the number of properties Alice had.

With the increased income from her new lands, Alice continued to act as a provider of loans to people at court. On 21 November two loans were recorded in the Close Rolls, one to a man named John de Multon, for £20, and the other to Anthony de Lucy, the baron who had given her some of her first property two years previously.[48] This was for a far more substantial sum of £600. John de Multon and Anthony de Lucy had various familial and landed ties, Multon having been the ward of Lucy's father. Just two days later, Multon wrote to his wife saying that he and Lucy were travelling on crusade to Lithuania with a company of men, explaining the need for a loan from Alice.[49]

Alice's past business dealings with Lucy had established a relationship between the two, and he clearly thought she was a reliable person to borrow money from. This explains why Multon also borrowed from Alice. Alice might well have regretted providing these loans, for both men died on their crusade the following year and she apparently did not receive the repayment of her money until ten years later.[50] Wardship of Lucy's lands passed to Queen Philippa upon his death.[51] In fact, Alice was not the only one lending money for this crusade, as in July Philippa had also lent money to some of the men who went abroad.[52]

In the spring of 1368, Alice made a bold move which was to show the support she had from the king. A knight named John de Cobeham had been granted the manor of Ardington in Berkshire by Edward as a sign of favour. Alice now decided that she wanted this desirable manor for herself, and so Cobeham agreed to rent the manor to her for £80 a year. Alice proceeded to enter the manor, but she had not obtained permission from Edward to do so; Cobeham had only been granted the manor for his lifetime, and Edward still ultimately owned it. Any change in ownership had to have his approval.

After Alice entered the manor Cobeham went on to quitclaim his right to it, giving it to Alice. Alice now held the manor without rent and without the king's licence. For the mistress of the king this was no obstacle, and on

1 May Edward granted her a pardon for acting illegally in this way.[53] Alice was allowed to keep the manor for herself, in exchange for the usual feudal dues owed to Edward. Alice had now gained another significant manor holding, and with it her wealth and power increased.

Confident in this favour from the king, Alice was quick to secure the manor under enfeoffment-to-use, which she had become familiar with several years before. In the middle of July, she gained a licence to enfeoff John de Hanneye, who had been her fellow feoffee in her first property deal, with the manor. At the same time, she enfeoffed two other men, John de Ploufeld and William Gresleye, who were both chaplains and trusted by her. On the same day as being granted this licence, the three men were granted a pardon for obtaining, and trespassing in, the manor of Menestoke in Southampton.[54] This was to become another of Alice's key manors held by the men on her behalf.

The favours did not end there. The same month, Alice was given a gift by Edward of two thirds of the manor of 'Monylawes' in Northumberland, which was to be held by her for life and passed on to her heirs.[55] This gift was notable because it was permanent: Alice's heirs could hold it for generations to come. Usually, the favours that royal servants received from the crown were for a limited period, and at most for the lifetime of the servant. Those who found particular favour might have received wardships, or be given annuities, but it was rare for those who served in the household to receive permanent grants of land unless they were already of a landed status in their own merit – knights and titled nobility. It was certainly rare for women to receive such gifts. Only one other damsel of Queen Philippa's received a grant of land from Edward during Alice's time at court, and this was just a temporary wardship given to her because she had surrendered a similarly valued annuity.[56]

This series of generous grants in the summer of 1368 confirms that Alice had become very close to the king and that he wanted to show favour in a firm way whilst still remaining fairly discreet. The grant of land in particular, for its unusual level of favour, could suggest that Alice had given birth to her second daughter, Jane, around this time. If John had been born around 1364, and the grant of wine to Alice in 1366 suggests the birth of Joan, then the birth of her third and final child in 1368 fits well.

By autumn, then, Alice probably had three young children and had been in a relationship with the King of England for around six years. This firmly placed her as an exception in English history. Although other English kings had had affairs, they were not usually considered serious relationships. Henry I (*c.* 1068–1135) did have a relationship with one mistress, Sybil, for well over a decade, but he also had many other relationships, and is known to have had at least twenty-four illegitimate children. Henry also lived over two centuries previously: of the three kings who had ruled since 1216, only Edward's father had fathered an illegitimate child, and this was prior to his marriage.[57]

In a century and a half, then, there was no real precedent for Alice's situation. If Edward had had a small indiscretion here or there, many might not have thought too much about it, although it would have called into question the image Edward had portrayed of a unified family and a strong relationship with his wife. That he was now having a long-term relationship with one of his queen's ladies-in-waiting, and had three children with her, would have caused great shock.

How much Alice and Edward's relationship was common knowledge at this time is unclear. It seems that many people – at least outside of the inner circle of the court – were not aware of it. The couple were very discreet, and as the affair developed Alice might have been kept at a greater distance from the court. Certainly, few contemporary commentators mention the relationship until the following decade, and it was only after Philippa's death that the age of Alice's children would have made it obvious to all that the relationship had been well established during the lifetime of the queen.

Alice and Edward might well have been wise to try to keep their affair quiet. Just a few years before their relationship started, King David II of Scotland was the subject of scandal because of his mistress. David had taken a woman called Katharine de Mortimer back to Scotland with him after his release from English captivity. David lavished favour upon Katharine, 'which display of favour was displeasing to some of the Scottish lords', and in June 1360 she was attacked whilst the couple were out riding. Katharine was stabbed with a dagger and thrown from her horse, dying in the attack.[58] The news of Katharine's murder would certainly have reached England, and so Edward would have wanted to be careful that he did not equally enrage his own nobles.

Alice was not listed among the ladies of Philippa's household who were given robes to celebrate Christmas with the royal family at court that year. This could be evidence that Alice was indeed being distanced from the court, and even that she had been removed from Philippa's service. On the other hand, if Alice had given birth to Jane that summer, or perhaps in autumn, her absence from the Christmas celebrations might simply have been due to her recovering from giving birth and caring for her three young children away from court.

The year 1369 was to prove an important and tragic one for the crown. The government turned its attention to war, and there were many fronts to consider; £40,000 was split between William Wyndesore, the newly appointed Deputy of Ireland, and Prince Edward for their respective campaigns in Ireland and Aquitaine.[59] Meanwhile, Edward III turned his focus back to France and the war he had waged for decades in order to claim the throne for himself.

In May, King Charles V of France had declared the 1360 Treaty of Brétigny between England and France to be null and void.[60] For nine years, this treaty had paused hostilities between the two countries which had been raging intermittently since 1337. Charles had decided it was time to resume the war. Edward still had around £100,000 left of the ransom money paid for Charles's father, John II, which he now dedicated to this new French campaign. As summer arrived preparations were well underway to cross the Channel before winter, which usually signalled the end of campaign seasons. But in August, this campaign was stopped in its tracks: Queen Philippa of Hainault, Edward's wife of forty-one years, had died at Windsor Castle.

The Church of St Laurence in Upminster, historically in the county of Essex, where Alice Perrers was buried. (Author's Collection)

Detail of the tomb brass of Alice's oldest daughter, Joan, at All Saints Church, Kingston. (All Saints Church, Kingston)

The tomb effigy of Queen Philippa of Hainault, modelled on her in life, at Westminster Abbey. (Dean and Chapter of Westminster)

The tomb effigy of King Edward III of England at Westminster Abbey, constructed during the reign of his grandson Richard II. (Dean and Chapter of Westminster)

One of the seals of Alice Perrers, attached to a grant of some of her lands to King Edward III, December 1371. (Author's Collection, reproduced with permission of The National Archives, E 40/5004)

Return to England of Isabella of France, by Jean Fouquet, in *Grandes Chroniques de France* c. 1460. The scene depicts Isabella landing with her army, prior to the downfall of her husband Edward II. (Bibliothèque nationale de France)

Reconstruction of the medieval mural painting in St Stephen's chapel, Palace of Westminster, showing the kneeling figures of Queen Philippa and one of her daughters (thought to be Isabella of Woodstock) by Ernest William Tristram. (Parliamentary Art Collection)

Philippa of Hainault and her army, from Jean Froissart's *Chroniques*, *c.* 1410. Froissart wrote that Philippa helped lead the army at the Battle of Neville's Cross on horseback, although this was not the case. (Bibliothèque nationale de France)

7

The King's Lover

With the death of the queen consort who had been so integral to the country, the government and the royal family, there was no question of Edward or his family continuing with the planned French campaign. The royal household immediately went into mourning, and Alice would have been at court helping with the extensive preparations for the queen's funeral – and conveniently placed to comfort her lover. If Alice had remained one of Philippa's damsels after 1366, then in death Philippa certainly showed that she had no love for her: Alice was not bestowed an annuity by the queen, unlike most other members of her household.[1]

But Philippa could not stop Alice attending her funeral as a mourner. Alice was listed alongside other ladies of Philippa's household as receiving 6 ells of long black cloth for their mourning outfits.[2] Perhaps members of Philippa's household who were close companions of the queen and were aware of Alice's status might have found Alice's presence distasteful. But either Alice was still officially one of the queen's damsels, and so was obliged to attend due to her position, or Edward was keen to have his mistress there as moral support. Regardless, most of the nobles of the realm were expected to attend the funeral of the queen who had been ruling for over forty years. There would be thousands in attendance, and so to prevent Alice's attendance would only draw attention to her.

The position of Philippa's ladies at court would have been debated in the months after her death. Some of them would have found their services no longer needed, whilst others would have been transferred into the households of other noblewomen at court. Most of Edward's children were married and starting families of their own, and so there would have been positions available attending to the wives and children of the English princes. Katherine Swynford, the sister of Philippa's lady-in-waiting Philippa Chaucer, had already found herself working as a governess for the children of John of Gaunt, and similar positions could have been found for other women.

However, many of the women of Philippa's households would have no place left for them at court other than as guests. Edward certainly would have wanted to keep Alice close, so she might have been found another position at court or in the royal household, but otherwise Alice would have based herself in London to remain close to Edward. She was now the only woman in his life, and she would be keen to make sure her position did not slip.

As May 1370 arrived, Alice began to feel comfortable exerting her influence further. On the 14th of the month, Edward confirmed a transaction between Alice and Sir Alan Buxhill, one of the knights of his chamber.[3] In December the previous year, Edward had granted Buxhill the wardship of a very valuable heiress, Mary Percy. Mary's parents were both dead by the time she was a year old, and her inheritance included at least nineteen properties in the east of England worth at least £360.[4] A significant grant, it reflected Edward's close relationship with Buxhill. Despite this, Buxhill was persuaded by Alice to pass this grant to her instead, presumably in return for other favours. Although Alice had apparently paid Edward money for this privilege, Edward had in turn increased her grant by not only granting the wardship of Mary Percy, alongside all the lands that her parents had owned, but by adding on a grant of the lands which had been owned by Mary's maternal grandmother.[5]

This purchase was a triumph for Alice. By the time of Philippa's death the previous year, Alice had obtained seventeen properties, an incredible portfolio for a woman of her birth.[6] This new grant, however, more than doubled her holdings and gave her a substantial income. Mary Percy's parents had been part of the aristocracy, her father being the 3rd Lord Percy of Alnwick, and her mother being Lady Orreby. Their properties and income reflected their status, particularly as a rising family at Edward's court. That Alice now controlled what had been theirs brought her own lifestyle in line with that of members of the nobility. It also proved that she was still firmly in Edward's affections nine months after the death of his wife.

Alice had clearly spent her time in the king and queen's household building up relationships with men at court who could be useful to her business deals. From the knights to whom she lent money, to those she persuaded to give her land in very beneficial deals, Alice was building up a network of contacts through her relationship with the king. Now that Philippa was dead, Alice's relationship with Edward became more widely known, and this might have encouraged others at court to make these deals with Alice in the hope of receiving favours from the king in return.

From 1370 onwards, hints begin to emerge of Alice's influence behind the scenes. John Bernes, one of the eight men to whom Alice regularly gave land under her enfeoffment-to-use scheme, was elected mayor of London for two consecutive terms between November 1370 and November 1372.[7] Perhaps it may be too much of a stretch to say that Alice held enough power in 1370 to influence the election of a position as significant as mayor of London, but it is certainly an interesting coincidence and shows that, even if Alice had no hand in his election, she had built allies in powerful places.

Another man whom Alice had started to become close to was William Latimer, the steward of the royal household. Latimer was a few years older than Alice, being born in 1335, and had been a part of the household since at least 1359.[8] He had served in a variety of Edward's wars, and as the 4th Baron Latimer he had some personal wealth – around this time he lent £1,133 to the crown to help fund the renewed French wars.[9] Latimer had become close to King Edward: he had been made a Knight of the Garter in 1361 and became chamberlain in 1371, one of the closest personal servants of the king. He became a key figure in organising the war effort, gathering money and inspecting military forces for Edward.[10] Latimer was certainly an influential man at court, and Alice was wise to get him on her side.

The London merchant Richard Lyons was also gaining importance in Alice's life from 1370 onwards. Despite their inauspicious start, Lyons was well placed to join Alice's supporters. As a merchant, Lyons had a reserve of wealth that was exceedingly useful to the English crown at a time when war with France was renewing. Lyons would be an important contact in the years to come.

Although many of the men that Alice was tying herself to were London merchants, they were not her exclusive source of interest. Despite her immoral status as a mistress, Alice had ingratiated herself with William Wykeham, a man of the Church who had been part of the royal household and government since 1361.[11] Wykeham came from humble beginnings himself, being the son of a Hampshire peasant villager. He had served Edward in various capacities since the late 1350s, and by the time Alice joined the royal household around 1362 Wykeham was known as 'the king's beloved clerk'.[12] The following year, the king wrote that Wykeham was 'by his side in constant attendance ... under the king's special protection' and Edward saw that his friend was amply rewarded for his service.[13] In 1367 he was made Bishop of Winchester and chancellor, and by this time he had been given so many benefices by Edward that his annual income from these appointments alone was just over £873, more than three times the amount of the next-highest-earning benefice-holder.[14] Wykeham was eager to use this wealth to help the king where he could, and when Edward had been looking for funds to restart the French war in 1369 and 1370 Wykeham had given a significant £3,000.[15]

Alice joined the household just as Wykeham was cementing his position by Edward's side, and she wisely recognised that his closeness to the king and his rising power in the royal household made him a significant ally for her. That both Wykeham and Alice had come from a lower class than many others in power in the household might have helped them form a reliance on each other, and the pair seem to have built a genuine friendship which would prove to be vital to their joint survival in the decades to come.[16]

Although Alice had become powerful at court and had benefits as the king's mistress, she was still subject to the king's will. In early December 1371, Alice surrendered lands in Kent to Edward because he wanted to give them to a religious house recently founded at Dartford. Alice used this as an opportunity to obtain far more valuable land. The land she had surrendered was worth £40, but in return for surrendering her land, and a £500 payment to Edward, she was granted the manor of Wendover in Buckinghamshire, together with all the benefits of the manor such as its knights' fees.[17]

Obtaining Wendover was highly desirable to Alice. The manor had, until July of that year, belonged to William Wykeham. Wykeham had been serving as chancellor for the past four years, but he was dismissed this year under accusations of mismanagement of funds. The manor of Wendover was a valuable property, worth over £80 a year, and was considered one of the most important manors in Buckinghamshire.[18] It was also in a prime location, being close enough to London that Alice could remain in the sphere of the royal court. Moreover, two of Edward's powerful sons, Prince Edward and John of Gaunt, had residences nearby.[19] If Alice wanted to stay close to those in power, and expand her social circle to include these powerful princes, then Wendover was a great base.

The events of the autumn of 1371 proved that knowledge of Alice's position as Edward's mistress had spread far and wide, and that she was considered to hold influence over the king. In October, Pope Gregory XI wrote from Avignon to many powerful members of government. Gregory had only been elected at the very end of the previous year, but before that point his brother, Roger de Bellofroti, had been held as a prisoner by Jean III de Grailly, a Gascon nobleman loyal to Edward III. Gregory was now attempting to use his influence as pope to secure the release of his brother.

Among those to whom the pope addressed letters were several of Edward's sons (Prince Edward, John of Gaunt and Edmund of Langley); leading nobles including Richard, Earl of Arundel, and Humphrey, Earl of Hereford; William Wykeham, Bishop of Winchester – and Alice Perrers.[20] Alice was the only woman sent a letter, and that she was included among a list of such illustrious and powerful men demonstrates that the pope was well aware of her relationship with the king and was happy to exploit it. It was expected that women would hold a mediating influence over the men in their lives. Previous popes had written to Philippa, as Edward's wife, and now that he was widowed it was hoped that Alice would do the same.

As the next year arrived, Alice continued to accept gifts and payments from Edward and his government. On 15 April 1372 Alice received hundreds of pounds 'paid to her own hands' from the exchequer at Edward's order. The entry notes that she was to receive £197 for jewels and other items that she had sold to the crown for Edward's own use during Christmas two years prior. She was to receive a further £200 for more jewels and items purchased for Edward's use for Christmas the previous year.[21]

By the summer of 1372 Alice's lands had grown significantly in size, and this came with a substantial income that would have allowed her to live a luxurious life. In fact, her wealth was enough that she was able to start lending even more sizeable amounts of money to others at court. On 25 June Alice lent £500 to a knight named Gilbert de Culwen.[22] Considering that knights usually had an annual income of between £40 and £400 in the early parts of the following century, this was a significant loan.[23] Despite this, Culwen was able to pay Alice back in full four years later, which Alice acknowledged on the Close Rolls. It was just as well, for Culwen had given his lands and chattels in Cumberland as surety.

Although Alice's wealth had grown exponentially since the death of Queen Philippa three years earlier, her notoriety was similarly growing. Around this time the *Prophecies of John Bridlington*, a collection of twenty-nine poems, were written. The text makes allusions to Alice's immoral position and how she was leading Edward and the court astray by referring to biblical stories of similar evil women who tempted strong men: Samson and Delilah, and David and Bathsheba.[24]

In the verses, the author refers to a woman, 'Diana', who seduced Edward during the siege of Calais of 1346–47, sleeping with him and giving birth to 'a robber' as a result. They go on to write: 'Love will trouble the Bull [Edward] and overcome him, while he fulfills the crafty desires of wild Diana … if I were to say more, I would make a woman my enemy.'[25] Although the author claims that this happened decades earlier at Calais, it certainly seems that they were referring to Alice's present situation with the king. Alice had given birth to a son by Edward, who could be seen as a thief of land and money from Edward's legitimate children, as well as a threat to their status. Alice's clear rise in power at this time would also mean the author would certainly want to avoid incurring her wrath.[26] The author's opinion of Alice's influence on Edward is clear: 'A whore is the doorway to death.'[27]

By this time, many of Edward's old friends and family had died and so he started to turn his attention to the new group of courtiers he had gathered around him, encouraged by Alice, who looked to promote the interests of her friends and allies. In 1372 Edward ordered that Alice's friend William Latimer was henceforth to have pure ermine trim on his Garter robes, a status marker that was worn by Edward's sons and his titled nobles but not a lower-ranking baron like Latimer.[28]

Others at court were not faring quite as well. William Wyndesore's expedition to Ireland funded by Edward two years previously had not worked out for him. In trying to raise funds for the military in Ireland and for the renewed French wars, he had clashed with the Irish parliament, even imprisoning representatives of County Louth when they denied him a subsidy.[29] By the spring of 1372, the government was receiving so many complaints about Wyndesore from Ireland that they made the decision to recall him and replace him with another man, Robert Ashton.[30] Now back in England, Wyndesore had a chance to become better acquainted with the woman at the heart of Edward's court. Something about Wyndesore clearly caught Alice's eye, and she decided he was a powerful man who needed to be added to her list of allies, even if he was temporarily disgraced. This decision would change the course of Alice's life.

On 14 January 1373, Alice received what would prove to be a significant gift from Edward, who had recently come into possession of a house and a shop in Thames Street, London. This property was located in the parish of All Hallows the Less, and its previous owners had forfeited the messuage and shop because they were in debt to Edward.[31] Edward now granted this property to Alice and her heirs as a permanent gift. It is possible that Alice already had property in the city after her marriage to Janyn, but she was determined now to make a statement with the land in Thames Street.

Alice wasted no time in building a row of houses on the site, which she leased out to tenants to provide an income.[32] However, this piece of land was not just to provide income to Alice and she decided to make it one of her main residences. Spending time at court with the king would have had many benefits, but Alice wanted to make her mark on the city and create a physical symbol of the power she held. She would never be queen, but she wanted to remind the City of London and all who visited that she was one of the most powerful women in the country – and one of the richest.

Alice therefore had a major residence built for herself on the site along-side the rented houses. An extensive inventory of items at the property from just a few years later shows that this house on Thames Street, which became known as the New Inn, was almost certainly Alice's main place of residence. Her son, John, was living there in 1377 and most likely had been since Alice constructed it as it was close to the court and his father.[33]

Quite how large the property was when Alice owned it is not clear, but as it was one of her main homes, and contained so many fine items, it must have been significant. After Alice's ownership, the house was granted to two princes: John of Gaunt, then his brother Edmund of Langley. Near the end of the following century, in 1485, a survey of the property showed that it had twenty-two rooms, a great hall and chapel.[34] Although some of these rooms would have been added or enlarged across the century since Alice had owned it, that it was considered fine enough to grant to two of England's princes shows that even in her time it must have been a significant home.

Alice gathered many high-quality pieces of furniture for the residence. The inventory of goods in the house is too extensive to list, but even a sample demonstrates the wealth that Alice had gained.[35] She had a tester and canopy for a feather bed made from luxurious white silk striped with gold and decorated with cords. She had multiple coverlets (bed sheets) for the bed made from a variety of materials including white fustian (a type of heavy cotton cloth), red silk and red camaca (a rich fabric, often made from silk). Another bed in the house had a coverlet of paned red cloth and blue wool which was lavishly decorated with half-pured miniver. Many more pillows, mattresses, sheets, testers, cushions and curtains are listed, showing that she had multiple sumptuously decorated bedrooms.

The inventory also gives an insight into the types of luxurious clothes Alice could afford. Alice was certainly dressing above the station into which she had been born, but her position as the king's mistress, as well as her rise to a major landholder, allowed her to transcend this in her clothing. Among the many items of clothing listed were a red and blue lined cloak, a russet gown furred with grey, and a short black cloak furred with expensive pured miniver. She had more cloaks of a variety of colours and cloths, as well as numerous gowns made from wool, velvet and camaca in a variety of colours. She also had a variety of mantles and tunics, kirtles and garters, buttons and gloves in her wardrobe, all in a rich variety of fabrics and often personalised and embellished.

There were a few religious pieces in Alice's goods that suggests either that she was allowed the privilege of having a portable altar, a benefit bestowed only upon the upper classes, or that the chapel described the following century was constructed in Alice's time. She had a tabernacle (for holding the consecrated host) with an image of the Virgin Mary on it, a wooden altar, a couple of altar cloths and a case containing a pillow for the altar. Other belongings hint at Alice's literacy, as she had a book on the life of St Margaret as well as multiple primers (prayer books) written in English. These religious books, alongside her provisions for a private altar, suggest that Alice could have been quietly devout. On the other hand, these were items that any good noblewoman was expected to have in her home, so Alice might simply have owned them as a status symbol, or they might even have belonged to her son, who was a teenager at the time the inventory was taken. Alice certainly did not donate to religious institutions as other pious noblewomen of her time did.

Alice was eating well at her home, with a gilt spice dish and salt cellar to season her food, and a dozen silver dishes to eat from. She had the luxury of an ivory chessboard with a set of chess pieces to entertain her in her leisure time. Alice also went horse riding, for she had numerous saddles: a basic one made from leather; one made from red cloth embroidered with the letters 'A' and 'P'; another made from red leather with a matching bridle; another made from black cloth embroidered with roses and birds, with a bridle; and a final saddle of unclear material and design.

Alice would have ridden as a status symbol, but she likely rode for pleasure too. Edward certainly loved riding and hunting, and even in his older age continued these pursuits. It would make sense for Alice to enjoy riding alongside Edward as a leisure activity. Noblewomen in fourteenth-century England certainly partook in hunting alongside men, and so there is no reason Alice did not do so as well, especially considering her own personalised 'Alice Perrers' saddle.[36] The total value of goods in this property in 1377 was over £119, a significant amount indeed.

This year also brings a rare example of Alice's interactions with Edward's children. On 1 May 1373, Alice was gifted a silver drinking vessel by

Edward's son John of Gaunt.[37] Alice was one of many receiving gifts from the prince that day, including his daughters and father. This gift showed Alice's importance within the royal family, and Gaunt's recognition of her relationship with his father. It is difficult to tell whether by giving Alice this gift he was showing his friendship and acceptance of Alice or if it was given out of duty, but there is little evidence to show that Gaunt disliked Alice, and certainly at times in the future he was seen to help her cause.

Gaunt could hardly dislike Alice simply for her position as a mistress, for by this time he had taken Katherine Swynford as his own mistress and had the first of four illegitimate children with her.[38] Perhaps he could have resented Alice for having been Edward's mistress during the life of his mother, Philippa, but he might not have found this too much of an issue when mistresses were not uncommon at this level of society. He had also seen the happiness Alice had brought his father after his mother's death, which might have compensated for this indiscretion. If Edward found Alice's qualities attractive, then there is no reason why Gaunt would not like her personality too, and Alice might have worked to ingratiate herself with this powerful prince who could be useful to her in the future.

There is no real evidence to assess how Edward's children viewed Alice. Certainly, none of them appear to have been close to her, for there are few gifts between them and they do not feature greatly in her life after Edward's death. But Alice was frequently by Edward's side, and his children must have spent a lot of time in her company as a result. Princess Isabella is often found side by side with Alice in gifts of clothing from Edward in the wardrobe accounts, showing that Alice was with Edward at many major court events when his children were also present.

This year, Alice was once again busy working behind the scenes with her allies at court to secure benefits for them and herself alike. In January 1373 she appears to have been at her manor of Pallenswick in Middlesex, her main residence outside of London, where she gathered a large group of men that she used as her feoffees to manage her extensive property portfolio. Here, one group of her feoffees granted many of Alice's properties to another group of feoffees, and this transfer was witnessed by several courtiers including Alice's friend William Latimer.[39] Meanwhile, Alice had perhaps been using her influence with Edward to secure a favour for her new friend William Wyndesore, who was sent back to Ireland to act as its lieutenant this year, despite his controversial leadership.

In the summer Alice received a public gift from Edward that has been used as evidence of her avarice and desire for power. On 8 August at the palace of Woodstock, Edward gave 'our beloved' Alice jewellery, goods and chattels that had belonged to him and Philippa.[40] Many historians have taken this as evidence that Alice had forced Edward to gift her the personal jewels of the late Queen Philippa. This was therefore seen to show that Alice not only demanded jewels befitting a queen, but wanted to destroy the sacred memory of Philippa and assert herself as Edward's only woman – and that Edward was so besotted in his senility that he accepted this.[41] However, the grant itself states that these jewels had already been given to another person, Eufemia, the wife of a knight called Walter de Heselarton. So, although the jewels had previously belonged to the royal couple, they were 'not treasured items from Philippa's undisturbed wardrobe' but smaller pieces that had already been separated from Philippa's memory.[42]

In fact, a record in the Patent Rolls from the previous month states that Philippa had originally gifted the jewels and goods to Walter.[43] He was dead by Easter 1367, and so he must have received the jewels from the queen prior to this point.[44] It was not unusual for gifts given by the royal couple to their subjects to be taken back and given to other people, so it is not necessarily noteworthy that Walter and Eufemia's gift was recalled and granted to Alice, who is referred to in the grant as Philippa's damsel. In fact, there is no evidence apart from supposition that Alice influenced Edward in any way to give this gift. True, she might have identified the jewels as something she wanted and spoken to Edward in private about them, but it could just as easily have been a genuine gift from Edward to his 'beloved' Alice that she had no hand in. Edward had always lavished his wife and daughters with jewels, and so Alice was no exception. To assume that the gift is evidence of underhand greed on Alice's part is unfair.

In February 1374, John de Southeray, Alice's son, received a generous annuity of £100 from Edward.[45] This might not quite have been solely Edward's idea, and Alice might have been planning for John to receive this gift for a while. A few months earlier, in September 1373, Alice had gained this £100 for herself by making a deal with the Countess of Atholl.[46] This grant was now passed, with Edward's permission, from Alice to John. A significant amount of money, it might well have been a symbol to those at court of John's status as Edward's illegitimate son, as two years previously the illegitimate son of Prince Edward had been gifted the same amount.[47] Regardless, John was now receiving a healthy income for a young boy, and Alice was clearly beginning to think about the future of her children.

This year was perhaps a celebration for Alice and Edward, as it is likely their son reached 10 years of age. This meant that their relationship had been going for at least a decade, and Alice had been the only woman in Edward's life for five of those ten years. Edward decided he wanted to gift his love a specially commissioned present to demonstrate his feelings: a gold brooch encrusted with pearls and decorated with blue and iron lacquer with the inscriptions *Pensez de moi* ('think of me') and *Sanz departir* ('never apart').[48]

This gift to Alice has been judged harshly, saying it showed 'the aged Edward's pitiful eagerness to play the role of ardent lover to the mother of his bastard'.[49] True, Edward was 62, and probably about twice as old as Alice. But although Edward's life had slowed somewhat, in the early 1370s he still seemed to be quite healthy and mentally aware, and he had continued to partake in ceremonial appearances. He continued to read petitions and grant patronage, and although the royal household began to stay closer to London, Edward continued to travel further from home and partake in sports and hunts.[50]

Perhaps Edward was trying to live up to his past reputation of a chivalric romantic, or perhaps he and Alice simply were in love and it was a gift that Alice cherished. She can certainly have been considered more than just the mother of his bastard by now. The true extent of Alice's feelings towards Edward are impossible to know, but whilst she clearly appreciated the material aspects of their relationship and the heightened status it had given her, it is a rather cynical view of her character and Edward's own judgement of how she thought of him to assume that she felt no love or tenderness towards him.

Contemporaries who were jealous of Alice's rise, and her close proximity to the king, suggested that she was a seductress who had tricked an old man with her youth and her way with words, that she was in it simply for the money and the gifts.[51] But Edward had been markedly restrained with the gifts and favour he had bestowed upon Alice, and although Alice gained much simply by association with him, it is far easier and more reasonable to assume that she did care for him and would have appreciated this personal gift. Edward also showed his affection towards her in other, more public, ways, for it is also in this year that a reference is found to a ship of Edward's, with sixty crew, named *La Alice*.[52] Edward was clearly happy to show his love for Alice on his own initiative.

Whilst Alice's family were receiving gifts from the king, the government as a whole was struggling for money. The renewal of the French wars a few years earlier, expenditure for stabilising Ireland and the personal wars of his sons (such as John of Gaunt's bid for the crown of Castile) had drained the coffers of the remaining riches from earlier triumphs and the ransoms of the Scottish and French kings. Whilst the kingdom continued to believe the crown had its own personal hoard of wealth, the reality was that it was running into great debt. Now the group of men at court and in the household who had built up Edward's trust – and become Alice's allies – offered to step in and give favours to the crown.

In August, Richard Lyons and another man, John Pyel, lent the crown the substantial sum of 20,000 marks, under agreement that the crown would pay them back 30,000 marks (around £20,000).[53] This was said to have come about 'by the counsel of the said Richard and of the other intimates close to the king', perhaps hinting at Alice's involvement in facilitating the loan. Alice and Lyons had certainly been working together for years, and Alice had also dealt with Pyel in the past, he granting her property in London back in 1367.[54] The terms of interest on the loan were especially excessive, though, and would be a cause of ire in the future.

It was no wonder that these 'new' men were gaining prominence in Edward's diminishing court. From the late 1360s, many of Edward's senior magnates had been retiring or dying of old age, and their replacements were away fighting in various English wars. This year, 1374, only thirteen of the twenty-four Garter knights made it to Windsor to join Edward and his eldest son for the Garter feast celebrations.[55] Naturally, Edward would start to rely more on his mistress now that he had no wife, and on the men of his household who were Alice's friends and allies. That they were often from the mercantile classes meant that they were a source of revenue when parliament was reticent to grant any, and it meant that they were not obliged under feudal dues to serve Edward abroad in the military, meaning they could stay close to court. These men seemed to be loyal to Edward, were helping to advance his interests and policies, and it was natural that Edward would have placed his trust in them. However, those who were not able to spend as much time at court and who were born into the nobility were always going to resent the growth in this new 'clique'.

Now that he was growing into an older boy, Alice's son joined Edward's court alongside other young nobles to begin his education. In October 1375, John de Southeray received a gift from his father – alongside three royal wards – of a gown made from russet cloth, with a hood lined in blue cloth.[56] The gown was part of the livery of the esquires who were part of Edward's household, showing that John was taking up an official position as his status deserved. The following month, John received another gift from Edward of a saddle with a white harness.[57] It would have been a stylish accessory for the young boy whilst out riding with the household and alongside his father.

Now that John had firmly found his place at his father's court and had an income to sustain him, Alice started to make provisions for his future landed estate. For such an important task, Alice gathered her closest allies to hold a group of properties in trust for him. In October, William Wykeham, William Latimer and other trusted men were granted a group of properties by the king.[58] Although Alice's name is not mentioned, later events show that she clearly orchestrated this grant and the men were holding the properties for her. Whilst John had no formal titles, and was the son of a goldsmith's daughter, he had royal blood in his veins through his father and this would raise his position in life. Royal bastards historically had been able to rise to a reasonable station in life either in the church or in the government, promoted by their fathers. If John were to capitalise on his connection to Edward III and be the success that his mother dreamed him to be, he would need a landed estate to demonstrate his power and cement his position within the nobility.

Alice had continued to receive small gifts from Edward. In October and November she was given robes by Edward alongside his eldest daughter, Princess Isabella.[59] That she was receiving clothes of the same quality as a princess demonstrates that Alice had risen further above her rank than anyone would have thought possible at this time. The discretion around their relationship from the previous decade was completely dropped, and Alice was taking her place at Edward's side. Although her low birth and Edward's position as king would mean that the couple could never entertain legitimising their relationship through marriage, Edward was happy to treat her as his queen in many respects.

That year, Alice continued to receive grants of land and make her own deals to build her property empire. This was not all plain sailing, and in the summer of 1375 her manor of 'Fynyngley' in Nottinghamshire was attacked by 'evildoers' who stole eight oxen, five cows and eleven calves. They chased the remaining cattle into her crops until they were trodden down and ruined, then cut the legs of six other oxen. Finally, they 'imprisoned her men and servants and kept them in prison until they made oath not to stay there any longer in her service'.[60]

Understandably, this has been taken as evidence that at lower levels of society animosity was growing towards Alice Perrers, the immoral mistress flaunting her position.[61] However, Queen Philippa too suffered numerous parkbreaks during her tenure. Moreover, on the same day that a commission was set up to investigate the attack on Alice's manor, Edward's son Edmund, Earl of Cambridge, had his own commission set up to investigate parkbreaks in twenty different properties in Yorkshire, where evildoers hunted in his parks and warrens, felled his trees, fished his fisheries, stole goods, hares, pheasants, partridges and deer, and assaulted his men and servants.[62] Although the men who attacked Alice's manor in Nottinghamshire might well have taken issue with Alice as an individual, it is more likely that the attack on her property was just one of many on those seen to be at the top of society. This year saw another outbreak of plague which took its toll on the population, and these attacks on wealthy parks and manors might have been a way to show frustration at the conditions of the lower classes, who were suffering from increased food prices.[63] What mattered was the property and the inequity of resources and land, rather than the individual who owned it.

Plague and a new treaty with France meant that Edward needed to leave the capital to protect his health, and he now had more time for leisure. Edward spent the summer travelling across numerous manors and castles, from Windsor, Sheen and Moor End into Northamptonshire, Leicestershire and Rutland. Although his advancing age would have led to heightened concerns for his health, it seems he was still fit enough to travel such distances. He also ensured that his entourage took part in sports and hunting, as he had always loved to do, paying for forty-eight bows for 'the ladies in our company upon the chase in this coming hunting season'.[64] Whether Edward was still physically capable of taking part in these hunts as he once did is not clear, but Alice was almost certainly among the ladies accompanying him. It would have been a chance for the couple to enjoy leisure time together and have some light-hearted activities to fill their days.

As winter set in, Alice and her children settled in at court with Edward. The gifts of clothing to Alice and John across October and November suggest the pair were largely living with Edward at this time – certainly John was, in his capacity as an esquire of the household – and it would seem logical that Alice and Edward's two daughters, Joan and Jane, were with them. John was around 11 years old, with Joan and Jane probably 9 and 7 respectively. There was much celebration for the midwinter feasts this year, and Princess Isabella and Prince Thomas of Woodstock joined Edward at Eltham for Christmas, and possibly Alice and her family by extension.[65]

Alice's children seem to also have spent time getting to know their royal relatives. John, in particular, became friendly with 8-year-old Richard, the only surviving son of Prince Edward and the future king of England. Their similar ages, and that John was Richard's half-uncle, meant that they were growing up together at the royal court. No doubt Alice also encouraged the friendship. Prince Edward's health was failing fast, and it was becoming clear that Richard would be heir to the throne in the not-too-distant future. If Alice and her family were to survive after the death of Edward III, Richard was their way to do so.

Christmas 1375 was spent in jubilation, and Alice might well have felt secure in her little family's position. This year she had started to secure a future for her son, with the prospect of many more grants to come as the boy grew up and proved himself to his father. As her young daughters moved ever closer to maturity, so too could Alice begin to think of equipping them with sufficient dowries and lands to lure noble families to marry them for their connection to Edward, thus ensuring all of her children would live at a far higher station in life than the mercantile class into which Alice had been born. So too was she secure in her relationship with Edward, whose love for her had never waned. With boats named after her and men as powerful as the pope petitioning her for help, all the while laden with jewels, gowns and lands, her previous life as wife to Janyn Perrers must have felt like a distant memory. But Alice's future was not as secure as she might have thought, and the following year was to see the start of a significant shift at court.

8

Danger at Court

The year 1376 was supposed to be auspicious for King Edward III. On 25 January he marked the start of his fiftieth year as King of England – a milestone only one previous English king, Henry III, had passed. With the growing hatred of the close-knit circle of courtiers around the king, it was decided that full advantage needed to be taken of this landmark year. Edward was still incredibly popular with the commoners of England. They loved the monarch who had strengthened the country, made it a force to be reckoned with on the Continent, and had been ruling for as long as most people could remember.

Festivities began almost immediately, with a week-long tournament held at Smithfield in February. The tournament was designed to remind the people of Edward's prowess and impressive martial history.[1] Unfortunately, it was Alice's appearance there which stuck in people's minds. Many have assumed that Alice's starring role in the tournament was her own doing – a way to remind the country of her central role in Edward's life and the court. Whilst this may very well be true, it is not unreasonable to think that Edward wanted to celebrate the start of his milestone year with the woman he loved.

Wherever the idea originated, Alice certainly stole the limelight. Her appearance at the start of the tournament was recorded by the *Chronicle of*

London: 'dame Alice Perrers' opened the tournament by riding from the Tower of London through Cheap dressed 'as lady of the sun'. Travelling with Alice was a procession of lords and ladies. The lords were riding horses, which the ladies led by their bridles.[2] It is not quite clear where the motif of 'lady of the sun' originated from, although it could have been a reference to Edward's own personal badge of a sunburst.[3]

Most have taken this extremely public participation of Alice in the tournament as Edward's woman to be crass, a bold statement showing her power and ambition. However, it isn't clear what contemporaries thought of Alice's place in the tournament. The *Chronicle of London* merely describes her involvement, making no positive or negative judgement upon Alice or the tournament itself, but by virtue of its mere mention, it could indicate that it was seen as extraordinary.

Alice's outfit was stunning. She wore a russet gown edged with ermine, a white fur supposed to be reserved for the royal family and upper nobility. On top of the gown she wore a cloak of gold tissue lined with red taffeta, and all of her clothes were embroidered with hundreds of seed pearls. She wore a leather cap which was also encrusted with jewels.[4] She must certainly have glistened like the sun. Every day a procession travelled from the Tower of London to the tournament field for several hours of jousting, then returned to the Tower for feasting afterwards. Alice had cemented her place as the woman at the centre of the royal court, and the crown had gained attention, whether that was for good or bad.

The next major event in the political calendar for Edward's fiftieth anniversary was to be the Garter feast of St George's Day. In recent years, the Garter feasts had lost some of their clout. Endless wars meant many of the members were often absent from the feast, and most of the original members had now died of old age. Despite this, the Order of the Garter was still the most prestigious knightly order of the kingdom, and being founded by Edward himself it was unquestionable that this jubilee year could pass without the most elaborate of celebrations.

The Garter feast was filled with esteemed guests, including many members of the royal family who had been absent in previous years. Edward presided in a red robe with the Garter's motif, and he was joined by his eldest son, Prince Edward, and two more of his sons, John of Gaunt and Edmund of Langley. King Edward's daughter, Princess Isabella, was given Garter robes for the occasion, alongside her husband Enguerrand de Coucy, who was a knight of the order.[5] The Duke of Brittany, who was the son-in-law of Prince Edward's wife, Joan of Kent, also attended as one of the knights of the order. The occasion was made even more significant by the election of six new knights to the order, filling the spaces which had become vacant.[6]

The impressive list of royals and nobles who attended, followed by their retinues, meant that the celebrations of 23 April 1376 were the largest social gathering at Windsor Castle in over a decade.[7] Alice is not recorded as ever having received Garter robes, the only women to be given this honour during Edward's lifetime being his Queen, Philippa, and his eldest daughter Isabella, but she must have been present at the feast in some capacity.

The spring of 1376 was full of excitement and festivities at the royal court. The Smithfield tournament and Garter feast had brought nobility together to celebrate the king and were lavished with wealth and entertainment. Plans were made to continue the festivities into the summer, with another tournament at Smithfield to be held during the Feast of Pentecost on 4 June. Alice Perrers was listed alongside Princess Isabella as a recipient of cloth of gold and taffeta to be crafted into fabulous gowns for the celebration as a gift from Edward.[8] In the end Alice never got to wear these robes, as the tournament was cancelled. Although the Garter feast had seemed like a triumph for Edward's court, just five days later parliament opened. It became known as the 'Good Parliament', but for Alice it was anything but.

The parliament was the first to have gathered since the end of 1373. The Commons were told that they had been called to provide taxes to support the defence of the realm under the threat of the wars with France potentially starting again. The Lords and Commons agreed to grant the crown taxes on wool and leather, as they had in the previous parliament, but they were reluctant to provide much further taxation. They asked Edward that they might be 'excused at this time from granting him any other subsidy in aid of his said wars, since they have been so ruined and destroyed previously' through disease and crop failure.[9]

The Lords and the Commons had been requested to hold their sessions separately, but this did not quite go to plan. The Commons decided to elect a spokesman, Sir Peter de la Mare, who is now viewed as the very first Speaker of the House of Commons.[10] It was then requested that a group of lords visit the Commons to discuss grievances raised during the initial sessions of the parliament. Edward agreed to this, and so on Monday 12 May a committee of lords came to the Commons to listen to their concerns. This is where the root of the Commons' refusal to grant extra taxation was revealed.[11]

The Commons – headed by de la Mare – claimed that the king would not need to rely on the taxation of his people to fund his government and his wars were it not for the 'irresponsible and corrupt behaviour of "certain councillors and servants" about the king'.[12] The people whom they viewed responsible for this squandering of the royal purse were Lord Latimer, Richard Lyons and Alice Perrers. Latimer and Lyons were accused of loaning money to the crown with extortionate interest rates, whilst Alice was guilty of receiving generous gifts from Edward which damaged the country as a whole.

In the minds of the Commons, these were reasonable claims. They raised the 'great amounts of gold which have been brought into the realm from the ransoms of the kings of France and of Scotland' which meant that Edward should have no need to tax his own subjects if he 'had always had loyal counsellors around him'.[13] They believed that the king had a goldmine of personal wealth that he should be using, and if that source of money had been depleted it was only down to greedy counsellors who had siphoned the wealth for themselves. In reality, of course, the crown had steadily been depleting its gold reserves over the years to avoid calling parliament for taxation, and to fund the French wars, which were not as profitable as they had been in the days of huge English victories.[14]

Latimer and Lyons had official roles in government from which it was possible for them to play the system, cheat the king, provide poor advice and enrich themselves. Alice being named in the grievances of parliament was unusual because it was less common for women to be dragged into complaints of poor governance due to their unofficial role at court. Of course, as Edward's mistress – and a powerful, semi-official one at that – Alice was an exception. The *Anonimalle Chronicle* highlights exactly the issue that the Commons had with Alice: she was receiving £2,000–£3,000 a year from Edward 'without any notable profit and in great damage to our lord the king'.[15]

The biggest problem with Alice was not that she was a woman, nor necessarily that she was a mistress. It was that she had carved out a new role for herself which had not been seen before. Kings had had mistresses and affairs, but they were usually nameless, and whilst they might result in bastard children and some monetary compensation for the mother, it had never amounted to such political power before. The only acceptable role for a female lover of a king was to be his queen, and a woman of noble or royal blood. Queens were entitled to an income by virtue of their position, but they worked for that money. Queens provided a channel for the kingdom to access the king, whether through requesting favours and intercessions or receiving patronage and gifts. Queens could temper a king's anger or help build alliances. They also provided heirs.

Alice, however, was not a queen, as much as she might hold a lot of the benefits. Her position as the king's lover meant people could try to obtain favours through pleasing her, but, unlike a model queen, Alice often went back on her word and left people out of pocket. Alice did not patronise institutions or fund religious orders. She was not an official channel for business to be conducted, and so she did nothing for the kingdom. Therefore, she was not deserving of receiving money from the crown.

The next record of proceedings does not come until Monday, 19 May, when witnesses were called to investigate the accusations against Lyons and Latimer. One of the former treasurers, Richard Scrope, was brought in and his testament was damning. He said that William Walworth, a representative of the City of London who had previously loaned the crown money, had been alienated by Latimer, Lyons and John Pyel. Walworth, he said, was willing to offer loans to the crown at far more reasonable terms, but he had been overlooked by the three men who held a monopoly on the king's attention and thus his loans.[16] The substantial loan of 20,000 marks to Edward provided two years earlier by Lyons and Pyel now came under suspicion.

Scrope's words were severe accusations, and Latimer and Lyons suffered further by the betrayal of John Pyel. Pyel was present whilst the evidence was being heard and, clearly desperate to distance himself from what was happening, he turned on his supposed accomplices. Pyel said that the high-value loans were the idea of Latimer and Lyons and, worse, he suggested that Latimer and Lyons had in fact stolen some of the money provided for the

loans out of the crown's own treasury.[17] A study of the receipts of the exchequer by historian Chris Given-Wilson reveals no evidence of theft on the part
of Latimer and Lyons, but these were powerful and shocking accusations.[18]

In the intervening period, Alice Perrers had also come under further scru-
tiny. Just the previous day, on Sunday 18 May, Bishop Brinton of Rochester
gave a sermon at St Paul's Cross in London which was damning of Alice's
position at court. In his speech, he told the crowd that 'it is not fitting nor
safe for all the keys of the kingdom to hang from the belt of one wife'.[19]
Although Alice was not Edward's wife, the implication was clear. Alice was
seen as the puppet master who was controlling the court for her own benefit,
and for a woman this was not a suitable position. The revelations in parliament the following day seemed to prove this, as Alice was closely tied to
Lyons and might have been the person to connect Lyons, Latimer and Pyel to
Edward for these extortionate loans.

The next few days were spent in tense anticipation of what would come
next. The Commons had called for the arrest of Lyons, and on 24 May de la
Mare appeared before the Lords and confirmed that the Commons were
refusing to proceed any further with parliamentary business and granting
taxation until Lyons and Latimer were removed from government. There
was also one other crucial term in their demands: Alice Perrers was to be
banished from court.[20]

This was a devastating blow for both Alice and Edward. Edward was to
lose his companion of many years, who had given him three children and
whom he cherished deeply. For Alice, it meant the loss of the status and
power to which she had become accustomed. She had successfully built up a
huge, landed empire and had more than enough income to sustain her lifestyle. But just a few months previously she had been the 'lady of the sun',
and she wasn't going to relinquish that easily.

Edward was in no easy position. He needed the money from parliament
and by the end of May he had bigger worries on his mind. His eldest son,
Prince Edward, had taken a turn for the worse. The ill health of his heir had
been weighing on Edward's mind for years, but the succession was now in
crisis. Edward was aware that he was ageing and was showing signs of infirmity himself. Were his eldest son to die, Edward's heir would be a child, his
grandson Richard.

There was no other choice: Edward was forced to agree to Alice's banishment from court. Alice was given a significant amount of leniency, for she was allowed to keep all of her lands and goods on the condition that she did not return to the king's presence. She was then largely left out of the rest of the proceedings, with one stark exception. Item forty-five on parliament's list of business specifically concerned Alice Perrers, and it shows the amount of fear that Alice's actions over the past decade had instilled into the Commons. Alice had not been put on trial, and was not accused of any particular crimes, but an ordinance had been made regarding her. The ordinance goes as follows:

> Because a complaint was made to the king that some women have pursued various business and disputes in the king's courts by way of maintenance, bribing and influencing the parties, which thing displeases the king; the king should forbid any woman to do it, and especially Alice Perrers, on penalty of whatever the said Alice can forfeit and of being banished from the realm.[21]

This is a fantastically intriguing piece of writing. Alice was accused of meddling with the courts of law and influencing the outcome of trials. The chronicler Thomas Walsingham elaborates this charge further, saying that Alice 'felt no embarrassment in taking her place on the bench of judges at Westminster'.[22] Far from being content with her status as mistress, and the benefits bestowed upon her by Edward, Alice was accused of acting nefariously for her own gain and the gain of her friends. Alice was specifically banned from doing so any longer by this ordinance. If she broke this, she would no longer simply be banished from court but she would have to leave the kingdom altogether and would have everything she owned confiscated.

The fear that Alice's actions struck into the hearts of the men responsible for the rule of the realm is clear. It was not just Alice who was a danger, but any woman who might come after her. Alice's actions were wrong not because they influenced the law of the land, but because she was a woman who was transgressing her expected place in society. The ordinance is specific in that it is forbidding any woman from doing so again, not just any person (and thus, any man).

Walsingham even slips in an accusation of witchcraft into his chronicle, claiming that during the Good Parliament a priest who was 'an evil magician, dedicated to evildoing', was arrested. This man was supposedly under the employment of Alice, who used him to bewitch the king into undertaking their affair and '[enabled] Alice to get whatever she wanted from the king'.[23] In reality, no such accusation exists in the official record. Walsingham simply inserted this fictional story to add to the evil, scheming persona of his version of Alice. The only way a woman could have gathered the power that Alice had, the only way she could possibly have charmed a great king like Edward, was through witchcraft.

Whilst Alice was banished from Edward's presence, she was otherwise free to live her life as she pleased. She retained control of all the lands she had gathered over the years and was able to continue operating as a *femme sole*. For the court, it seems that this was considered satisfactory. The evil influence of a grasping mistress was removed from the king's presence, and now business could focus on punishing the men around him who were seen to be far more dangerous. Latimer and Lyons had supposedly stolen from the crown and had impoverished the kingdom for their own personal benefit. It was time for them to face the consequences of their actions.

Whilst it was traditional for unhappy subjects to blame evil advisors who surrounded the king, to avoid placing any blame on the king himself, in the case of the Good Parliament it seems that the country at large genuinely did believe that the crown's problems were due to greedy, selfish advisors taking advantage of an ailing king. The Commons were now ready to proceed against Lyons and Latimer. By the end of May both men were arrested, their goods confiscated and their trials awaited.[24]

However, the kingdom was dealt a huge blow on 8 June when Prince Edward, heir to the throne, died at Westminster Palace. The death of this universally loved man was devastating to all sides involved in the Good Parliament. The prince had been seen as a defender of the common man, a symbolic leader for the rebels in the Good Parliament. They had confidence to act against Edward III's advisors because they knew the prince would be on their side.[25] Moreover, the succession was now in crisis. The heir to the throne was a 9-year-old boy and, though no one wanted to say it, it was clear the king would not live long enough to see Prince Richard out of a minority rule. When Edward died, England would be left with a child king.

Edward was devastated by the loss of his eldest son. He left London in his grief and travelled to his manor at Havering, staying there for the rest of June and into July.[26] His son was dead, his mistress was banished from his presence, and his court was falling apart from in-fighting and parliamentary trials. Following the dying wishes of Prince Edward, King Edward immediately acknowledged Prince Richard as his heir and brought him into the royal household.

After a delay in proceedings due to the death of Prince Edward, the Commons pushed on with the trial of Lyons and Latimer. In another innovation, the two men were impeached by parliament. Although impeachment already existed in common law courts, it had yet to be used in parliament.[27] It meant that in future, parliament could use impeachment to initiate trials against individuals, rather than having to wait for the agreement of the crown. Inevitably, both men were found guilty. They were imprisoned upon payment of a fine, and banned from ever again holding office. But parliament pushed further against Lyons, claiming his 'crimes were so great and horrible that this did not suffice to make satisfaction' and thus he should be punished as if he had committed treason. With no other choice, the crown was forced to agree, and all his goods and lands were confiscated.[28]

With two successful trials under its belt, parliament decided to push on and try to impeach numerous other men of the household for similar crimes of corruption and the ruin of the kingdom. Finally, on 10 July – nearly eleven weeks after starting – the Good Parliament drew to a close. The Commons had destroyed the court clique that had dominated for most of the decade, and they were confident that with a new advisory council in place the kingdom would recover and go back to its glory days.

At the close of parliament, King Edward was at Eltham Palace. He was unable to travel back to Westminster due to illness, which had plagued him since the death of his son. Alice Perrers's whereabouts is a mystery, as no evidence survives to say where she retreated to after her banishment during parliament. It is clear, though, that she stuck to the orders for a time. Edward was left alone. Meanwhile, the men of the Good Parliament were hailed as heroes and popular songs were composed celebrating the speaker, Peter de la Mare.[29]

Over summer an eerie silence drew over the country and the government turned its attention to a suitable funeral for Prince Edward. John de Southeray had not been affected by his mother's banishment, for he was granted clothing to attend the prince's funeral.[30] King Edward's health finally seemed to be recovering, and he spent the rest of July and August on a small progress across Kent and Essex.[31] As he mourned his son and faced his own mortality, Edward finally turned to finishing off the tomb of his late beloved wife, Philippa. At the end of May, he paid a stonemason of London for making angels to adorn her tomb, and this was followed by another payment on 28 June to the same mason 'for divers costs and expenses incurred about the tomb of Philippa, late Queen of England'. These included pieces of ironwork, copper angels and two effigies representing two of their children who died in infancy, William of Windsor and Blanche of the Tower.[32]

But by the end of August 1376 Edward III was seriously ill. The nature of his illness during this period is not fully known to us today. Walsingham snidely suggested that he was lovesick for Alice, saying that his illness was 'not, as is believed, typical of the feebleness natural to old men, but one which is said to occur generally in young men who have been deeply smitten by love'. If his readers were to be left in any doubt as to his meaning, he makes it completely clear that Edward 'had incurred this weakness because of his longing for this harlot, Alice Perrers, in that she had been banished from his presence'.[33] More persuasively, another chronicler claimed that Edward had a type of ulcer or cancerous growth.[34] A final possibility is that Edward had suffered a stroke. Whatever the cause, Edward was severely incapacitated and this was a huge worry.

Edward's condition was so severe that he was not even able to attend the funeral of Prince Edward at the end of September and he had to send cloth of gold to be offered to the funeral procession on his behalf instead.[35] As September progressed his health worsened, with six different doctors attending to him. With the arrival of October it seemed like Edward might die any day. The Archbishop of Canterbury sent a letter to his diocese on 2 October from London ordering 'special prayers' to be said for the 'healthy state' of the king, and over the next few days Edward's affairs were put in order.[36]

On 7 October 1376, King Edward III drew up his will at his manor of Havering-atte-Bower, certain that death was near. Appropriate grants were bestowed to his family, including to his 'dearest daughter' Princess Isabella.[37]

In the end, the king lived to see another day. Perhaps shaken by the close call with death, John of Gaunt decided to bring some comfort to his father in his final days, and he recalled Alice to court. Taking her chances, Alice hastened to the manor of Havering, where Edward was still resting. However, Alice was now keenly aware of the dangers caused by her place by the king's side, and she swiftly had a general pardon issued to her. On 22 October at Havering, it was declared that Alice was to be pardoned of all of her debts for money and precious objects 'received or delivered by her or by others by her supervision in the king's chamber, the receipt of the Exchequer or elsewhere, for all time past'. She was further pardoned for any actions 'real, personal or mixed' which anyone in the royal family might have against her, as well as for all felonies, quarrels or trespasses she might be under suspicion of.[38]

Gaunt was not merely being generous to Alice; he had decided that the over-stepping of authority of the Good Parliament needed to be rectified. The crown was in crisis, and he viewed himself as its saviour. The only way to fix the problems the country was experiencing was to reinstate crown authority, and this meant no bowing to the whims of the common man. It was the king's prerogative to choose his own courtiers, and so Gaunt decided those condemned by the parliament needed restitution.

Edward was persuaded to issue pardons to all those impeached and convicted during the Good Parliament, with the exception of Lyons. Latimer had his fine of 20,000 marks wiped clean, and he was restored to his previous estate. He was fully pardoned of any felonies, treasons or conspiracies he might have partaken in. Gaunt was not the only one working to reinstate the previous court clique, and Alice seems to have taken a particular interest in the fate of William Wyndesore, the disgraced Lieutenant of Ireland.

Wyndesore's time in Ireland had been a thorn in the side of the English. Whilst he was a powerful man and capable military commander, he was despised by the Irish for his harsh, bordering on tyrannical, rule. This had not changed during his second term as lieutenant. So bad had the complaints become that a coffer had to be specially purchased 'to contain the rolls and memoranda of the accusations against William de Windsor'.[39] When Wyndesore returned to England from Ireland in the summer, he was arrested and imprisoned in the Tower of London, but just four days later he was released.[40]

As the king began to recover, plans were put in place to start securing the succession. Near the end of November, Prince Richard was invested as Prince of Wales and Duke of Cornwall, and by March the next year he had been given an increased income to suit his new status as heir to the throne.[41] The court came together in December to celebrate Christmas, and after the difficulties that 1376 had thrown at the crown, it was decided huge celebrations were needed. It was, after all, still Edward's jubilee year.

The whole kingdom was said to have gathered together, with the chronicler Froissart explaining that 'all the prelates, earls, barons and knights of England were commanded to attend'.[42] Edward was still recovering his strength at his manor of Havering for the festive season, with his beloved Alice by his side. Alice and Edward's son, John, was also with them at Havering and was gifted a sleeved doublet made from eastern silk brocade for the celebrations.[43] Their two daughters, Joan and Jane, were also with them.

With Christmas over, and most of the disgraced courtiers returned to Edward's presence, John of Gaunt felt confident enough to officially discredit the disaster of the Good Parliament. A new parliament was summoned for 27 January, and due to the fragile health of Edward, who had 'been in great peril of his life', parliament was informed that Prince Richard would preside over the session in his absence.[44] Tensions had been rising with France, and war once again seemed imminent, so it was necessary to obtain the taxes from parliament which had been refused during the Good Parliament to secure England's defences.

With the threat of France, and the need to restore the natural order, John of Gaunt had taken it upon himself to make sure the Commons would fall into line this time. Some form of election fixing had clearly taken place, with very few of the MPs who had sat in the Good Parliament being returned.[45] This new group of men fulfilled their duty, and repealed most of what the Good Parliament had achieved. It was also forced to agree to pardon those who had been convicted.[46] Although Alice had already secured a personal pardon from Edward, it was now conceded that 'in the last parliament, by false accusation and without due process, Alice Perrers was deprived of the common liberty which each loyal liege of the king, men as well as women, should enjoy and have freely'. It was also noted that Alice had not been present at the previous parliament and thus was unable to defend herself. As a result of these considerations, MPs petitioned Edward and his council to 'cause her to be entirely restored to her first estate'.[47]

It was a significant victory for Alice. Although she had been returned to Edward's presence for a few months, and had received a pardon from him, it was now confirmed in parliament that she had done no wrong. Her prospects were looking far better, especially as by early February Edward was finally well enough to leave Havering-atte-Bower and return to his palace at Sheen, via Westminster Palace. He travelled by barge and as he passed through London, the nobles who had boats and barges of their own joined him on the water.[48]

Meanwhile, Alice had quickly reverted to scheming at court and enjoying her power as the woman by the side of such a powerful king. In fact, she was seemingly almost constantly in his presence. In December, she had interfered in important council business regarding Ireland. Although William Wyndesore had escaped any punishment for his handling of the Irish lieutenancy, it had been decided by the council that they should still look into the accusations against him. It was ordered that a knight, Sir Nicholas Dagworth, should go to Ireland and open enquiries. William had become an ally of Alice's, and so she tested her newly returned position to help out her friend. She persuaded Edward to cancel the order, arguing that Dagworth was a known enemy of William and 'it was unreasonable that one enemy should be the judge of another'.[49] To the frustration of the council and the court, Edward acquiesced and the commission was cancelled.

Shortly after this, Alice had one of her greatest victories yet. On 7 January 1377, her son John married Mary Percy, Alice's ward. Alice had held Mary's wardship for nearly seven years, and she now decided to use this control to her advantage. John de Southeray held royal blood, and this gave him a heightened status, but the mar of bastardy meant he would be limited in how far he could rise. By marrying into an established, powerful noble family, Alice was securing a bright future for her son. Any children that John and Mary would have would be legitimate nobles, and combined with the wealth and favour Alice had already secured for John through his father, John's prospects were safeguarded. Alice Perrers, who had come from obscure beginnings, was now the mother of children of royal blood, and she had ensured her future descendants would be of a far higher status in life than she had come from.

The wedding was most likely held at the manor of Havering.[50] Edward was still resting there at the time, and Alice would have wanted John's father to witness his wedding – and to have the legitimacy of the king presiding over the celebrations. It was also just a few weeks after Christmas, when the family had been together there, so it is unlikely they had moved away so soon. The bride was around 9 years old, and the groom 12 going on 13. The couple were lavished with expensive, sumptuous clothes for their wedding. For the ceremony, John wore a lined gown made from cloth of silver, and a hood of scarlet. Mary had a long mantle with a train which was lined with pured miniver, a beautiful addition to her outfit.[51]

At least one of John's sisters appears to have been involved in the ceremony, for Edward bestowed further generous gifts of clothing to Mary and an unnamed sister of John for the occasion. John's sister's outfits were to be 'of the livery of his aforesaid wife', suggesting that this sister had perhaps been designated as a female attendant for Mary. Alice's elder daughter, Joan, was around 10 years old, and her younger daughter, Jane, was around 8; as the more senior, it is more likely that Joan took part in the celebrations.

The girls were each gifted a fine trousseau by Edward: a corset and a hood, both lined with pured miniver and trimmed with ermine; a silk cloth kirtle; gowns of silks lined with miniver, with ermine at the collar and cuffs; a mantle of scarlet cloth and pured miniver; a mantle of blood-red cloth lined with grey squirrel fur; and a further corset and kirtle made from blood-red cloth lined with pured miniver. This was an extremely generous gift, and over 3,500 squirrel furs were used to provide these items of clothing.[52] Less than two weeks later, Edward extended his gift-giving further, sending Mary a bed made from silk cloth.[53] Edward was obviously joyous at the wedding of one of his children, and it must have been a happy occasion to raise his spirits after his brush with death. One has to suggest, though, that Alice might have been involved in the procurement of such gifts, especially when her daughter benefited as well as her son. With the marriage secured, Mary moved in with Alice and her family.[54]

On 2 March 1377 parliament – shortly to be known as the 'Bad Parliament' for its undoing of the work of the Good Parliament – closed its session. A feast had been held on Sunday 1 March to celebrate its conclusion, as was customary, but those in England probably felt they had little to celebrate.[55] After a brief presence on the River Thames, the king had been hidden away at his palace of Sheen, and now his health once again took a turn for the worse, with further medicines required for his use.[56] It seems likely that by this point, Edward had suffered a stroke. He was said to have sat still 'like a statue in position, unable to speak'.[57]

During this period, so Walsingham says, 'that evil woman began to obtain, contrary to the will of the people but with the king's blessing, a shameful increase in possessions', and it does indeed seem as though Alice Perrers was desperately trying to take whatever favours she could get out of Edward, knowing her time was limited.[58] In Edward's lucid moments, Alice continued to obtain grants of land and other favours. On 24 February, an order was sent to Edward's butler to send Alice the tuns of wine which had fallen into arrears from his grant to her for her 'good service to Queen Philippa' back in 1366.[59]

In the middle of March, Alice once again used her influence to restore her friends at court, and Edward issued an order for Richard Lyons and Nicholas Carew to come to him at his palace of Sheen. Although Lyons had received a pardon from the Bad Parliament, he had not been fully forgiven for his crimes and had been ordered to pay back debts he owed to the crown. Carew was the Keeper of the Privy Seal and seemingly a friend or at least an ally of Alice. When Carew got to Sheen he found Edward in his bed and Lyons already there. Alice was sitting at the head of Edward's bed. Carew was then told that Edward had decided to pardon Lyons for the £300 debt he owed, perhaps a reasonable request. Edward's instructions went even further, saying that he wanted to gift Lyons 1,000 marks of treasure and restore the lands which had been confiscated from Lyons and granted to Edward's sons Edmund of Langley and Thomas of Woodstock.[60]

Perhaps aware that this request was problematic, Carew requested various knights and squires who were in the room to come within the king's curtains to hear Edward's order for themselves. After this had been done, Alice instructed one of the knights, Sir Alan Buxhill, to tell Edward's children of his orders, and inform them that they were to vacate the properties. Buxhill, perhaps indignantly, said that he would gladly do so as long as the king ordered him to. So, 'at the instance of the said Alice the king ordered him to do it at once'.[61] Accordingly, on 17 March 1377 Richard Lyons received his official pardon from the king and had the judgements against him overturned and his lands and rents returned to him.[62] Once again, Alice had demonstrated the power she held through the king, and her ability to bend the court to her will.

Despite the king's increasingly poor health, as spring arrived plans were made to hold a grand Garter celebration on St George's Day. The celebration of the previous year had been successful in restoring morale to the king, his court and the country, and after the disaster of the past year it was thought the crown could do with capitalising on this once again. At the start of April orders were issued for two Garter robes to be given to Prince Richard and Henry, Earl of Derby (son of John of Gaunt), to fill the slots left in the order by the deaths of Prince Edward and another knight since its last meeting. Two days later, on 6 April, another order was given for the issuing of Garter robes to the rest of the knights of the order, in preparation for the forthcoming celebrations. The previously disgraced Lord Latimer was among the men receiving their robes.[63]

More robes were issued on 12 April, this time made from scarlet cloth. These were to go to a group of young men who were to be knighted as part of the celebrations: Thomas of Woodstock, Henry, Earl of Derby, 'the son of Dame Alice Perrers' and the heirs of various other nobles.[64] This list, provided by the author of the *Anonimalle Chronicle*, is one of the most notable contemporary suggestions that John de Southeray was indeed the child of Edward III. No contemporary document ever explicitly states this, but the order of the boys listed makes it clear. First on the list was Edward's own, legitimate son. Next was his grandson, who later became King Henry IV. Next was Alice Perrers's son – no father listed – who came above the heirs to the greatest lords in the land. It was an implicit statement that the king was his father.[65]

On the feast of St George, 23 April 1377, John de Southeray was knighted by King Edward III, alongside members of the nobility and two future kings. Alice Perrers had triumphed. Her son was now a knight, married to a daughter of one of the great noble families of England. His prospects in life could not look brighter. Edward's reign had been marked by knights from humbler backgrounds making their fortunes and rising in status due to their military prowess and their dedication to the king. John now had all the tools he needed to do the same, and with a mother like Alice championing his cause, success would seem all but guaranteed.

John even seemed to be ingratiating himself with the young Prince Richard, his half-nephew, for there is a record from Richard's household accounts relating to the day of his knighting which shows him gifting two saddles to 'the bastard', presumed to be John.[66] The boys were a similar age, John probably only being a few years older than Richard, and would have grown up at court together. If John could keep Richard's friendship, then favour on Alice's family could continue into the next reign.

Alice now decided to make her final moves in securing the future of her son. On 13 May, John was granted the manor of 'Lowystoft' near Yarmouth and the hundred of 'Luddynglond' in Suffolk with all of its income and profits, as well as the reversion of several other manors including: Bolton near Carlisle; two manors which at that time were held by Edward's daughter Isabella and her husband; the manors of 'Faxflete', 'Hicchyng' and 'Walton upon Trente'; as well as all the lands held by a knight named John de Nowers.[67] These were the lands that Alice had gathered with her trusted allies two years previously, who had loyally held them until she was ready to use them. Now these lands were formally granted by the king to his son. The grant of an interest in seven manors and even more land was a significant gift for a teenage boy, and would have given him a good income in his own right until he was old enough to gain the income from his new wife's inheritance. Alice was making sure her son had property in his own right, to guard against any future attacks on her.

June saw Alice continue to '[steal] from the king anything she could pluck from his grasp' as his life teetered on the edge.[68] She was by his side at Sheen on 5 June when he granted her wood for life from Whittlewood forest for fuel for whenever she stayed at the castle of Moor End in Northamptonshire, as well as further wood for timber needed to repair the castle and its buildings. The following day, Edward confirmed Alice's interest for life in Moor

End Castle and the manor of the same name in Oxford.[69] It had not even been fifteen years since Edward had bought Moor End Castle for himself, spending nearly £1,000 on its buildings.[70] Now it was for Alice's use. Edward also bestowed Alice and John with further items of clothing as his life hung in the balance. Alice was gifted sumptuous ermine-trimmed gowns and hoods of scarlet and sanguine cloth, whilst John received a satin coat of arms.[71]

Aware the end was near, and that she was increasingly alienating those at court with her desperate attempts to secure her future after Edward's death, Alice felt it necessary to obtain a further pardon from Edward. She had, of course, already received one the previous October, as well as one from parliament earlier in 1377, but Alice must have been sensing more and more that this might not be enough to help her once she had lost the king's protection. Her actions over the past few months had clearly met with great disapproval.

On 4 June Alice was granted another full pardon by the king. This pardoned her from 'all debts, prests [loans] and accounts in which she is bound to the king on account of any sums of money, or for gold, silver, jewels, cloths or other things'. Alice's paranoia of the dangers posed by all her past deeds was clear, as the pardon tried to cover every eventuality. Anything which she might have done in the present, 'as well in the king's time as when she was with the late queen Philippa', was to be covered by the pardon, and it ends with another long list of potential crimes to be pardoned from: 'all felonies, receiving of felons, confederacies, conspiracies, ambidextries, champerties, maintenances of false quarrels, conventicles, allegiances and other trespasses whereof she is indicted or appealed, and of any consequent waivers'.[72] Her real fear is evident, but the grants of further favours to her across the next two days show that she couldn't resist trying to get every last benefit from the king.

Alice was seemingly guilty, as Thomas Walsingham accuses her, of being 'like a dog waiting expectantly at the table for a morsel to be tossed to him by his master's hand', but to an extent her actions are understandable.[73] Alice was a single woman who held the tainted reputation of being a mistress. She had three children to look after who were all under the age of 15, and life was difficult for women in her position who had been legitimately married, let alone a mistress. The Good Parliament had shown Alice that there was at least a section of the Commons and the court who resented – even hated – her, and she must have known she was going to face a battle once Edward died.

Alice was not a member of the nobility who had authority and power through virtue of her birth. She did not have powerful family members to call upon who worked in government and could support her, as noblewomen would have. She was not a man who could make his own way in the world, who could rise through the ranks through military prowess as so many of the self-made men at Edward's court had done through the decades. Everything she had become had relied upon Edward's favour. Yes, she had built her own empire using her wits and clever business dealings, but little of that would have been available to her without him. Whatever Alice had when Edward died might well be all she would have for the rest of her life, and with the odds so weighed against her, it is easy to see why she desperately took the last pieces she could. She needed to protect herself and her children.

There was now no more that Alice could do. Froissart lamented: 'On 21 June 1377, the gallant and noble King Edward III departed this life, to the deep distress of the whole realm of England.'[74] In his final days, Edward had apparently talked jovially of hawking and hunting, but as the end had neared he had suddenly lost the power of speech.[75] He almost certainly suffered a stroke, and might well have suffered a few smaller ones earlier in the year. Alice was likely by his side as he died, but he was also almost certainly surrounded by members of his family: his three surviving legitimate sons, John, Edmund and Thomas, and his daughter Isabella. As Edward's health had declined, it was noted that Alice and Princess Isabella 'would spend the whole night with him', showing that both women took care to attend on him.[76] Members of his court, lords and knights of the land would all be at Sheen waiting to hear the news, ready to begin serving the next king. Those who were not with the king would have been at Kennington Palace waiting on Prince Richard and his mother, Joan of Kent.[77]

Thomas Walsingham attempts to portray a scene of the king's death very different to the reality. According to him, Edward was almost entirely alone upon his death. He says that Alice was with Edward as he was dying, but as 'she perceived that the king stood on the threshold of death' she decided to take one more thing from Edward: 'She artfully removed from the royal hands the rings, which the king wore on his fingers to display his royalty … so, in this way bidding the king farewell', she fled. She had shown the world that she had never loved Edward for himself, but solely for the possessions he had given her. Edward was left alone with no one but a priest to hear his confession and absolve him of his sins as he died.[78]

The scene is dramatic, and it is a story that has marred Alice's name for centuries. Many have believed the story through the years, and it is still sometimes quoted as fact in modern history books. It ignites the fires of negativity which surround Alice's character – that she was a greedy social climber who took advantage of a senile old man and twisted his once-noble character into a shell of a man who showered her in gifts. But it is the version of a religious man angry at an immoral king, his mistress and his grasping courtiers, who was seeking to use the tale as a moral warning to his readers. It was simply out of the question for a medieval king to be left alone at his time of death like that. Moreover, it was not within the character of Edward's family and their relationship for his children to have abandoned him at the time of his death.

If further evidence was needed, then no rings belonging to Edward were ever found in Alice's possession after his death – nor were they ever accused of having been in her possession in the official record. If, as Walsingham claims, these rings were there to show Edward's royal authority, then they would have been recorded in his wardrobe and would have been passed on to Richard, and so somebody would have noticed they were missing.

Alice was probably at Edward's side as he died, but she most likely would have left court soon after. There was no place for her there without him, and she might have wished to distance herself from grieving family members and courtiers who might be reminded of everything she had taken in recent months. She was almost certainly grieving herself. Whilst her relationship with Edward had been financially beneficial, and there is no doubt she took plenty of material wealth from Edward – even taking advantage of him when he was near death – she must surely have had at least fondness for him, if not love.

Whilst the last year or so of Edward's life had been marked by infirmity, senility and strokes, Alice and Edward had been in a relationship to some extent for thirteen years or more. When Alice had first started a romantic relationship with Edward, although he was several decades older than her he was still a handsome, strong king who commanded the respect and admiration of everyone in his own kingdom and beyond. He was a charming, caring man, who had earned the love of his courtiers, his wife and his children, and there is no reason why his character would not have been appealing to Alice, too. She was the mother of three of his children and it is extremely unlikely that after more than a decade by his side she viewed him solely as a means to wealth and not as a friend and even lover.

Whether Alice was still at court for the king's funeral is unclear, but it is likely that her son John was part of the funeral. John was, after all, the king's son, half-uncle to the new king, and half-brother to the men who were now organising the kingdom. He was a member of Edward's household as a young knight, and so he had every right to be part of the funeral cortège. Edward's gift of a silk coat of arms to John was recorded just four days before his death, suggesting that John was with his father as he died. Around 550 members of Edward's household and administration were provided with black mourning liveries for Edward's funeral, and there is no reason why John would not have been part of this.[79] John was mourning a father too, so Edward's family surely would have shown pity on the boy and allowed him to attend. They might even have allowed his sisters to attend, too.

Edward's funeral was bound to be one of the grandest that century; it might even have been the most expensive funeral that England had ever seen.[80] The king was embalmed, and a wooden effigy was created in his image. In fact, it seems to have been modelled on a death mask, and the drooping on the left side of the mouth provides further evidence that Edward had suffered at least one stroke before he died.[81] His body stayed at the palace of Sheen for two weeks, until it was brought through London in a solemn procession which lasted a couple of days. Over 2,000 people took part in the funeral cortège, and the country was overcome with grief at the death of their constant king.[82] Froissart exclaimed that 'to witness and hear the grief of the people, their sobs and screams and lamentations on that day, would have rended anyone's heart'.[83] Edward was interred near the body of his most beloved wife, Philippa of Hainault, in Westminster Abbey, just as he had promised on her deathbed.

Edward was buried on Sunday 5 July 1377. The second-longest-reigning English monarch up to that point in time, Edward quickly became a king of legend, and it was not exaggerated flattery that led Froissart to say that 'his like had not been seen since the days of King Arthur'.[84] Edward had brought the warring baronage together and unified the country that had become broken and bitter during the reign of his father and regency of his mother. He launched one of the greatest wars in history against France to claim the throne for his own, and he brought many improvements to the court and government. He was a generous man willing to reward his subjects on merit as well as birth, and his reign saw the establishment of many great noble families. He created the Order of the Garter, the most prestigious knightly order in the country, and his court was known throughout Europe for its chivalry and revelry, but his final years had been marked by tragedy as almost all of his close friends and family died around him.

Alice had truly been the second love of his life. Philippa had filled his heart for over forty years, and no woman would ever take her place. But it is exceedingly clear that Alice was not just a fling for an ageing king. The attention he lavished upon her, the thoughtful gifts he gave her – such as the brooch inscribed 'think of me' and 'never apart' just a few years before his death – and that he seems to have remained faithful to her all show that for Edward, at least, Alice was his love. Their relationship was always going to have met with disapproval. It had begun in the lifetime of his queen, and as much as he adored Alice, her position in life meant he knew he would never be able to marry her. If Alice had been a noblewoman, and Edward had been able to make her his legitimate wife, then the story might have ended very differently, and Alice might have received far less vitriol than she did both at the time and in subsequent centuries. As it was, Alice was now alone in the world with three children to look after, and a court full of people who were against her. Her life was about to get very dangerous.

9

Downfall of a Lady

As the dust settled after the funeral of Edward III, the court was quickly busy with preparing for the coronation of the young King Richard II. Less than a month after Edward III's death, Richard of Bordeaux was crowned King of England in Westminster Abbey on 16 July 1377. The court and the country at large were filled with a tantalising mix of mourning for their heroic king of fifty years and excitement at the prospect of a new, young, invigorated king. Though it would be some years before Richard could truly exercise power, the old court clique run by Alice Perrers, Lyons and Latimer would have no currency with the new king. Trusted, loyal men could be placed around Richard during his minority, with the hope that they would continue to influence him for good as he came of age. For Alice, though, this meant a renewed danger.

How Alice spent the lead-up to Richard's coronation is uncertain. It is probable she did not show her face at court, but she was almost certainly still in the capital, living with her children and daughter-in-law, Mary Percy, at her manor in Thames Street. Alice must have wondered how to proceed with her life now. Undoubtedly, she was in mourning for the loss of her partner, but perhaps more pressing than that was her uncertainty of how the court and country would react to her now that she didn't have the king's protection. The Good Parliament of the previous year must have massively shaken her confidence. Now that Edward was dead, what would happen to her?

Despite this, Alice would have had a degree of assurance in her circumstances. Much of the property she owned she had tied up under enfeoffment-to-use, meaning it was safe from any bid that could be made against her. Her son had a respectable income of his own from the crown, and he owned property in his own right. He had also been knighted and was married to a very eligible heiress. Certainly, the future of her son was secure, and Alice probably thought she could ride out any storm that would come her way. Perhaps she even hoped she would come out of the transfer of power unscathed.

If these had been Alice's hopes, then she was sorely mistaken. The new regime of Richard II wasted no time in taking action against those it had failed to persecute the previous year. People across the country were invited to submit petitions against those at court they felt had wronged them or owed them a debt, and Alice Perrers was number one on this list. Peter de la Mare had been returned to parliament, and he was bringing back the spirit of the Good Parliament. Parliament opened on 13 October, and plaintiffs were informed that they had to present their petitions by 21 November ready for proceedings against Alice. With all the complaints gathered, a trial against her was launched in parliament on 22 November 1377.[1] Unlike the Good Parliament, where Alice was given an informal warning against her actions, Richard II's government was ready to punish her fully for her perceived crimes.

Despite everything, only two formal charges were levied against Alice: firstly, she was to be charged for acting against the council's order that Sir Nicholas Dagworth was to be sent to Ireland to investigate the accusations against William Wyndesore; and secondly she was charged with persuading Edward III to pardon Richard Lyons, restoring his property and cancelling the fine he was ordered to pay after the proceedings of the Good Parliament. These charges laid bare the overwhelming influence that Alice was said to have had over Edward III, particularly in the last few months of his life, for Alice 'so importuned the said grandfather [Edward], in his court at Sheen, that by her singular pursuit and procurement' Lyons was pardoned of his crimes. Unlike the informal proceedings against Alice in the Good Parliament, Alice was present in this parliament in front of the Lords and Commons of the land to answer the charges against her. When asked how she wished to respond to the charges against her, Alice replied:

> Saying that she was not guilty of those articles of accusation, and that she was ready to vouch for and prove this by the testimony of Sir John Ypres, then steward of the household of the said grandfather, and William Street, then controller of the said household, Sir Alan Buxhill, knight, and Nicholas Carew then keeper of the privy seal of the said grandfather, and others who had been in the said grandfather's entourage and with him at the time when she was supposed to have committed the offence, and who best knew the truth of the matter.[2]

In the event, almost all the men whom Alice called upon as witnesses betrayed her. Sworn in and questioned in front of Edward's sons John of Gaunt and Edmund of Langley, as well as the earls of March, Arundel and Warwick, they all gave evidence supporting the accusations against Alice. Roger Beauchamp, Edward's chamberlain, swore on the Holy Gospels that Alice had submitted a bill for him to take to Edward which recalled Dagworth from Ireland. Beauchamp recounted that he and Alice had an argument over the bill, as he did not want to take it to the king because it contradicted the council's order. The argument attracted the attention of Edward, who asked what the bill contained. When Beauchamp informed him of its contents, Edward 'at once said that the petition was reasonable'.[3] This suggests that whilst Alice was indeed using her influence to help her friend William Wyndesore, the king was not being completely controlled by Alice and was using his own judgement in the matter.

Another man, Sir Philip de la Vache, stated that he never heard Alice speak directly with Edward about Dagworth, although she had created 'a great stir in the king's household' by saying it was unreasonable for him to go to Ireland when he was an enemy of Wyndesore's. He did, however, confirm that he was in the king's chamber when Lyons was pardoned and had heard what had happened. Going into far more detail about the pardoning of Lyons were Nicholas Carew and Alan Buxhill, who explained how Alice had been sitting at the head of Edward's bed and orchestrated Lyons's pardon, even pressuring the king to comply.[4] Again, both men stated that they knew nothing of Alice causing Dagworth's recall from Ireland, although Buxhill had heard Alice talking about the matter on many occasions.

William Street also turned on Alice, saying that whilst he had heard another person, William of York, raise with the king the matter of Dagworth's mission, Alice agreed it was unreasonable to send Dagworth and, 'according to his knowledge, the said Lady Alice had been the principal instigator of the said matter, or so he believed'. The only man questioned who vaguely acted neutrally in the charges against Alice was John Beverley, who 'said that he had never heard the said Alice speak with the king concerning either matter; because she was wary of him, and never spoke of anything in his presence'. Whilst he did not provide concrete evidence of Alice's misdeeds, he 'believed in his own mind that she was the instigator of the said business, because he knew of no other who could have pursued it'.[5]

In total, seven knights and nine squires of Edward's household were questioned before the panel of noblemen who all swore on oath that 'Alice was, for gain, the principal instigator' in the recalling of Nicholas Dagworth from Ireland and that she 'was wholly willing to advise and promote' the pardon of Lyons whilst she was at Sheen that May. The evidence was damning, and Alice was found guilty of the charges. It was agreed that Alice had therefore broken the ordinance from the Good Parliament against women interfering in court business, and as such Alice was subject to full confiscation of her lands, tenements, goods, chattels and all other possessions.[6]

The testimony of the men during Alice's trial, the stories of her evil personality as told by Walsingham, and her perceived greed and immorality by subsequent historians mean that Alice has gained a terrible reputation. She is thought to have alienated everyone at court, beyond her few lackeys who carried out her business, and to have been universally hated, as epitomised by the proceedings against her in the Good Parliament and her subsequent trial during Richard II's reign. However, Alice's defence right at the start of her trial that she could prove her innocence through the testimony of the men who ultimately betrayed her may reveal a different story.

Alice had captured the heart of Edward III, a man who had only had eyes for one woman for a large part of his life, and she was at least on cordial terms with his son, John of Gaunt, who had given her gifts and supported her return to court after the Good Parliament. She even had a friendship with Bishop William Wykeham, a powerful man of the Church. But unless Alice was completely oblivious to those around her – which considering her clear intelligence and perceptiveness is obviously not the case – she must have had at least some indication from many members of Edward's household that she had some allies and even friends among them.

It could be argued that Alice was unaware of how her actions were chafing against men at court, although the testimony of John Beverley shows that she was careful around those whom she did not trust to be on her side. It follows that she had enough self-awareness to know which members of Edward's court and household were more sympathetic to her and her influence. That Alice believed that men like Buxhill, Carew, Ypres and Street would defend her shows that she must have had enough evidence from her time in Edward's household that they would. Carew, for example, had even been one of the trustees of land held in trust for Alice's son, John.[7] This suggests a friendly relationship with the men prior to her trial, even if sometimes they were cautious of the orders given to them on her behalf, and thus that Alice cannot have been as abrasive to those around her as previously imagined. Even Walsingham notes that many lords and lawyers 'made appeals on her behalf not only in private but in public', although he attributes this to Alice having bribed them.[8]

It is not that Alice was innocent of the crimes she was accused of; it makes complete sense that Alice was using her influence to help her friends and allies and that others at court had less incentive to do so. It is very likely that events did transpire as the men described at her trial. But that they did not defend Alice and instead aided her conviction probably says more about the mood at court than it does about Alice's personality. Richard's new regime had made it clear very early on that they were determined to sort the problem of Alice Perrers out once and for all, and so the men called to testify were either with the new government, or with Alice. It made complete sense for their survival to choose the government.

The crimes Alice was convicted of once again highlight that the problem with Alice Perrers was that she was a woman wielding power in a male-dominated world. By the fourteenth century, queens were expected to hold influence over their husbands, but they were not expected to be involved in the everyday decision-making of the king and his council. If a queen interceded in a particular case, it was to be a rare occasion and it was to be done in a feminine way. This is why the symbol of a pregnant Philippa pleading with her husband to spare the lives of the burghers of Calais held so much currency. Queens were meant to be submissive to the authority of their husbands. They were not to seek power for themselves but were to protect the vulnerable in society.[9]

Philippa had fulfilled this expectation of her as an English queen, and in fact far surpassed it. She had given birth to many children, she had never sought to hold power in her own right, and she had always followed her husband in his decisions. The rare times she interceded in events were within the prescribed role given to her as queen. Any other persuasion that Philippa might have enacted on Edward had been behind closed doors, where no records were kept.

Alice subverted this model of ideal female authority. Alice was not a queen quietly pleading with the king to pardon a common thief who had stolen some jewellery: she was a mistress who was blatantly using her position to obtain favours for men who had been judged guilty by parliament and the council. She was directly questioning the decisions of men who helped the king rule the country, doing so at court in front of anyone who would listen, and she was even directing the king himself how to act. That the men during her trial noted how Alice was sitting on the king's bed was an uncomfortable reminder to everyone at court that Alice slept in that very bed. The sexual power of a woman around the king was always suspect, even that of a queen, and for Alice to highlight the power she held by being the king's mistress was an uncomfortable confrontation for the men around her.

With a guilty verdict, Alice was subject to full forfeiture of her goods and banishment from the realm. But Alice caused problems for her judges. She had tied up almost all her land under enfeoffment-to-use, which historically had been protected when their owners had been found guilty of crimes which warranted confiscation. But now that parliament had finally found a solution for Alice, they could not allow her to get away with keeping her wealth.

Parliament thus had to issue a special decree that even all of her enfeoffed lands should be taken from her 'because of the fraud and deceit which can be presumed'. However, parliament was very cautious that this should not set a precedent and that the rights of enfeoffment should be protected. They specifically stated that 'it is neither the king's nor the lords' intention that this ordinance or decision made for so odious a crime in this particular case should apply to any other person, or be taken as an example in any other case'.[10]

Everything that Alice had gained in the last fifteen years was now taken from her. On 3 December 1377, a writ was issued by parliament instructing escheators in counties across the realm to confiscate any lands and goods owned by Alice within their region.[11] As the list of Alice's empire trickled back to the crown, the shocking extent of her holdings was revealed. Alice held fifty-six manors across the country, and although the value of these holdings is unclear, the twenty-six manors listed in surviving valuations from the period gave her a total income of over £480.[12] This was not to mention a variety of other tenements and smaller pieces of land she owned, as well as the vast array of goods, clothing and jewels. A note in the Issues of the Exchequer describes the confiscation of well over 21,000 pearls owned by Alice as part of her jewellery, which came to the staggering value of £468 18s 8d.[13]

When all of this is taken into consideration, it is clear that Alice must have had an income of well over £1,000 a year, making her one of the richest people in the country. At this time, £1,000 was generally the minimum income required to uphold a man of the rank of an earl, the highest level of nobility outside of the royal family other than that of a duke (and the only dukes at this time were Edward III's sons, in any case).[14] Even sixty years after Alice's downfall, just seventy families in England had an annual income of between £300 and £2,500, with the majority of them earning less than £1,000.[15] Alice might never have been able to become Edward's queen, but she was certainly living a lifestyle as close to one as possible.

As the inquisitions were carried out, and the reports were sent back to the government, rumours started to circulate. When the sheriffs of London returned their report into Alice's lands in the city, including the extensive inventory of her goods at her manor on Thames Street, they mentioned

that they had launched an investigation, taking oaths from her neighbours. During the course of their questioning, they discovered something
shocking: 'The said Alice was espoused to William Wyndesore, knight, and
was his wife long before the arrival of the writ.' Unsure how to proceed,
the sheriffs decided that 'as it was not stated in the writ, nor could the jurors
determine, whether the said Alice was the wife of the said William or not,
they took her [goods] which they found into the king's hand'.[16]

This revelation was to change the course of Alice's future. At some point,
Alice had married William Wyndesore, the Lieutenant of Ireland whom she
had saved from investigation, and who was ultimately part of her downfall
during this parliament. When exactly Alice married William has been a source
of contention for historians and contemporaries alike. Thomas Walsingham
claimed in his chronicle that Alice's marriage to William had been discovered
the previous year during the Good Parliament, and that was the reason for
Edward banishing her from his presence; it made him an adulterer and endan-
gered his soul.[17] Although numerous historians have taken this at face value, it
is evident that this was not the case, and Walsingham was probably conflating
the events of the next two years with that of the Good Parliament.[18]

Alice had no need to marry – even in secret – before Edward's death,
and certainly before the Good Parliament. Under medieval law, a woman's
property came under the control of her husband when she married.[19] Alice
had shown how much she valued her independence and ability to control
her own affairs, and before the Good Parliament there had been no hints
of a threat to her position. Marrying before then would have made abso-
lutely no sense for her future. Even after the Good Parliament had shown
her vulnerability, she had been allowed to keep full control of herself and
her property as long as she stayed away from court and Edward. If Alice had
never returned she could have stayed a wealthy, independent woman for as
long as she wished, and a man would only threaten this lifestyle.

On 26 December, the king's council ordered a sale of Alice's goods that
had been taken from her properties in London, giving first refusal to William
as her husband.[20] But the seizure of Alice's goods caused some problems, as
it soon transpired that not everything that had been confiscated belonged to
her. At the end of the London sheriffs' report of Alice's goods in Thames
Street they noted that there were servants and other interested parties who

wanted to claim some of the items.[21] Alice was not living in her manors alone, after all.

In the new year, Richard's government had to make several grants to members of Alice's household returning their goods to them. On 13 January 1378, John de Southeray petitioned for restitution of his goods and furniture that had been in Alice's Thames Street house. A list of his goods was submitted to the king and council itemising which pieces belonged to him and this ran to quite an extensive list on its own, including many pieces of clothing, two collars for two little dogs, two of the primers, and some of the dishes and cutlery.[22] This list was extended and resubmitted two weeks later on 27 January to include a much larger list of goods – perhaps an attempt by a son to save some of his mother's items?[23]

John was noted as living at the time with Thomas, Bishop of Exeter, who was the Lord Treasurer, rather than with his mother. This was probably organised by the royal family as a way to keep an eye on the boy. The placement might not have been all bad for John, as the bishop seems to have been friends with William Wykeham, Alice's trusted ally. The two men had been part of Edward's government together, and the bishop left Wykeham gifts in his will of 1393.[24] By helping John to submit his petition for the return of his goods, the bishop does seem to have been looking out for the young boy. John's goods were duly returned to him, and on 28 January the government also confirmed Edward's patent letters granting John his £100 annual income.[25] Whilst parliament had been keen to punish Alice to the full extent of the law, the royal family seems to have been a lot more sympathetic to her young son.

On 17 January an order was given to the sheriffs to deliver to Digeo de Ware, 'executor of Joan Dachet late damsel of Alice Perers ... all goods and chattels seized into the king's hand ... which the said executor may prove to have been of the said Joan'.[26] Although Alice's wealth and position meant she would have had numerous everyday servants to attend to her, cooking her meals and cleaning her houses, this is a rare insight to her rank and household. Alice had once been a damsel to Queen Philippa, and now she had risen high enough to have damsels of her own.

February saw the government having to wade through more complaints which had arisen from the confiscation of Alice's lands. Because Alice had used enfeoffment-to-use so widely, she had a huge network of men controlling her various manors, farms and tenements for her and now these men had also lost their positions through the confiscation. Alice had people renting premises from her or her feoffees, she had people working her land, and these people were now out of their jobs and homes. The king and council therefore granted many of these rights back to the plaintiffs.[27]

With many of the problems of Alice's confiscation ironed out, the government started to gift Alice's remaining lands and goods as rewards to its loyal allies. Servants of the king, such as his damsel Reymunda de Bourk, his yeoman Adam de Colton and his servant Robert Bulwyk, were given grants of timber, gardens, dovecotes and small dwelling houses that had been Alice's, whilst more important members of the court were given much larger gifts: John of Gaunt was granted Alice's manor at Thames Street alongside all the other houses she had built in the area, whilst King Richard's half-brother, John Holland, was given two manors worth £100 a year.[28] Princess Isabella also received restitution for manors that had belonged to her and her estranged husband, Enguerrand de Coucy, which Alice had taken from the couple 'with subtlety and without reasonable cause'.[29]

Throughout 1378, parliament received dozens of petitions from across the country from people who had grievances against Alice Perrers. At least forty of these petitions survive today at the National Archives, hinting at how many people felt aggrieved by Alice. For comparison, though, during the downfall of the powerful Despensers (the favourites of Edward II) fifty years previously there were hundreds of petitions submitted, suggesting that Alice's wrongdoings were not as widespread as has been portrayed.[30]

On 20 October 1378 the second parliament of Richard II's reign opened at Gloucester. The still-pressing need for money for the young king's government, depleted from the last years of Edward's reign, meant that the Commons had come to the session already hostile, believing that the subsidies granted by the 1377 parliament had been partially siphoned by John of Gaunt for his own uses.[31] The petitioners against Alice expected their business to be dealt with during this parliament, but this was not to be. Most of the petitions have no answers written on them.

Although rumours had circulated since the end of the previous parliament that Alice and William Wyndesore had married, no official proclamation had been made as to this fact. Therefore, the petitions that poured in between the first and second parliaments of Richard's reign all refer to Alice as a single woman, Alice Perrers. This was now to cause an obstruction to the pursuit of justice. At the Gloucester parliament William Wyndesore submitted a petition to the king regarding the judgement against Alice in the 1377 parliament, stating that 'various errors are to be found' and asking that 'the judgment passed against his said wife might be reversed'.[32]

The biggest error in the judgement against Alice was that she had been tried as a *femme sole*, when William was claiming that he and Alice had been married at the time of her trial.[33] Under medieval law, married women could not be tried for a crime in their own right as they were legally tied to their husband. Upon marriage, everything a woman owned became the legal property of her husband, even if she had obtained it in her own right, and her actions were also covered by her husband. If she got into personal debt with another person, the husband was liable for the repayment. If she were accused of a crime, she had the right to have her husband tried alongside her in a joint litigation. Alice had not been extended the luxury of having her husband as a joint defendant – as the marriage had not been known by the court – and so the trial against her, William argued, was legally invalid.

This crucial bit of information is one of the strongest pieces of evidence that their clandestine marriage did not come out during the Good Parliament. William was not clutching at straws with this claim, and the fact that Alice had been tried incorrectly was a huge legal headache for the government and could lead to the need for a second trial of Alice, this time with William alongside her. Alice as a single woman was easy to deal with, but Alice allied with a powerful man like William Wyndesore was a much stronger force to be reckoned with. If the government had known beforehand that she was married, they would have tried her correctly in the parliament of 1377.

The most likely date for Alice and William's marriage was sometime between Edward's death in the summer of 1377 and the point at which it became clear that Alice was going to be put on trial that November. Although Alice had been removed from court after the Good Parliament in 1376, there was no need for her to align herself with another man so soon. The informal judgement had allowed Alice to keep her lands and property, and so she was far stronger – and more independent – staying as a single woman. When Edward nearly died and Alice was recalled to court, Alice might have started to enter into discussions with Wyndesore about a possible marriage alliance, especially considering how hard she worked over the next few months to stop Dagworth from being sent to investigate William's actions in Ireland. William would not make a useful ally if he had been removed in disgrace. But whilst the king was alive it still did not make sense for Alice to actually marry Wyndesore. The only time Alice would be willing to hand over control of her assets would be when Edward died and she knew that she was at risk. She was safer in marriage to Wyndesore than alone.

William's petition to parliament was given a reply by the king's sergeants, who stated that Alice's banishment could not be pardoned in the present parliament, 'nor was it known whether she was outside the kingdom or within the same kingdom'. Either scenario presented a problem for Alice, for if she had complied with the banishment then she needed Richard II's permission to re-enter the country, and if she was still in the country then she was acting against the law. Regardless of Alice's location, the sergeants continued to say that they 'certainly did not intend that by the law she should be allowed to make this plea or any other … until she had the grace of the king himself'.[34]

If parliament hoped that this would dissuade William and Alice then they were sorely mistaken, for the next item on the parliament rolls records that William subsequently submitted another petition to the king asking that the couple be allowed to pursue their case in parliament. The couple finally met with success, and King Richard forwarded their petition to his great council in parliament, commanding that they be allowed to continue with their case.[35] The young Richard was clearly sympathetic to Alice, and the friendship he might have struck up with John de Southeray could well have paid dividends to Alice.

Despite this breakthrough for Alice and William, parliament closed without a decision being made on the judgement against Alice in the previous parliament. Alice was still officially a fugitive who had been convicted of her crimes. Fortunately, the couple did not have to wait too long to try again. The third parliament of Richard's reign was called just a few months later, in April 1379. This gave the couple a chance to submit another petition to the government asking that the trial against Alice be looked at because it had been undertaken in error.[36]

Although the couple's petition once again went unanswered, some headway was made at the end of the year when, on 14 December, William was pardoned for having harboured Alice during her banishment, and Alice herself was pardoned 'for having stayed in the realm since her said banishment, with licence for her to remain as long as she and her husband please'.[37] Alice had never left the country and had in fact been kept by her husband, almost certainly along with her daughters.

Although the first parliament of Richard's reign had been so determined to convict Alice, and the government had indeed benefited from taking custody of Alice's vast possessions, the impetus for punishing Alice had seemingly come from members of parliament looking to settle scores. Many of the men who came to that parliament were the same men from the Good Parliament, including the Speaker, de la Mare, and Walsingham states in his chronicle that Alice was only convicted 'because of the diligence and the wisdom of these knights'.[38]

Now that Alice was under the control of a husband, and not acting as a powerful mistress influencing an ageing king, she was of little threat to the government. The young King Richard had already shown that he was sympathetic to Alice's cause, and the government 'with the assent of the magnates of the realm' was happy to grant pardons to Alice and William for breaking the terms of the banishment. Alice's fate was no longer in the hands of men looking for revenge for the overturned work of the Good Parliament, but instead in those of the royal family with whom she had spent almost two decades.

The pardon highlights Alice's wisdom in allying herself to a man like William Wyndesore, as it was spurred by a private deal made between William and the government two months earlier. In October, William agreed to become constable of the territory of Cherbourg in Normandy at a time when English-controlled territories in France were coming under increasing attacks from the French.[39] William was a capable military commander who had been entrusted with the rule of difficult Ireland, and the government needed men of his expertise to help hold on to English lands. In taking over control of Cherbourg, William also agreed to join a military campaign in Brittany that was going to be launched the following year by Thomas of Woodstock, the youngest child of Edward III. He would lead 200 men-at-arms and 200 archers, funding 100 of the men-at-arms for half a year from his own money, and in return Alice's lands would be given to him.[40] To further sweeten the deal, in November the great council confirmed a grant of £100 a year that Edward III had given to William Wyndesore back in 1367.[41]

William and Alice would have known how much the government needed William's help, and this was a chance to levy his own wealth and military experience in exchange for progress on Alice's case. As well as her husband, Alice was able to call upon the help of one of her old friends and allies, William Wykeham. Wykeham had been made a member of the king's council the previous year, and so was in a position to privately champion Alice's cause. If Walsingham is to be believed, Wykeham even owed Alice a favour. Towards the end of 1376, Wykeham had been removed from office in disgrace under accusations of mismanagement of funds during his time as chancellor.[42] Then, just three days before Edward III died, Wykeham was pardoned and restored to his episcopal estates. According to Walsingham, Wykeham begged Alice for help and she agreed to intervene with the king in return for a large monetary reward.[43] Alice probably did help her friend, although she might not have needed a bribe to do so as the two had often done favours for each other in the past.

Between William Wyndesore agreeing to undertake a significant military expedition, and William Wykeham working behind the scenes at court, in January 1380 Wyndesore felt confident enough to submit another petition to the newly convened parliament. This time, William employed a different tactic and submitted the petition in his own name, instead of jointly with Alice. In it, William mentions how long he had been petitioning for the restoration of Alice's property and that he was looking for the matter to be settled during this parliament.[44] Finally, after two years of campaigning, there was success. In March 1380, William Wyndesore was granted almost all of the lands that had been confiscated from Alice at the end of 1377.

Three months later a suggestion of Wykeham's hand in helping with this restoration is found. On 26 June, Wyndesore granted one of Alice's manors, that of Menestoke in Southampton, to Wykeham and a collection of other men.[45] In fact, just days before the first restitution of Alice's property, William Wykeham founded Seinte Marie College of Wynchestre, later known as New College, Oxford. After Alice and William regained most of Alice's property portfolio, they went on to sell several more pieces of land and rents to Wykeham, which he in turn used to endow New College.[46] This certainly suggests a collusion of some sort. Wykeham might have owed Alice a favour, but in the dangerous world of courtly power, even friends could twist deals to their benefit.

Alice had finally had a small victory. Although she was now required to share her lands with her husband, she had at last seen the return of most of what she had worked hard to gain. But fate was not yet done with Alice. Whilst the king, with the assent of his council and parliament, had given William custody of Alice's property, they had not in fact granted the request in all the couple's earlier petitions, which was to overturn the decision of the 1377 parliament. Whilst Alice had formally been pardoned for ignoring her banishment, had been given indefinite leave to stay in the country, and her property had been returned to her husband, she was still technically convicted of the crimes accused of her. William and Alice had originally asked that the judgement against her be cancelled in the light of the information that she was married at her trial. But this was never done, and Alice's legal status was in limbo as a result.

Although spring had seen success for Alice, January had brought a devastating blow to the future of her son: on 5 January 1380, Pope Urban VI appointed Thomas Arundel, Bishop of Ely, to proceed in an annulment of the marriage of John de Southeray and Mary Percy.[47] After Alice's trial in November 1377, and the confiscation of her lands in early December, Mary Percy's half-brother, Henry Percy, had been granted Mary's estates, which had been under Alice's keeping as her guardian and mother-in-law. Henry Percy had risen significantly in power that year, being made Earl of Northumberland in July and taking part in Richard II's coronation, and he was now to turn his attention to secure a brighter future for his half-sister.[48]

The Percy family had never been happy with the marriage of their young heiress to Alice's illegitimate son, but with the assent of the king they were powerless to protest. They could have potentially seen future advancement by being tied to a relative of the monarch. But with Edward dead and Alice's entire estate forfeit, the marriage to John was a disaster for the family. They urgently needed to reclaim Mary and her fortune. In their petition to the pope, the family told how Mary had been 'influenced and cunningly led astray by her guardian' to marry a man 'of defective birth'. They emphasised that she stayed with Alice 'unwillingly' and 'as soon as possible she seized an opportunity to turn aside from her and flee to the house of her relatives, where she publicly expressed and proclaimed her disagreement with the de facto contracting of this aforesaid marriage'.[49]

The noble future that Alice had thought she had secured for her son in the new year of 1377 had crumbled. John still had his annual income from the crown, he was still a knight, and he still had status as the king's illegitimate son, but with his father dead and no noble bride to secure his place in society, his prospects were looking bleak. The likelihood that John would now achieve a high estate in life was small. As a result, John perhaps decided he needed to make his way in life through military endeavours. John was 15, due to turn 16 that year, and so he was seen to be old enough to start looking at joining the wars with France as a knight. Perhaps William also wanted to ensure that his stepson was not sitting by idly and was able to support himself. As such, John joined his stepfather on his campaign to Brittany in 1380.[50]

For Alice to see her only son leave to fight in a dangerous war with her new husband must have been difficult. Though William was an experienced and capable military commander, war was treacherous. As the men left on campaign, Alice was left behind to care for her two daughters, Joan and Jane, who were themselves entering their teenage years. In the end, both William and John returned unharmed, and John had experienced his first taste of war.

The year 1381 was not to bring peace for Alice's family; in fact danger was to return to their doorstep. As the last days of spring were fading, discontent was bubbling across the country. The parliaments of Richard's reign had been dominated by the need for taxation to replenish the empty royal purse, but the country was still suspicious of the crown's claims of poverty. During the Good Parliament, blame had been placed on Alice, Latimer, Lyons and the rest of the court clique around the king for draining the coffers for their own benefit. With Alice and her allies removed from court, the 1378 parliament had instead turned its suspicions to John of Gaunt.

Regardless, parliament had granted various taxes to the government, including an unpopular poll tax. But there were still accusations of evil counsellors surrounding the young king, and the crown's lack of money seemed to confirm this.[51] Discontent was also being stirred by figures such as the priest John Ball, who had been preaching in Kent against the social inequalities between the classes. Whilst the lords were 'clothed in velvet and camlet furred with grise, and we be vestured with poor cloth: they have their wines, spices and good bread, and we had the drawing out of the chaff and drink water'.[52]

At the end of May, tensions finally came to a head and the infamous Peasants' Revolt began. The revolt started around Kent, Essex and London, though it soon spread across the country, and the rebels were determined to remove all those around the king whom they deemed to have an evil influence. Many high-status officials were attacked and killed during the uprising. The vast quantity of silver, gold and furniture kept at John of Gaunt's Savoy Palace in London was smashed or thrown into the river before the palace was set on fire and burnt to the ground.[53] Luckily Gaunt was not in the city, or he might have found his life in danger from the rebels.

Other members of the king's government were not as fortunate. The rebels broke into the Tower of London, where they seized the Archbishop of Canterbury and other men and beheaded them. Most importantly for Alice, the rebels seemed to consistently target men who had been convicted during the Good Parliament and subsequently pardoned. Richard Lyons was murdered in the street by one of the rebel leaders, Wat Tyler. Froissart claims that this was because Lyons had beaten Tyler when he was a valet in his service, but it is certainly striking that many others connected to Lyons and Alice were attacked during this rebellion.[54] An associate of Lyons's, John Leicester, had his property in Kent destroyed, whilst Sir Robert Salle, a close friend of Lord Latimer, was murdered. Meanwhile, two burgesses who had faced charges in the Good Parliament were attacked in Yarmouth and their property looted.[55]

With such violence circulating in the areas Alice and William held much of their property, and the targets being those connected to the Good Parliament, Alice was in real danger for her life. It is unclear which of their many properties Alice and William resided in, but William was called upon by the government to help quash the rebels in Cambridge and Huntingdon, so it might be that the couple were staying close to these towns. William was called again to help settle insurrections in Cambridgeshire in December 1382, which certainly suggests he was often in the area.[56]

Despite her proximity to the heart of the Peasants' Revolt, there is no evidence that Alice, her family or any of her properties were attacked. This is certainly very striking considering the certainty of many historians that Alice was universally despised. Why were Alice and her family not targeted? She turns up in chronicles and had taken a public role in courtly events like the tournament at Smithfield where she was Lady of the Sun, so it cannot be that commoners simply had little knowledge or opinion of her. The impetus for persecuting Alice in the Good Parliament and the parliament of 1378 came from those called to parliament, confirming that she had a level of notoriety among at least the knightly class.

It may be that Alice was considered to have been sufficiently punished, unlike the men attacked during the rebellion who were seen to be still wielding power over the king and country. It could be that Wyndesore was a respected figure in the area, as a powerful man and capable military commander who had had his own run-ins with the government, and so the rebels felt no need to target him. Or it could be that many people did not object too passionately to Alice's position as Edward's mistress, even if they might have morally disapproved. Whatever the reason, Alice and her family emerged from the rebellion unscathed.

For his help in protecting Cherbourg, for funding soldiers for the Brittany campaign whilst also fighting himself, and for quelling rebels in East Anglia, William once again saw his power and status rise. In the parliament that convened at Westminster on 3 November 1381, William Wyndesore was called to sit as one of the lords temporal in the House of Lords.[57] William was beginning to cement his position as a trusted member of the ruling class, bolstered by his increased wealth through his control of much of Alice's former empire and his own military prowess. The days of his questionable actions in Ireland were firmly behind him, and he was becoming more indispensable to Richard's regime as each month passed.

Alice, too, had been ingratiating herself with Richard II. On 10 November 1383, 'at the supplication of Alice', the king granted her those of her goods which had been forfeited to him after her trial in 1377 that he was 'not yet possessed of'.[58] Although this meant that not everything taken from Alice was to be returned, probably including her many expensive jewels, it was a small victory to have some of her possessions back. A month later, Alice received another significant grant of favour. A week before Christmas, Richard granted her four tuns of Gascon wine yearly for life from the port of London.[59] This was double the amount that Edward had given her two decades earlier and perhaps suggests that Richard had sympathy for how Alice had been treated in the years since Edward's death.

As 1384 arrived, Alice had built herself a precarious life that was a shadow of her previous glory. Her son was a knight who was building a reputation in England's wars. Her husband was often abroad serving the government in a military capacity, and so the couple probably spent little time together – although there is no evidence that either party minded this situation. Their marriage was certainly not one of love. Through this marriage, Alice had seen the return of most of her goods and lands. But her legal status had never been fully resolved after her trial, and everything that had been returned to her relied on her marriage to William and his use to those in power. This fine balance of Alice's life was soon to come crashing down around her.

On 15 September 1384, William Wyndesore died. Alice had now been widowed for the second time in her life, and her situation this time was no more secure – in fact, it was probably more uncertain. In the inquisition post mortem taken of William's lands, his three sisters, Christina, Margery and Isabel, were named as his heirs, confirming that Alice and William had never had children together.[60] As his widow, Alice would be legally entitled to a portion of his lands – usually around a third – and William certainly had a significant amount of personal wealth and estates. Just two months before his death, he had been granted a licence to enclose 2,000 acres of his land, wood and pasture in Westmorland into a private park.[61] Regardless, Alice's greatest concern was probably with her own landed empire, which legally had been in William's hands. There was no saying whether the government would allow her to keep these lands now that William was gone.

If William's death was not difficult enough for Alice, fate was to deal another cruel blow; it seems that around the end of this year, her son John also died. The last known record of John finds him in Aragon in autumn, but he is not heard of again. It is probable he died of an unknown malady, for he was due to return to England and seemingly never made it.[62] In just a few months, Alice had lost her husband upon whom her security was based, and her only son in whom she had placed all her hopes for her future. Her dreams and ambitions had been destroyed.

Alice was a fighter, and her treatment since Edward's death had only hardened her resolve to assert what she felt were her rights. She had spent much of her life as a single woman in a man's world, and she vehemently believed that everything she had built during the 1360s and 1370s was rightfully hers. In November 1384, a parliament was held at Westminster and Alice wasted no time in presenting a petition to the newly assembled Commons and Lords. Now that William was dead, it was more important than ever to have her legal status resolved, as it was only by doing so that Alice could hope to see the return of her lands.

Alice petitioned the king, 'humbly' requesting that the 1376 ordinance and 1377 judgement against her 'be completely annulled in this parliament and declared invalid and held at nought' meaning that Alice and her feoffees could be 'fully restored to their former condition'. Finally, Alice had a breakthrough. Parliament responded to her petition, saying that King Richard had 'thoroughly considered the request' and 'by the advice and assent of the prelates, lords and commons in full parliament' agreed that the ordinance against Alice was to be officially repealed. Alice was to be 'restored to the peace and common law of the land' from that point onwards.[63] Alice was once more a lawful citizen of the English crown, a *femme sole* who was allowed to own her land and make transactions in her own name. Seven years after her trial, Alice had a small victory.

It was indeed just a small victory, for William's death had left her in significant difficulty. Despite his own substantial estate and wealth, William had died in debt to the crown. A month after his death, Richard's government had ordered the confiscation of 'all the jewels, tallies and other goods' of William and asked that the Chancery be informed of their price and true value, 'the king having learned' that William was 'bound to him in many and divers great sums of money'.[64] Many of William's possessions that Alice might have expected a share of would now be confiscated by the crown to cover his debts.

More seriously for Alice, the terms of William Wyndesore's will were to cause problems for the rest of her life. William's will stated that his goods, chattels and lands were to be given to a group of men that included his nephew, John Wyndesore, so that they could pay his debts and provide for his soul. Though William's sisters were his heirs, his nephew John ended up inheriting most of William's estate.[65] Tied up in this estate were some of Alice's lands. Upon William's death, these lands should technically have reverted to Alice, but he had instead given them in trust to a group of men spearheaded by his nephew. When William died, Alice had not yet received the parliamentary revocation of the ordinance and judgement against her, and so she had no legal claim to her own lands. The lands had only been returned to William, not to William and Alice.

Alice had in fact been given many of her landed estates upon William's death, and this was confirmed and extended by the judgement in parliament in November. But some of her former manors were tied up in William's trust, and John Wyndesore now claimed this inheritance for himself. This bid for William's lands seems to have been supported by Richard II, for in May the following year he received a pardon for taking possession of them.[66] John was now depriving Alice of some of her former property, and Alice was furious.

Quite why William set up this trust for his lands is something of a mystery. Although there is no evidence that William and Alice were close, and their marriage was clearly a mutually beneficial transaction, it would have been exceedingly cruel of William to deprive Alice of her hard-fought lands. One suggestion is that William might have planned to use the trust as a safety net for Alice.[67] Much like how Alice had relied upon enfeoffment-to-use to protect her lands from confiscation, William might have created this trust to avoid the penalties of his debt to the crown. After his death, his goods and his land in Ireland had been confiscated by the crown to pay for these debts, but by placing his English lands in a trust they became exempt from confiscation. William might have intended the men whom he placed in charge of the trust to give the profits to Alice.

This theory certainly makes sense, although it places a lot of trust in William's character and in his care for Alice. It may simply be that William had not thought much about Alice's fate, and he was instead looking out for his Wyndesore relatives. Alice herself seemed to suggest in one petition to the government that William acted underhandedly when dealing with her estates. In a petition to the king and parliament some time after William's death, Alice claimed that she had still not received four manors that the couple had been promised in 1380 in exchange for William supplying men for the Brittany campaign. Alice requested the return of these manors, but she also mentioned that 'when the charter for these lands should have been made to William and Alice and their heirs, William arranged for it to be made to himself and his heirs only ... so that she is disinherited'. Alice even claimed that rather than William supplying the troops, it was in fact 'she and her friends' who had paid the full cost of the men.[68]

After William Wyndesore's death, Alice's tone in many official documents seems decidedly bitter. She felt that William and John had disinherited her and stolen lands that were rightfully hers. Although she still had plenty of means to support herself, she was not going to be satisfied until she was fully pardoned and restored, and the government had no incentive to do this. Although Richard had shown sympathy for Alice, the reality was that someone like John Wyndesore was going to be far more useful to his government than a twice-widowed single woman. With her only son now dead too, Alice had little hope of seeing her desires fully realised. If John de Southeray had lived, then as her male heir and a blood relative of the king, he could have pushed for Alice's full and proper restitution. As it was, she was just an angry woman who was something of a minor nuisance.

John's death was the greatest tragedy of Alice's life. He was 20 years old, on the cusp of adulthood, and by all accounts he had been living up to his mother's great expectations. Just two years before his death he had joined English troops in Portugal, proving himself a capable military commander despite his youth. During one attack it was said that John was 'the first in to the fray', and although he received a severe injury, 'he got up, and summoning his strength, returned to the battle with the same determination as before'.[69] Through his brave conduct, John was earning the respect of those around him.

This respect was demonstrated in the summer of 1382, when John de Southeray led a revolt of soldiers against Prince Edmund of Langley. The English army had been abroad for nearly a year without pay, and so a group of lesser nobles gathered 'to speak and make their complaints known to each other', and 'louder than all the rest' was John. Because of his royal birth, his courage and his obvious charisma, the soldiers all rallied behind him, shouting his name and calling him a 'valiant bastard'. John led 700 men to Prince Edmund, demanding they received their money. Eventually, the Portuguese king agreed to pay the soldiers.[70]

Though he had rebelled against his royal half-brother, John had shown exemplary conduct during the war and was trusted and revered by his fellow knights. This incident highlighted John's confidence and capability, and shows that Alice would have had far better prospects had John lived. Her family would likely have been able to hold on to Alice's lands, and John could have built a powerful future.

Even now, suspicion of Alice continued and was weaponised in government. At the start of 1385, Alice's old friend William Wykeham was ordered to 'keep in his own hands ... all the jewels of great value placed in his hands' by Alice.[71] Wykeham had fallen from grace, and Alice was now being used to implicate him in underhand dealings. He was accused of hiding some of Alice's jewels and thus concealing them from the forfeiture of her goods that was proclaimed in 1377. Wykeham managed to return to favour by the end of the year, and the charges against him faded away, but in 1389 he made sure to properly quash these rumours. He came before the council saying that he had never received any jewels from Alice, and she corroborated his story, swearing on oath that she had never given Wykeham any jewels 'after the said judgement or before'.[72]

After William's death and Alice's petition to parliament, she largely disappeared from the record. In 1393, a record in the Close Rolls demonstrates that Alice had, temporarily, had some luck in her battle with John Wyndesore. On 10 January, the sheriffs of London were ordered to set John Wyndesore free from his imprisonment at Newgate jail. The record explains that John had been imprisoned 'at suit of Gauter de Bardes citizen of London in a plea of debt for 660l in the city court' but also 'at suit of Alice who was wife of William de Wyndesore knight in a plea of trespass, namely concerning goods of hers to the value of 3,000l by him carried away'.[73] Over eight years after her husband's death, Alice was still claiming that John had stolen her lands and goods, and thus was trespassing in his possession of them.

Claiming that he owed her £3,000 was quite bold, considering the huge value of this amount of money.

Intriguingly, this entry also demonstrates that Alice had now got one of her daughters involved in her legal quarrels. The record states that as well as being imprisoned for his debt and trespass with de Bardes and Alice, he was imprisoned 'at suit of Joan Wyndesore in a like plea of trespass concerning goods of hers to the value of 4,000l'.[74] It is not quite clear which of Alice's daughters brought this case, for Joan and Jane have very similar names when written in French or Latin for official documents. In Alice's will, both daughters are called Johanne, Johanna and Ioanna interchangeably. Their distinction as Joan and Jane has been implemented by historians to help distinguish between them as likely English translations, but names could be quite fluid in the medieval period. Alice's will seems to suggest she favoured her younger daughter, Jane, or at least that Jane had more interest in fighting for Alice's cause, and so it may be that it is in fact Jane who is taking part in her mother's scheme here.[75]

The combined claims of Alice and her daughter amounted to John Wyndesore owing the Perrers women £7,000, a staggering amount. The women were claiming that John owed them seven years' worth of an earl's income. Considering Alice's estimated wealth at the time of her forfeiture in 1377, this is perhaps not unrealistic, but it would depend on just how much of Alice's former lands John was actually in possession of, and how much Alice was owed from William's lands as his widow. It seems that Alice's success was short lived. Although she and her daughter had succeeded in imprisoning John, ultimately the entry notes 'vacated, because nothing done thereupon' and they seemingly received no recompense from John, nor their longed-for lands.

Despite this, Alice's daughter seems to have inherited her fighting spirit. Within the next year, *Johane la fille de Dame Alice Wyndesor* ('Joan/Jane the daughter of Lady Alice Wyndesore') submitted her own petition to King Richard and his parliament.[76] She stated that when Edward III had been alive, he had granted her the marriage of the Earl of Nottingham 'in aid and advancement of the said Joan' but that this grant had passed to William Wyndesore and Alice after their marriage. William then sold the marriage for 2,000 marks (over £1,300), and after William's death John

Wyndesore 'without right' took all of his goods including this money. Joan or Jane had tried to recover this money for herself, but she was being obstructed by John's clerk and attorney, as well as the under-sheriff and judge of London, who, she alleged, had altered the record of an inquisition held into the matter. She was now asking the government to intervene on her behalf to recover this money.

It is not clear if Alice's daughter was granted the money owed to her, but after this the Perrers women once again go quiet in the official record. Alice reappears in 1397, once again clamouring for her rights to be reinstated. In the parliament called in September that year, Alice submitted another petition to parliament regarding the error made in the trial against her in 1377.[77] She asked for a review of the appeal in error that she and William had made back in 1378, and, 'having been read in parliament and fully heard', the king and parliament agreed that once the parliament had ended, Richard 'upon thorough deliberation should determine and fully conclude the matter of the said petition'.

That Alice was asking this may seem strange when thirteen years previously Richard had already annulled the judgement and ordinance against her and restored her to her position. The answer lies in her ongoing legal dispute with John Wyndesore, for he and his associates had been holding on to Alice's land using legal loopholes left behind by the fact that Alice and William's 1378 appeal had never been concluded.[78] Although Richard had promised Alice that he would fully conclude her petition, he obviously took advantage of the idea that he would 'thoroughly' deliberate it: two years later, in 1399, Alice was forced to submit another petition to the new king Henry IV, asking again that the errors of the 1377 judgement be corrected and annulled.[79] Richard had clearly never answered her. It seems the new king was far too busy securing his own rule to answer Alice, for no endorsement accompanies the petition.

Alice had not been entirely forgotten by those in power. Her old friend, William Wykeham, was still looking out for her. This same year, Wykeham returned the manor of Compton Mordak in Warwickshire to her.[80] Alice had granted Wykeham the manor back in 1374, and it was now a valuable property for Alice, whilst Wykeham was in possession of vast amounts of land and wealth of his own.

Alice had also spent some time looking to the futures of her daughters. Joan and Jane were in their early thirties as 1400 arrived, and at some point Alice had arranged marriages for them. The marriages were respectable for their social rank, although Alice perhaps felt bitterness at how lowly they were in comparison to the grand lords that she would have originally envisaged them marrying. Joan, the eldest, married a man named Robert Skerne and Jane married Richard Northland.

Robert Skerne was a lawyer from Kingston-upon-Thames in Surrey; he owned the manor of Downhall in Kingston, a not insubstantial building, where the couple might have based themselves.[81] Through his profession, and his family connections in Surrey, Robert was fairly wealthy, and the marriage would have provided Joan with the comforts she had grown accustomed to as Alice's daughter. Little else is known about Robert and how he became acquainted with Joan and Alice, although it could have been through his work, considering the amount of legal transactions and challenges Alice undertook.

Whilst Joan had married a wealthy professional, Jane had married Richard Northland, a knight of good social standing. Richard had distinguished himself in military service during the 1370s, serving in the Portuguese campaign for part of 1373 and leading men of his own.[82] At the end of that year, he was granted protection to go to Ireland in the company of William Wyndesore, leaving in early 1374 and thus forming the link between Richard and Alice's family.[83] Richard was rewarded for taking part in these military expeditions in March 1374, when Edward III granted him several parcels of land in the Welsh Marches, including over 30 acres of land in Minsterworth, Gloucestershire.[84] As well as enriching Richard's landed wealth, Edward was placing an experienced knight in what had always been a contentious region.

In 1377–78 Richard had been responsible for the protection of the Isle of Wight, where he was in charge of 100 men-at-arms, showing the trust placed in Richard by the king and council, for this was a time 'of peril then threatening'.[85] A petition dated to early 1377 also mentions Richard Northland acting as Captain of Bourg, just north of Bordeaux in France, again showing his rank and the trust in him as a knight and military commander.[86]

Both of Alice's daughters, therefore, were married to men of good standing, who had their own reasonable personal wealth and landed estates and could support the women. This was to be a comfort to Alice, for it appears that her health was beginning to falter. As 1400 arrived, Alice was reaching 60 years old. She was living at her manor of Gaynes in Upminster, Essex, and seems to have been living there for quite a few years. Her younger daughter Jane might possibly have moved in with her mother in December 1399 to care for her, as a record from 1402 notes Jane Southeray as having occupied Gaynes since this time, and Alice went on to leave Jane the manor in her will.[87]

On 15 August 1400, Alice Perrers made her will at Upminster, suggesting she had become quite sick.[88] Alice requested that she be buried in the parish church of Upminster, St Laurence, before the altar of the Virgin Mary. Alice seems to have had an affinity with Mary through her life; a seal of hers from *c*. 1374 shows an image of the Virgin Mary and child, her tabernacle seized in 1377 had an image of the Virgin Mary on it, and now she wished to be buried before Mary's altar.[89] To endow St Laurence in exchange for her burial in such a prestigious location in the church, Alice gifted them one of her best oxen, money to pay for wax candles to burn around her body, and another 10 marks to pay for ornaments in the church. She also gave the chaplain 10 marks, the priest 3*s* 4*d*, and 40*s* was left for someone to say prayers for her soul.

Alice also showed significant generosity to the people of Upminster, which had been her home for so long. On the day of her burial, Alice had instructed 10 marks to be distributed to the poor, and she left another 20*s* to the poor of the parish as a whole. Alice also left 40*s* to repair the town's roads. The final beneficiaries of Alice's will were her household servants – Richard, Thomas and Janyn received 20*s* each, and a maid named Alice was given 2 marks (just over 26*s*). It is certainly striking that one of her servants shared the unusual name of her first husband, but whether there is any connection between the two is unclear.

The generosity of Alice's will is overshadowed by her bitterness of spirit in her dying days. Alice left her manor of Gaynes to her younger daughter, and split all her other manors and lands between both Joan and Jane. John Wyndesore had occupied some of these manors, she claimed, without her consent. She passionately asked that her heirs and executors recover them and share them between her daughters, 'for I say on the pain of my soul that the said John has never had a right there'.[90] Sixteen years after the death of William Wyndesore, and on her own deathbed, Alice was still furious at her lost lands and how she had been treated.

Alice seems to have survived into the winter, for her will was not proved until February 1401. Alice, the notorious, great mistress of King Edward III of England, was dead. Despite holding such vast power in the 1370s, despite the fears of her wealth and influence, Alice had died in obscurity. No chroniclers recorded her death, and even some contemporary legal records seem to be confused about when she died.[91] From the heights of her power as Edward's unofficial consort, Alice had died with much of her empire dismantled by the men around her. Whilst she had received some gifts from Edward, and benefited from connections due to their relationship, Alice had built up the majority of her wealth and lands through her own intelligence, ingenuity and astuteness. But, ultimately, as a single woman she was vulnerable to the powerful men around her, who viewed her as an intruder in the ruling of government.

She was forced to rely on a man – her husband – to have any hope of having these lands returned to her, but he ultimately betrayed her too in failing to resolve her legal status and not having her lands placed in her name, leaving the door open for his nephew to steal them from under her. Her only salvation could have been with one final man, her son, but he died on the cusp of manhood and greatness, leaving these hopes vanquished. Alice had done her best to restore her position, both for her own pride and for the legacy of her two daughters, and now, in death, she had to leave the fight to them. Alice Perrers was one of the richest, most powerful women of her time, but as a medieval woman she was powerless against men.

The terms of Alice's will seem to have been carried out by her executors, and she would have been buried in Upminster church as she wished, although her tomb has sadly not survived. Alice's daughters duly made efforts to reclaim their mother's lands, helped by their husbands. In July 1401, it appears that Jane teamed up with her brother-in-law, Robert Skerne, to obtain the manor of Philiberts in East Hanney, Berkshire.[92] Alice had owned the manor prior to her marriage, and in the first restitution of Alice's lands in 1380 it had been promised to William upon the death of Richard II's half-brother, John Holland. Now, just months after her death, her children had been successful in obtaining it.

In her will, Alice had requested that her manor of Compton Mordak, given to her by William Wykeham a few years previously, be sold to help pay for her bequests. It seems that her eldest daughter Joan might not have been happy at this idea, because Alice warned her that if she tried to prevent the sale of the manor then she was to be forbidden from receiving a share of Alice's valuable London properties.[93] Interestingly, in January 1401 the manor was granted to Joan and her husband Robert Skerne jointly with the Bishop of Salisbury and a few other men, seemingly predating Alice's death in late January or early February. It has been suggested that Jane might have died between Alice making her will and dying herself, thus explaining why the manor then passed to Joan when Alice had been so resolute not to give it to her.[94] The grant in July 1401 suggests that Jane was in fact still alive, but there are few surviving records regarding Jane after this year.

One of the only records that mention Jane after this point is a 1404 grant by the king, given at the request of Jane's husband Richard, 'to Thomas his son of the custody of all manors, lands, rents and services which the said Richard had as of the right of Joan his wife in the city of London and in Compton Moredok'.[95] The language of this does not make it clear whether or not Jane was alive. Frustratingly, this grant also does not make it clear whether Thomas was the son of both Jane and Richard, or if Thomas was a son from a previous marriage of Richard's. Richard had in fact earlier that month granted the same pieces of land to the king for twenty years, to revert to him 'or to the right heirs of his body by his said wife'.[96] Again, this does not make it clear whether the couple already had children, or whether Jane was in fact still alive and they were still hopeful they might yet have children.

An answer may possibly be found in the inquisition post mortem of William Wykeham, who died a few years after Alice in 1404. In the inquisition of tenements that William was renting out in All Hallows the Less in London, mention is made of a 'tenement formerly of John Weston and now of Richard Northlode, knight, and Joan his wife, daughter and heir of Alice Perers'.[97] If the 'now' is taken literally, then that certainly suggests that Jane had in fact outlived her mother.

Joan or Jane inherited Alice's manor of Gaynes as per the terms of her will, but this inheritance was not without controversy. There were other parties who had claim to part of the manor, including a follower of John of Gaunt. Although Alice had passed the manor to her daughter in her will, it had been granted to another person after Alice's death, and Joan or Jane had been left to fight for it.[98] After battling for control of the manor, in 1406 Alice's daughter finally reached an agreement where she surrendered her interest in the manor in exchange for 40 marks a year.[99]

After this deal, both of Alice's daughters disappear from the record. Whilst Jane's date of death is unknown, it appears that Joan lived until around 1430. In January 1431, Robert Skerne was admitted into the fraternity of Osney Abbey, where he arranged for prayers to be said in memory of Joan.[100] Robert was eventually buried in All Saints' Church in Kingston-upon-Thames next to Joan, and he had commissioned a beautiful monumental brass to go over their tomb.

The brass depicts both Robert and Joan, making it the only surviving visual record of any of Alice's family. Joan is shown to be a wealthy woman by her fashionable horned headdress with a large veil. The headdress is sumptuously decorated, and she wears a necklace with a large ornamental pendant. She has a close-fitting dress with tight sleeves, and a fur-lined mantle is held in place over her shoulders with two large brooches in the same style as her necklace. In the four corners of the monumental brass are spaces for coats of arms, which could have depicted Alice's heraldry, passed on to Joan, but these have not survived. Sadly, although the brass is accompanied by twelve verses in Latin, the words are solely in honour of Robert, with Joan's name not even being mentioned; she is referred to simply as 'his wife'.[101]

Joan and Robert appear to have had no children together, or certainly none that outlived them, and so if Jane too had no children with Richard, 1430 saw the end of Alice Perrers's line. The start of 1377 had seen such high hopes for her dynasty. With three children who had the blood of one of England's greatest kings running through their veins, Alice must have envisioned her legacy living on for centuries to come, with each generation rising higher than the last. Ultimately, Alice died seeing much of these plans laid to waste.

Alice had seen one of the greatest transformations of fortune of the century. From the obscure daughter of a goldsmith she managed to find her way to the glittering court of Philippa of Hainault and Edward III, a place filled with music, art and luxury. Through her relationship with the king she built up her own personal empire as a single woman, a feat unheard of, to become one of the richest people in the entire kingdom. The relationship brought not only financial benefits, but love and children too. Ultimately, Alice's power and influence aroused too much jealousy and suspicion in the men around her, and this was to lead to her downfall. Alice was to spend the last decades of her life fighting desperately to reclaim what was hers, to mixed success. Her daughters ultimately found reasonable marriages with honourable men, and lived their lives in relative wealth and luxury – even if it was not the great heights Alice desired. Alice had forged her own path in life, but those around her had not been ready for it.

Conclusion

The Queen and the Mistress

Life for women at court in the fourteenth century was generally one of lei-sure and pleasure. If they were lucky enough to be a damsel to the queen, or a visiting noblewoman, then they would have enjoyed beautiful gowns, luxurious jewels and endless feasting. Edward III hosted countless jousts and tournaments where ladies played a starring role, leading knights to the field at the start of the day, inspiring them to perform great feats and dancing through the evenings. With the close relationship between Edward and his queen, ladies at court also travelled widely, keeping Philippa company whilst she waited for Edward to conquer his latest city.

Philippa herself certainly enjoyed this lifestyle to the fullest, but she was ultimately rivalled by a social upstart. Alice Perrers should never have had access to the glamour of this chivalric dream, but Edward's desire through-out his reign to reward men on their service and not just on their blood opened the door for Alice's ascendency. These two women came from com-pletely different backgrounds in life, but both ultimately won the love of the same man.

As the daughter of a count, Philippa would only have dreamed of fall-ing in love with a handsome man, but the reality was that her marriage was always going to be a political business deal, and not a romantic fairy tale. Her eldest sister was wedded to a man more than three times her age, who had already been married and fathered six children, the eldest of whom was a girl almost the same age as his new bride. Philippa was lucky that her chosen husband was her own age, but this did not guarantee success. Her own marriage was contracted because her new mother- and father-in-law were warring with each other. This bitter fighting would eventually lead to the presumed murder of one of them. Politics in the fourteenth century was a dangerous game.

Alice was born into a family of goldsmiths, a more privileged birth than many of her contemporaries', but a difficult life nonetheless. Born just a few years before the horrors of the Black Death descended on the country, she survived and flourished, marrying a man of her status who was successful enough to provide jewels to the king himself. She settled into a comfortable lifestyle, treating herself and her husband to cloths that women of her status would previously not have dreamed of wearing, but all too soon she was left a widow, fighting for her survival in a world unkind to single women. Luck saw her find her way into service to the queen, the greatest honour she could have imagined, but her beauty, wit and intelligence found her something more: the attention of the great King Edward III of England.

Though many women of the medieval period grew to love husbands that had been chosen for them, this was not always a guarantee, and so Philippa of Hainault and Alice Perrers would have counted themselves very lucky that they found love in a man such as Edward. Hailed by his contemporaries as 'the flower of this world's knighthood ... excelling almost all his predecessors in goodness and mercy', the athletic, chivalrous Edward was quite a man indeed.[1] But these were formidable women in their own rights, not mere ornaments to this great king.

Philippa and Alice have not always been given their due places at Edward's side, often appearing as mere footnotes in his life, if they are mentioned at all. But these women were at the core of Edward's being. Philippa provided Edward with the loving family he had dreamed of as a child, blessing him with many children who rallied around him when he needed help, and cared for him in his old age. But Philippa was also brave in her love for Edward, and accompanied him across Europe in his conquests. She spent Christmas in the cold reaches of Scotland, gave birth in monasteries in the Low Countries, and provided company during months-long sieges in France. Without her unwavering support, many of Edward's greatest triumphs might never have been possible.

Philippa extended this support to anyone she met, patronising university colleges, musicians, poets, artists and writers, interceding for criminals sentenced to death for stealing pieces of cloth, and welcoming into her fold a plethora of women and children who needed a home. This gave her an unblemished name among her contemporaries who did not have a single bad word to say about her. This reputation was so great that chroniclers even imagined Philippa undertaking great feats that never happened, such as charging into battle at Neville's Cross. Philippa was a queen who would do anything for the poor and needy, and for her family, and she did.

It is no wonder, then, that Alice Perrers attracted so much vitriol. Whilst Philippa had been the model queen for close to half a century, Alice Perrers was her opposite. A woman who overtly cared for power and money, she seemingly held none of Philippa's virtues. Where Philippa supported the arts, Alice gathered jewels. Where Philippa obtained pardons for criminals, Alice committed subterfuge and lied to obtain favourable business deals. Where Philippa had many children blessed by the church and the sanctity of marriage, Alice was an immoral mistress, causing her king to sin with her. Alice never stood a chance.

And whilst Alice did commit many wrongs, one wonders how evil a woman she truly was. Many of her acts were carried out simply because fourteenth-century England was not ready for an independent woman such as her. She used her sexuality with the king because, as a woman, she could not advise him in his government or win battles for him, as the self-made men before her had. She played the legal system, using enfeoffment in a way none before her had, because her hold on the lands she had so carefully worked to obtain could be taken away from her at any moment. As a woman, her legal recourses were few.

Though many claimed that she alienated those at court with her haughtiness and wickedness, there is very little concrete evidence of this. Alice had many friends who stayed by her side right up until her death, decades after her great downfall. Whilst many testified against her at trial, their incentive might have been to save their own skin, rather than to see the downfall of a woman they supposedly hated. There is no doubt that there was a sizeable group of men at court, and across England as a whole, who disliked Alice and wished to see her removed from power, but the evidence points to this being down to her position as a powerful, uncontrolled, single woman in the king's bed rather than any of her personal failings. King Edward himself, the man who had only ever loved one woman, fell in love with Alice Perrers, and there must have been good reason for him to do so.

So whilst these two women seem so far apart, they must have held similar personal qualities that appealed to Edward. Both were confident and headstrong, both almost certainly attractive, both intelligent and charming, and both savvy to the politics of the court. Whilst Edward had scorned his mother and her lover, parading in costumes harking to an Arthurian tale of unfaithfulness, in his later life he bestowed a gift on his own lover asking that they be 'never apart'. The surviving records will never allow us to be privy to their deep, personal relationship.

Philippa and Alice, then, need to be viewed in a new light, one with the context and politics of their time, their similarities to each other, and in their link as lovers of the same man. The women were more complex than history has previously painted them, boxing them into angel and devil figures. Both had admirable qualities, but also made questionable mistakes. Both enjoyed the finer things in life a little too much, but also fiercely protected the rights of their children and of their own position. These women were expected to navigate a complex social system that at once demanded the participation of women and questioned their right to be there. Philippa, as a queen, and Alice, as a mistress, came from different stations in life, but both lived life to its fullest, allowing us to peer momentarily into their lives from over 600 years later.

Notes

Introduction

1   Jean Froissart, *The Chronicles of Froissart*, trans. Geoffrey Brereton (Harmondsworth: Penguin Books, 1968), 195–6.

Chapter 1

1   Jean Froissart, *Chroniques de J. Froissart*, vol. 1:2, ed. Siméon Luce (Paris: Mme Ve. J. Renouard, 1869), 287.

2   Kathryn Warner, *Philippa of Hainault: Mother of the English Nation* (Stroud: Amberley Publishing, 2019), 25–8.

3   See Janet van der Meulen, '"Sche sente the copie to her daughter": Countess Jeanne de Valois and Literature at the Court of Hainault-Holland', in *'I Have Heard about You': Foreign Women's Writing Crossing the Dutch Border*, ed. Suzan van Dijk (Hilversum: Verloren, 2004), 61–83.

4   *Foedera*, vol. 2:1, 381 dated December 1318 specifies 'Margaret daughter of the Count of Holland'; *The Register of Walter de Stapeldon, Bishop of Exeter, (A.D. 1307–1326)*, ed. Rev. F.C. Hingeston-Randolph (London: G. Bell & Sons, 1892), 169.

5   Leopold Devillers, *Monuments pour servir à l'histoire des provinces de Namur, de Hainaut et de Luxembourg*, vol. 3 part 1 (Brussels: F. Hayez, 1874), 51.

6   Warner, *Philippa of Hainault*, 41.

7   Van der Meulen, '"Sche sente"', 65.

8   Ibid.

9 Helen Castor, *She-Wolves: The Women Who Ruled England before Elizabeth* (London: Faber & Faber, 2011), 283–4.

10 CFR, Edward II, vol. 3, 300–1.

11 *Chronicles of Froissart*, Brereton, 40; *Chronicon Galfridi le Baker de Swynebroke*, ed. Edward Maunde Thompson (Oxford: Clarendon Press, 1889), 15–18.

12 Castor, *She-Wolves*, 284.

13 *Vita Edwardi Secundi: The Life of Edward the Second*, ed. Wendy R. Childs (Oxford: Clarendon Press, 2005), 239; *Chronicon Galfridi le Baker*, 18–19.

14 *Vita Edwardi Secundi*, 243.

15 *Foedera*, vol. 2:1, 617.

16 Mark Ormrod, *Edward III* (London: Yale University Press, 2013), 38.

17 Castor, *She-Wolves*, 292; *Chronicon Galfridi le Baker*, 20–1; Robertus de Avesbury, *Adæ Murimuth Continuatio chronicarum … De gestis mirabilibus regis Edwardi Tertii*, ed. Edward Maunde Thompson (London: Eyre & Spottiswoode, 1889), 46.

18 Henry Stephen Lucas, *The Low Countries and the Hundred Years' War, 1326–1347* (Philadelphia: Porcupine Press, 1976), 55.

19 Jean Froissart, *Oeuvres de Froissart*, vol. 2, ed. Kervyn de Lettenhove (Brussels: V. Devaux, 1867), 54.

20 See for example Warner, *Philippa of Hainault*, 56–8.

21 *Chronicon Galfridi le Baker*, 21; Ormrod, *Edward III*, 41.

22 *Chronicon Galfridi le Baker*, 24; *Chronicles of Froissart*, Brereton, 42; CCR, Edward II, vol. 4, 655; *Foedera*, vol. 2:1, 646.

23 Anne Crawford, *Letters of the Queens of England, 1100–1547* (Stroud: Alan Sutton Publishing, 1994), 88–9.

24 CCR, Edward II, vol. 4, 655–6.

25 *Foedera*, vol. 2:1, 650.

26 CCR, Edward III, vol. 1, 100.

27 Warner, *Philippa of Hainault*, 61–2.

28 CPL, vol. 2, 258–63.

29 'Edward III: November 1330', PROME, item 1.

30 Ormrod, *Edward III*, 68–9.

31 CPR, Edward III, vol. 1, 179.

32 Warner, *Philippa of Hainault*, 64.

33 *Foedera*, vol. 2:2, 724.

34 Van der Meulen, '"Sche sente"', 76.

Chapter 2

1 *Annales Paulini, Chronicles of the Reigns of Edward I and Edward II*, vol. 1, ed. William Stubbs (London: Longman, 1882), 338–9; Jean le Bel, *Chronique de Jean le Bel*, vol. 1, ed. Viard and Déprez (Paris: Librairie Renouard, 1904), 80.

2 Ormrod, *Edward III*, 70.

3 Great Britain Exchequer, *Issues of the Exchequer: Being a Collection of Payments Made Out of His Majesty's Revenue, from King Henry III to King Henry VI Inclusive*, ed. Frederick Devon (London: John Murray, 1837), 140.

4 Dates in chronicles vary, but the 25th is the most favoured date among them: see for example *Annales Paulini*, Stubbs, 339; Thomas Walsingham, *Historia Anglicana AD 1272–1381* (London: Longman, 1863), 192; *Chroniques* 1:2, Luce, 287; *The Anonimalle Chronicle, 1307 to 1334: From Brotherton Collection MS 29*, ed. Wendy R. Childs and John Taylor (Leeds: Yorkshire Archaeological Society, 1991), 139.

5 CPR, Edward III, vol. 1, 231; Edwin S. Hunt, 'A New Look at the Dealings of the Bardi and Peruzzi with Edward III', *Journal of Economic History*, 50 (1990), 151.

6 Michael A. Michael, 'A Manuscript Wedding Gift from Philippa of Hainault to Edward III', *The Burlington Magazine*, 127 (1985), 582–600.

7 Ian Mortimer, *The Perfect King: The Life of Edward III, Father of the English Nation* (London: Vintage, 2008), 67.

8 Ormrod, *Edward III*, 70–1.

9 *Chroniques* 1:2, Luce, 76, 287.

10 Ibid., 287.

11 Caroline Dunn, 'All the Queen's Ladies? Philippa of Hainault's Female Attendants', *Medieval Prosopography*, 31 (2016), 194.

12 Ibid., 193.

13 Dunn, 'All the Queen's Ladies?', 181; Warner, *Philippa of Hainault*, 73–4.

14 Kathryn A. Smith, *The Taymouth Hours: Stories and the Construction of the Self in Late Medieval England* (London: The British Library and University of Toronto Press, 2012), 22.

15 Caroline Shenton, 'Edward III and the Coup of 1330', in *The Age of Edward III*, ed. J.S. Bothwell (York: York Medieval Press, 2001), 14; Ormrod, *Edward III*, 64–6.

16 Mortimer, *The Perfect King*, 68.

17 John Carmi Parsons, 'The Pregnant Queen as Counsellor and the Medieval Construction of Motherhood', in *Medieval Mothering*, ed. John Carmi Parsons and Bonnie Wheeler (New York and London: Garland Publishing, 1996), 42.

18 CPR, Edward III, vol. 1, 257.

19 Ibid., 270.

20 CPL, vol. 2, 489.

21 Warner, *Philippa of Hainault*, 73 fn28.

22 Ormrod, *Edward III*, 73.

23 'Memorials: 1328', in *Memorials of London and London Life in the 13th, 14th and 15th Centuries*, ed. H.T. Riley (London: Longmans, 1868), 169–71.

24 'Edward III: October 1328', PROME, introduction.

25 Richard Barber, 'Edward III's Arthurian Enthusiasms Revisited: Perceforest in the Context of Philippa of Hainault and the Round Table Feast of 1344', *Arthurian Literature*, 30 (2013), 63–4.

26 Ormrod, *Edward III*, 74.

27 'Edward III: October 1328', PROME, introduction.

28 *Calendar of the Plea and Memoranda Rolls of the City of London: Volume 1, 1323–1364*, ed. A.H. Thomas (London: HMSO, 1926), membrane 31b.

29 Ormrod, *Edward III*, 76–7.

30 Warner, *Philippa of Hainault*, 70.

31 CPR, Edward III, vol. 1, 389.

32 Lisa Benz St John, *Three Medieval Queens: Queenship and the Crown in Fourteenth-Century England* (New York: Palgrave Macmillan, 2012), 83.

33 CPR, Edward III, vol. 1, 66–9.

34 Christopher Dyer, *Standards of Living in the Later Middle Ages: Social Change in England, c. 1200–1520* (Cambridge: Cambridge University Press, 1998), 31.

35 Warner, *Philippa of Hainault*, 79.

36 *Oeuvres*, vol. 17, 37.

37 C.M. Woolgar, *The Senses in Late Medieval England* (London: Yale University Press, 2006), 148.

38 Ormrod, *Edward III*, 613; Warner, *Philippa of Hainault*, 81.

39 Laura Slater, 'Defining Queenship at Greyfriars London, *c*.1300–58', *Gender & History*, 27 (2015), 53–4.

40 Carmi Parsons, 'The Pregnant Queen', 42; John Carmi Parsons, 'Introduction: Family, Sex, and Power: The Rhythms of Medieval Queenship', in *Medieval Queenship*, ed. John Carmi Parsons (New York: St Martin's Press, 1993), 8.

41 Stella Mary Newton, 'Queen Philippa's Squirrel Suit', in *Documenta Textila: Festschrift für Sigrid Müller-Christensen*, ed. M. Flury-Lemberg and K. Stolleis (Munich: Deutscher Kunstverlag, 1981), 342; Ormrod, *Edward III*, 84.

42 Caroline Shenton, 'Philippa of Hainault's Churchings: The Politics of Motherhood at the Court of Edward III', in *Family and Dynasty: Harlaxton Medieval Studies IX: Proceedings of the 1997 Symposium*, ed. Richard Eales and Shaun Tyas (Donington: Shaun Tyas, 2003), 118.

43 Carmi Parsons, 'The Pregnant Queen', 39, 42.

44 Newton, 'Squirrel Suit', 342.

45 John Carmi Parsons, 'Ritual and Symbol in the English Medieval Queenship to 1500', in *Cosmos Vol. 7, Women and Sovereignty*, ed. Fradenburg (Edinburgh: Edinburgh University Press, 1992), 61–3.

46 Newton, 'Squirrel Suit', 343.

47 Woolgar, *The Senses*, 246.

48 Newton, 'Squirrel Suit', 343.

49 CPR, Edward III, vol. 1, 501, 508, 512, 541.

50 Ibid., 523.

51 Warner, *Philippa of Hainault*, 87.

52 For example Ian Mortimer has done a lot of work exploring the theory that Edward II was not murdered in 1327 but lived on. His arguments can be seen in *Perfect King* and *The Greatest Traitor: The Life of Sir Roger Mortimer, Ruler of England, 1327–1330*, among others.

53 Ormrod, *Edward III*, 85.

54 *The Brut; or, The Chronicles of England*, vol. 1, ed. Friedrich Brie (London: Kegan Paul, 1906), 263.

55 *The Brut*, vol. 1, 264–7; *Chronicon Galfridi le Baker*, 43–4; *Anonimalle 1307 to 1334*, 143.

56 *The Brut*, vol. 1, 267.

57 Ormrod, *Edward III*, 88.

58 *Rotuli Parliamentorum, ut et petitiones, et placita in Parliamento*, vol. 2 (Great Britain: Parliament), 52a.

59 Mortimer, *The Perfect King*, 75.

60 Nicholas Orme, *From Childhood to Chivalry: The Education of the English Kings and Aristocracy 1066–1530* (London: Routledge, 2017), 11–12.

61 CPR, Edward III, vol. 2, 74.

62 Shenton, 'Philippa of Hainault's Churchings', 107.

63 Ibid., 105–6.

64 Shenton, 'Philippa of Hainault's Churchings', 107; Woolgar, *The Senses*, 236.

65 K. Staniland, 'The Great Wardrobe Accounts as a Source for Historians of Fourteenth-Century Clothing and Textiles', in *Textile History*, 20 (1989), 278.

66 Newton, 'Squirrel Suit', 344–6, 348; Shenton, 'Philippa of Hainault's Churchings', 107.

67 *Scalacronica: The Reigns of Edward I, Edward II and Edward III, as Recorded by Sir Thomas Gray*, trans. Sir Herbert Maxwell (Glasgow: James Maclehose & Sons, 1907), 105.

68 *Chronicon Galfridi le Baker*, 45; *Anonimalle 1307 to 1334*, 145.

69 *Chroniques* 1:2, Luce, 88.

70 'Edward III: November 1330', PROME, introduction.

71 *Scalacronica*, 105.

72 *Scalacronica*, 105; *The Brut*, vol. 1, 270.

73 Shenton, 'Edward III and the Coup', 17.

74 *Chronicon Galfridi le Baker*, 46; *Scalacronica*, 105; *The Brut*, vol. 1, 271.

75 'Edward III: November 1330', PROME, item 1.

76 Ormrod, *Edward III*, 91.

77 John Rylands University Library Manchester (JRULM) MS Latin 234, f. 2r.

78 CPL, vol. 2, 498–506.

79 Warner, *Philippa of Hainault*, 92.

80 Mortimer, *The Perfect King*, 85; Ormrod, *Edward III*, 124.

81 CCR, Edward III, vol. 2, 80, 86.

82 CPR, Edward III, vol. 2, 37.

83 Anne Crawford, 'The Queen's Council in the Middle Ages', *English Historical Review*, 116 (2001), 1203.

84 Warner, *Philippa of Hainault*, 93.

85 JRULM MS Latin 234, f. 32r.; Woolgar, *The Senses*, 233.

Chapter 3

1 Woolgar, *The Senses*, 236, 240.

2 TNA SC 8/265/13210.

3 CPR, Edward III, vol. 2, 78, 85.

4 Ibid., 84–5, 106.

5 'Edward III: November 1330', PROME, introduction.

6 *Scalacronica*, 107.

7 Woolgar, *The Senses*, 241.

8 CCR, Edward III, vol. 2, 262; litres of wine calculated using Susan Rose, *The Wine Trade in Medieval Europe 1000–1500* (London: Bloomsbury Academic, 2011), xvi.

9   *Foedera*, vol. 2:2, 823; Lucas, *The Low Countries*, 95.

10 Smith, *The Taymouth Hours*, 9–11.

11 *Anonimalle 1307 to 1334*, 147.

12 CCR, Edward III, vol. 2, 380.

13 CPR, Edward III, vol. 2, 236.

14 For identification of the Taymouth Hours with Philippa and Eleanor, see Smith, *The Taymouth Hours*.

15 Smith, *The Taymouth Hours*, 13; A.K. McHardy, 'Paying for the Wedding: Edward III as Fundraiser, 1332–3', in *Fourteenth Century England IV*, ed. J.S. Hamilton (Woodbridge: Boydell Press, 2006), 43–60.

16 Shenton, 'Philippa of Hainault's Churchings', 112.

17 Hilda Johnstone, *The English Government at Work 1327–1336, Volume I: Central and Prerogative Administration* (Cambridge, MA: Mediaeval Academy of America, 1940), 264.

18 Crawford, 'The Queen's Council', 1196.

19 CCR, Edward III, vol. 2, 553.

20 Johnstone, *The English Government at Work Volume 1*, 264.

21 Susan Crane, *The Performance of Self: Ritual, Clothing, and Identity During the Hundred Years War* (Philadelphia: University of Pennsylvania Press, 2011), 12; TNA Currency Converter, available online at www.nationalarchives.gov.uk/currency-converter/

22 Staniland, 'The Great Wardrobe Accounts', 278–9.

23 Woolgar, *The Senses*, 233.

24 Ibid., 233–5.

25 Ibid., 235–6.

26 Shenton, 'Philippa of Hainault's Churchings', 108.

27 Mortimer, *The Perfect King*, 97–8.

28 *Scalacronica*, 107; *Chronicon Galfridi le Baker*, 49; *The Brut*, vol. 1, 274–5; Ormrod, *Edward III*, 149–50.

29 CPR, Edward III, vol. 2, 322–3; Mortimer, *The Perfect King*, 90; Ormrod, *Edward III*, 151.

30 *Scalacronica*, 111; *Chronicon Galfridi le Baker*, 49; *Anonimalle 1307 to 1334*, 153.

31 Ormrod, *Edward III*, 152.

32 Mortimer, *The Perfect King*, 100.

33 Mortimer, *The Perfect King*, 100; Ormrod, *Edward III*, 152–3.

34 Amanda Richardson, '"Riding like Alexander, Hunting like Diana": Gendered Aspects of the Medieval Hunt and its Landscape Settings in England and France', *Gender & History*, 24 (2012), 262.

35 CPR, Edward III, vol. 2, 386.

36 'Edward III: December 1332', PROME, item 1.

37 Ormrod, *Edward III*, 129.

38 Barber, 'Edward III's Arthurian Enthusiasms', 59.

39 CPR, Edward III, vol. 2, 408, 415, 425.

40 CPR, Edward III, vol. 2, 399, 408; CCR, Edward III, vol. 3, 10, 23.

41 Mortimer, *The Perfect King*, 103.

42 Ibid., 104–5.

43 *Chronicon Galfridi le Baker*, 51–2.

44 *Scalacronica*, 115.

45 Warner, *Philippa of Hainault*, 111–12.

46 Joan was identified in some contemporary accounts as Joan of the Tower, leading to the idea she was born at the Tower of London, but Warner (*Philippa of Hainault*, 113) has argued she might have been mixed up with Edward's sister who was known by the same name and that she was instead born at Woodstock. That Philippa's churching was at Woodstock lends credence to the idea.

47 Shenton, 'Philippa of Hainault's Churchings', 109; Ormrod, *Edward III*, 615.

48 Shenton, 'Philippa of Hainault's Churchings', 109–10.

49 CPR, Edward III, vol. 2, 523.

50 CPR, Edward III, vol. 2, 541, 546; CPR Edward III, vol. 3, 33.

51 CPR, Edward III, vol. 3, 63.

52 Ormrod, *Edward III*, 616.

53 Ibid., 164–5.

54 CPR, Edward III, vol. 3, 79, 84.

55 Warner, *Philippa of Hainault*, 116.

56 CPR, Edward III, vol. 3, 201.

57 *Original Letters Illustrative of English History Etc.*, vol. 1, ed. Sir Henry Ellis (London: R. Bentley, 1846), 33–9.

58 Ormrod, *Edward III*, 616.

59 Benz St John, *Three Medieval Queens*, 136.

60 CPL, vol. 2, 529–33.

61 James Bothwell, 'An Emotional Pragmatism: Edward III and Death', in *Monarchy, State and Political Culture in Late Medieval England: Essays in Honour of W. Mark Ormrod*, ed. Gwilym Dodd and Craig Taylor (York: York Medieval Press, 2020), 54; Shenton, 'Philippa of Hainault's Churchings', 110–11.

62 Ormrod, *Edward III*, 617.

63 Mortimer, *The Perfect King*, 131.

64 W.M. Ormrod, 'The Personal Religion of Edward III', *Speculum*, 64 (1989), 855.

65 *Chronicon Galfridi le Baker*, 58; Ormrod, *Edward III*, 617.

66 Ormrod, *Edward III*, 174.

67 Shenton, 'Philippa of Hainault's Churchings', 110–11.

68 Warner, *Philippa of Hainault*, 121.

69 Jean Devaux, 'From the Court of Hainault to the Court of England: The Example of Jean Froissart', in *War, Government and Power in Late Medieval France*, ed. Christopher Allmand (Liverpool: Liverpool University Press, 2000), 11–12; Jean de le Mote, *Li Regret Guillaume, Comte de Hainaut*, ed. A. Scheler (Louvain: Imprimerie de J. Lefever, 1882), viii.

70 Ormrod, 'Personal Religion', 867.

71 CPR, Edward III, vol. 3, 464, 486.

72 Ibid., 387, 397, 425, 429.

73 Ormrod, 'Personal Religion', 866.

74 CPR, Edward III, vol. 3, 534, 537.

75 Dyer, *Standards of Living*, 31.

76 Lucas, *The Low Countries*, 283; CPR, Edward III, vol. 4, 113.
77 *Knighton's Chronicle 1337–1396*, trans. G.H. Martin (Oxford: Clarendon Press, 1995), 7; Mark Ormrod, 'The Royal Nursery: A Household for the Younger Children of Edward III', *English Historical Review*, 120 (2005), 404.
78 Lucas, *The Low Countries*, 283; *The Wardrobe Book of William de Norwell: 12 July 1338 to 27 May 1340*, ed. Mary Lyon, Bryce Lyon and Henry Lucas (Brussels: Palais des Académies, 1983), lxxxvii.
79 *Scalacronica*, 123; *Knighton's Chronicle*, 9–11.
80 *Oeuvres*, vol. 2, 360.
81 Barber, 'Edward III's Arthurian Enthusiasms', 69–70; Caroline Shenton, 'Edward III and the Symbol of the Leopard', in *Heraldry, Pageantry and Social Display in Medieval England*, ed. Peter Coss and Maurice Keen (Woodbridge: Boydell Press, 2008), 79.
82 CPR, Edward III, vol. 4, 313; *Foedera*, vol. 2:2, 1102.
83 Warner, *Philippa of Hainault*, 136.
84 *Knighton's Chronicle*, 9.
85 See Henry S. Lucas, 'Diplomatic Relations between England and Flanders from 1329 to 1336', *Speculum*, 11 (1936), 59–87.
86 Ormrod, *Edward III*, 208; Attila Bárány, 'The Participation of the English Aristocracy in the First Phase of the Hundred Years' War, 1337–1360', *Hungarian Journal of English and American Studies*, 3 (1997), British Studies Issue, 219.
87 Ormrod, *Edward III*, 204–5.
88 *The Wardrobe Book of William de Norwell*, lxxxiv–lxxxv.
89 Hunt, 'A New Look', 157–8.
90 Lucas, *The Low Countries*, 364.
91 *The Wardrobe Book of William de Norwell*, lii.
92 CCR, Edward III, vol. 6, 467.
93 CPR, Edward III, vol. 4, 546.
94 Mortimer, *The Perfect King*, 171.
95 Ormrod, *Edward III*, 225.
96 Lucas, *The Low Countries*, 403.
97 For details, see Ormrod, 'The Royal Nursery', 398–415.
98 Warner, *Philippa of Hainault*, 142.

Chapter 4

1 Ormrod, 'The Royal Nursery', 405–7.
2 CPR, Edward III, vol. 5, 236, 569.
3 Ormrod, 'The Royal Nursery', 407.
4 Jessica Lutkin, 'Isabella de Coucy, Daughter of Edward III: The Exception Who Proves the Rule', in *Fourteenth Century England VI*, ed. Chris Given-Wilson (Woodbridge: Boydell Press, 2010), 134.
5 Woolgar, *The Senses*, 224–5; R.A. Brown, H.M. Colvin and A.J. Taylor, *The History of the King's Works*, vol. 2 (London: Ministry of Public Building and Works, 1963), 731.

6   J.R.L. Highfield, 'The Early Colleges', in *The History of the University of Oxford Volume 1: The Early Oxford Schools*, ed. J.I. Catto (Oxford: Clarendon, 1984), 238.

7   CPL, vol. 3, 87.

8   Ibid.

9   John H. Harvey, 'Mediaeval Plantsmanship in England: The Culture of Rosemary', *Garden History*, 1 (1972), 14–21.

10 George R. Keiser, 'Through a Fourteenth-Century Gardener's Eyes: Henry Daniel's Herbal', *The Chaucer Review*, 31 (1996), 73–4.

11 Van der Meulen, '"Sche sente"', 79.

12 Bárány, 'Hundred Years' War', 222.

13 Ormrod, *Edward III*, 247.

14 *Knighton's Chronicle*, 39; Ormrod, *Edward III*, 248.

15 See for example Mortimer, *The Perfect King*, 199; Ormrod, *Edward III*, 130.

16 Ormrod, *Edward III*, 619.

17 Warner, *Philippa of Hainault*, 152–3.

18 Shenton, 'Philippa of Hainault's Churchings', 112–13.

19 Warner, *Philippa of Hainault*, 155; Juliet Vale, 'Philippa [Philippa of Hainault]', in *Oxford Dictionary of National Biography* (2010), accessed online at oxforddnb.com.

20 Mortimer, *The Perfect King*, 203–5.

21 E. Déprez, 'La mort de Robert d'Artois', *Revue Historique*, 94 (1907), 65.

22 Déprez, 'La mort de Robert d'Artois', 66; Warner, *Philippa of Hainault*, 153.

23 Barber, 'Edward III's Arthurian Enthusiasms', 60–1.

24 Avesbury, *Adæ Murimuth*, 135–6.

25 CPR, Edward III, vol. 6, 103–4.

26 Slater, 'Defining Queenship', 67.

27 Mortimer, *The Perfect King*, 208.

28 CPR, Edward III, vol. 6, 117–18, 139.

29 CCR, Edward III, vol. 5, 510; CCR, Edward III, vol. 6, 429, 559, 565–6, 583, 596, etc.

30 Mortimer, *The Perfect King*, 212.

31 Avesbury, *Adæ Murimuth*, 231.

32 Warner, *Philippa of Hainault*, 164; Ormrod, *Edward III*, 254.

33 Barber, 'Edward III's Arthurian Enthusiasms', 70–2; Walsingham, *Historia Anglicana*, 263.

34 Lutkin, 'Isabella de Coucy', 134–5; *Foedera*, vol. 3:1, 25.

35 CPR, Edward III, vol. 6, 457, 549.

36 Orme, *From Childhood to Chivalry*, 12.

37 Dunn, 'All the Queen's Ladies?', 205.

38 Warner, *Philippa of Hainault*, 170.

39 CPR, Edward III, vol. 6, 552.

40 Lucas, *The Low Countries*, 535–6.

41 CPR, Edward III, vol. 7, 70–1.

42 Ormrod, *Edward III*, 271.

43 *Knighton's Chronicle*, 63.

44 *Foedera*, vol. 3:1, 86.

45   CPR, Edward III, vol. 7, 200 notes Philippa being in Calais on 21 September.
46   Michael A. Penman, 'The Scots at the Battle of Neville's Cross, 17 October 1346', *Scottish Historical Review*, 80 (2001), 157–80.
47   *Chroniques* 4, Luce, 22–6.
48   *Chronique de Jean le Bel*, vol. 2, 126–7.
49   Lucas, *The Low Countries*, 558.
50   Ibid., 558–9.
51   *Chroniques* 4, Luce, 29.
52   *Knighton's Chronicle*, 65.
53   Ormrod, *Edward III*, 287–9.
54   Lutkin, 'Isabella de Coucy', 135.
55   Jean Froissart, *Sir John Froissart's Chronicles of England, France, Spain, Etc*, vol. 2, ed. Thomas Johnes (London: William Smith, 1844), 179–81.
56   Warner, *Philippa of Hainault*, 177.
57   *Knighton's Chronicle*, 77.
58   Ormrod, *Edward III*, 291.
59   *Chronique de Jean le Bel*, vol. 2, 166–7; see also *Chroniques* 4, Luce, 61–2.
60   *Knighton's Chronicle*, 85; *Chronicon Galfridi le Baker*, 91–2.
61   Philippa had been reunited with Edward in September the previous year, and so she could have subsequently fallen pregnant and been so during the fall of Calais in August 1347. But there is no record of Philippa giving birth again after Princess Margaret until late May 1348 – nine months from the fall of Calais (Staniland, 'The Great Wardrobe Accounts', 228). For Philippa to have been heavily pregnant at Calais, she must have given birth almost immediately afterwards, and instantly fallen pregnant again, with the baby leaving no trace.
62   Carmi Parsons, 'The Pregnant Queen', 42.
63   For a discussion of the comparison of these accounts, see Gemma Hollman, *Royal Witches: From Joan of Navarre to Elizabeth Woodville* (Cheltenham: The History Press, 2019), 32–3.
64   Ormrod, *Edward III*, 621.
65   *Chronique de Jean le Bel*, vol. 1, 156.
66   Kay Staniland, 'Medieval Courtly Splendour', *Costume: The Journal of the Costume Society*, 14 (1980), 12.
67   *Register of Edward, the Black Prince*, vol. 4, ed. M.C.B. Dawes (London: HMSO, 1930–3), 69.
68   Staniland, 'Medieval Courtly Splendour', 10.
69   George Frederick Beltz, *Memorials of the Most Noble Order of the Garter, from its Foundation to the Present Time Etc* (London: William Pickering, 1841), xxxii; Ormrod, *Edward III*, 303.
70   Woolgar, *The Senses*, 237.
71   Shenton, 'Philippa of Hainault's Churchings', 110; Mortimer, *The Perfect King*, 259.
72   Kay Staniland, 'Clothing and Textiles at the Court of Edward III 1342–1352', in *Collectanea Londiniensia: Studies in London Archaeology and History Presented to Ralph Merrifield* (London and Middlesex: Archaeological Society, 1978), 228.
73   Mortimer, *The Perfect King*, 256–7.

74 Ormrod, 'The Royal Nursery', 412–13.
75 *Foedera*, vol. 3:1, 171.
76 Mortimer, *The Perfect King*, 261.
77 Staniland, 'Clothing and Textiles', 229.
78 Mortimer, *The Perfect King*, 261–2.
79 *Chronicon Galfridi le Baker*, 99.
80 Ormrod, 'Personal Religion', 856.
81 Woolgar, *The Senses*, 243–4.
82 Shenton, 'Philippa of Hainault's Churchings', 120–1.
83 Veronica Sekules, 'Dynasty and Patrimony in the Self-Construction of an English Queen: Philippa of Hainault and Her Images', in *England and the Continent in the Middle Ages: Harlaxton Medieval Studies VIII* (Stamford: Shaun Tyas, 2000), 165–7.

Chapter 5

1 Brown, Colvin and Taylor, *The History of the King's Works*, vol. 1, 236.
2 CPR, Edward III, vol. 8, 530, 552, 571.
3 Warner, *Philippa of Hainault*, 200.
4 Richard Barber, *Edward III and the Triumph of England: The Battle of Crécy and the Company of the Garter* (London: Penguin Books, 2014), 138, 417.
5 *Chronicles of Froissart*, Brereton, 114–15.
6 Ibid., 116–17.
7 Barber, *Edward III*, 417–18.
8 CPR, Edward III, vol. 9, 72–3, 136, 161.
9 Warner, *Philippa of Hainault*, 205.
10 Ibid., 206.
11 CPR, Edward III, vol. 9, 287.
12 'Edward III: September 1353', PROME, item 40.
13 Mortimer, *The Perfect King*, 303–7; Ormrod, *Edward III*, 623–4.
14 Warner, *Philippa of Hainault*, 208.
15 Avesbury, *Adæ Murimuth*, 422.
16 Warner, *Philippa of Hainault*, 200.
17 Ibid., 212.
18 CPR, Edward III, vol. 10, 269.
19 Ormrod, *Edward III*, 624.
20 *Scalacronica*, 147; *Chronicon Galfridi le Baker*, 146–53; *Knighton's Chronicle*, 143–5.
21 *Knighton's Chronicle*, 151.
22 Mortimer, *The Perfect King*, 329.
23 CPR, Edward III, vol. 10, 508, 530–1, 602.
24 See for example ibid., 492, 517, 520, 594.
25 Ormrod, *Edward III*, 314.
26 Michael Bennett, 'Isabelle of France, Anglo-French Diplomacy and Cultural Exchange in the Late 1350's, in *The Age of Edward III*, ed. J.S. Bothwell (York: York Medieval Press, 2001), 215; Mortimer, *The Perfect King*, 329.
27 *Knighton's Chronicle*, 159.

28 James L. Gillespie, 'Ladies of the Fraternity of Saint George and of the Society of the Garter', *Albion: A Quarterly Journal Concerned with British Studies*, 17 (1985), 262.

29 Warner, *Philippa of Hainault*, 217.

30 Bennett, 'Isabelle of France', 223.

31 Mark Ormrod, 'Queenship, Death and Agency: The Commemoration of Isabella of France and Philippa of Hainault', in *Harlaxton Medieval Studies XX: Memory and Commemoration in Medieval England* (2010), 89.

32 Warner, *Philippa of Hainault*, 219.

33 Ormrod, *Edward III*, 391.

34 *Eulogium (Historiarum Sive Temporis)*, vol. 3, ed. Frank Scott Haydon (London: Longman, 1863), 227.

35 Ormrod, *Edward III*, 314.

36 John Le Patourel, 'The Treaty of Brétigny, 1360', *Transactions of the Royal Historical Society*, 10 (1960), 19–20.

37 Sharon Bennett Connolly, *Heroines of the Medieval World* (Stroud: Amberley Publishing, 2019), 28.

38 Patourel, 'The Treaty of Brétigny', 20–4, 31–2; Ormrod, *Edward III*, 405.

39 Ormrod, *Edward III*, 406.

40 Benz St John, *Three Medieval Queens*, 65–9.

41 For example CPR, Edward III, vol. 11, 209, 215, 237, 244, 249.

42 Chris Given-Wilson, 'The Merger of Edward III's and Queen Philippa's Households, 1360–9', *Historical Research*, 51 (1978), 183–7.

43 Benz St John, *Three Medieval Queens*, 82.

44 Ibid., 83; Woolgar, *The Senses*, 223–4.

45 Warner, *Philippa of Hainault*, 227–8.

46 Ibid., 228–9.

47 W.M. Ormrod, 'Edward III and His Family', *Journal of British Studies*, 26 (1987), 412.

48 Staniland, 'Clothing and Textiles', 228.

49 David Green, 'Lordship and Principality: Colonial Policy in Ireland and Aquitaine in the 1360s', *Journal of British Studies*, 47 (2008), 8.

50 Thomas Walsingham, *Chronicon Angliae, Ab Anno Domini 1328 Usque Ad Annum 1388*, ed. Edward Maunde Thompson (London: Longman, 1874), 50.

51 Sekules, 'Dynasty and Patrimony', 168.

52 Mortimer, *The Perfect King*, 352.

53 Devaux, 'From the Court of Hainault', 13–15.

54 Sekules, 'Dynasty and Patrimony', 161.

55 Bothwell, 'An Emotional Pragmatism', 53.

56 Warner, *Philippa of Hainault*, 236.

57 Mortimer, *The Perfect King*, 360.

58 Warner, *Philippa of Hainault*, 239.

59 For a discussion of these accusations, see Antonia Gransden, 'The Alleged Rape by Edward III of the Countess of Salisbury', *English Historical Review*, 87 (1972), 333–44.

60 For example Warner, *Philippa of Hainault*, 240; Frederick George Kay, *The Lady of the Sun: The Life and Times of Alice Perrers* (London: Muller, 1966), 67.

61 CPR, Edward III, vol. 12, 388, 392, 408.

62 Ibid., 288, 361, 369, 371.

63 Mark Ormrod, 'Queenship, Death and Agency', 97.

64 Joel Fredell, 'Late Gothic Portraiture: The Prioress and Philippa', *Chaucer Review*, 23 (1989), 183–5.

65 Sekules, 'Dynasty and Patrimony', 170.

66 Ibid., 172–3.

67 Ormrod, *Edward III*, 316.

68 Warner, *Philippa of Hainault*, 243.

69 Lutkin, 'Isabella de Coucy', 137–8.

70 National Archives currency converter, www.nationalarchives.gov.uk/currency-converter/

71 Ormrod, 'Queenship, Death and Agency', 101; Mortimer, *The Perfect King*, 360; Ormrod, *Edward III*, 628.

72 Ormrod, 'Queenship, Death and Agency', 101.

73 There are two payments recorded, for £100 and £50, though it isn't clear if the £50 was part payment for the £100, or an additional payment: *Issue Roll of Thomas de Brantingham*, ed. Frederick Devon (London: John Rodwell, 1835), xlii–xliii.

74 Mortimer, *The Perfect King*, 363.

75 CPR, Edward III, vol. 14, 6, 26; Warner, *Philippa of Hainault*, 245; CPR, Edward III, vol. 13, 382, 421.

76 *Knighton's Chronicle*, 197; *Oeuvres*, vol. 7, 251; *Testamenta Vetusta*, vol. 1, ed. Nicholas Harris Nicolas (London: Nichols & Son, 1826), 70–1.

77 Warner, *Philippa of Hainault*, 250–1.

78 *Chroniques* 1:2, Luce, 286; *Chroniques* 7, Luce, 181.

79 Ibid., 7, Luce, 182.

80 'Edward III: January 1377', PROME, item 6.

81 Ormrod, *Edward III*, 470; Ormrod, 'Queenship, Death and Agency', 94–5.

Chapter 6

1 Walsingham, *Chronicon Angliae*, 95.

2 E.g. Kay, *Lady of the Sun*, 18–19; Mark Ormrod, 'Who Was Alice Perrers?' *Chaucer Review*, 40 (2006), 221.

3 Historian Mark Ormrod discovered the petitions and realised their significance. His findings were detailed in his article 'Who Was Alice Perrers'; the petitions are found under TNA SC 119/5917, SC 8/119/5932 and SC8/104/S165.

4 Mark Ormrod, 'Alice Perrers and John Salisbury', *English Historical Review*, 123 (2008), 378–93; historian Laura Tompkins made the connection that Alice was linked to a London goldsmith family in her article 'Alice Perrers and the Goldsmiths' Mistery: New Evidence Concerning the Identity of the Mistress of Edward III', *English Historical Review*, 130 (2015), 1361–91.

5 'Edward III: October 1363', PROME, items 25–32.

6 Tompkins, 'Goldsmiths' Mistery', 1378.

7 *Calendar of Inquisitions Miscellaneous (Chancery) Volume IV 1377–1388* (London: HMSO, 1957), 13–16.

8   Kay, *Lady of the Sun*, 41.
9   Tompkins, 'Goldsmiths' Mistery', 1378.
10 Ibid., 1364.
11 Ormrod, 'John Salisbury', 378.
12 The London Metropolitan Archives, CLA/023/DW/01/087 (62) transcribed and translated in Tompkins, 'Goldsmiths' Mistery', 1390–1. See also ibid., 1363 for a discussion of Janyn's nationality.
13 Tompkins, 'Goldsmiths' Mistery', 1375.
14 Ormrod, 'Who Was Alice Perrers?' 226–7; TNA SC 8/119/5932, SC 8/119/5917.
15 Dyer, *Standards of Living*, 75.
16 Tompkins, 'Goldsmiths' Mistery', 1364; CPR, Edward III, vol. 12, 278.
17 *Calendar of the Plea and Memoranda Rolls of the City of London: Volume 2, 1364–1381*, ed. A.H. Thomas (London: HMSO, 1929), 11; Haldeen Braddy, 'Chaucer and Dame Alice Perrers', *Speculum*, 21 (1946), 226 claimed that Alice was in the household since at least 1359, but this was a misreading of a footnote in Walford Selby, *Life-Records of Chaucer* (London: Kegan Paul, Trench, Trübner & Co., 1900), 155 n1, which is referring to accounts of 1366.
18 Dunn, 'All the Queen's Ladies?', 175.
19 Ibid., 179–88.
20 Tompkins, 'Goldsmiths' Mistery', 1381.
21 Given-Wilson, 'The Merger of Households', 184.
22 CPR, Edward III, vol. 12, 278.
23 Ormrod, *Edward III*, 457.
24 Mortimer, *The Perfect King*, 88.
25 Bennett Connolly, *Heroines*, 28.
26 Ormrod, *Edward III*, 461.
27 Ibid., 462–3, 461.
28 *Plea and Memoranda Rolls*, vol. 2, 11.
29 Chris Given-Wilson, *The Royal Household and the King's Affinity: Service, Politics and Finance in England 1360–1413* (London: Yale University Press, 1986), 149; George Holmes, *The Good Parliament* (Oxford: Clarendon Press, 1975), 79.
30 Chris Given-Wilson and Alice Curteis, *The Royal Bastards of Medieval England* (London: Routledge & Kegan Paul, 1984), 139–41.
31 E.g. Given-Wilson and Curteis, *Royal Bastards*, 138; Ormrod, 'John Salisbury', 391; Mortimer, *The Perfect King*, 361; CPR, Richard II, vol. 1, 77, 102.
32 *A History of the County of Surrey: Volume 4*, ed. H.E. Malden (London: Victoria County History, 1912), 17–24.
33 CCR, Edward III, vol. 12, 198.
34 Ibid., 200.
35 Ormrod, 'Queenship, Death and Agency', 101.
36 CPR, Edward III, vol. 13, 321.
37 Rose, *The Wine Trade*, xvi.
38 Rod Phillips, *Alcohol: A History* (Chapel Hill: University of North Carolina Press, 2014), 78.
39 Dyer, *Standards of Living*, 10–32 passim.

40 Rose, *The Wine Trade*, 113–23; Phillips, *Alcohol*, 78–9.
41 Dunn, 'All the Queen's Ladies?', 205.
42 CPR, Edward III, vol. 13, 336, 311.
43 Ormrod, *Edward III*, 464. The source he quotes (Selby, *Life-Records*, 162–70) only gives a livery list for Christmas 1368, and the 1369 list mentioned is in fact restating the list of ladies from Christmas 1368.
44 Selby, *Life-Records*, 172–3.
45 CFR, Edward III, vol. 7, 349; the grant is repeated in November 1368, CPR, Edward III, vol. 14, 183.
46 CPR, Edward III, vol. 13, 396.
47 Ibid., 418.
48 CCR, Edward III, vol. 12, 396.
49 Alexander Grant, 'The St Bees Lord and Lady, and Their Lineage', Working Paper (Lancaster: University of Lancaster, 2013), 16.
50 CCR, Edward III, vol. 12, 396 notes it was cancelled on payment acknowledged by Alice 'on the files of chancery for the 50th year'.
51 CFR, Edward III, vol. 7, 389; CPR, Edward III, vol. 14, 210.
52 E.g. CCR, Edward III, vol. 12, 389; CPR, Edward III, vol. 14, 58.
53 CPR, Edward III, vol. 14, 125.
54 Ibid., 147.
55 Ibid., 146, 292.
56 James Bothwell, 'The Management of Position: Alice Perrers, Edward III and the Creation of a Landed Estate', *Journal of Medieval History*, 24 (1998), 37.
57 Given-Wilson and Curteis, *Royal Bastards*, 135.
58 *Scalacronica*, 162–3.
59 Ormrod, *Edward III*, 525; T.R. Gambier-Parry, 'Alice Perrers and Her Husband's Relatives', *English Historical Review*, 47 (1932), 273.
60 Barbara Tuchman, *A Distant Mirror: The Calamitous 14th Century* (London: Macmillan, 1979), 246.

Chapter 7

1 Bothwell, 'The Management of Position', 37–8.
2 Selby, *Life-Records*, 172–3.
3 CPR, Edward III, vol. 14, 437.
4 Laura Tompkins, 'Mary Percy and John de Southeray: Wardship, Marriage and Divorce in Fourteenth-Century England', in *Fourteenth Century England X*, ed. Gwilym Dodd (Woodbridge: Boydell Press, 2018), 138–40.
5 CPR, Edward III, vol. 14, 437.
6 Tompkins, 'Mary Percy', 140.
7 Tompkins, 'Goldsmiths' Mistery', 1389–90.
8 Given-Wilson, *The Royal Household*, 148.
9 Ormrod, *Edward III*, 526.
10 Given-Wilson, *The Royal Household*, 71, 148.

11 Laura Tompkins, '"Said the Mistress to the Bishop": Alice Perrers, William Wykeham and Court Networks in Fourteenth-Century England', in *Ruling Fourteenth-Century England: Essays in Honour of Christopher Given-Wilson* (Woodbridge: Boydell Press, 2019), 213.

12 Virginia Davis, 'William Wykeham's Early Ecclesiastical Career', in *European Religious Cultures: Essays Offered to Christopher Brooke on the Occasion of His Eightieth Birthday* (London: University of London Press, 2020), 48–9, 53.

13 CPR, Edward III, vol. 12, 444–5.

14 Davis, 'William Wykeham', 60.

15 Ormrod, *Edward III*, 526.

16 Tompkins, '"Said the Mistress"', 210.

17 CPR, Edward III, vol. 15, 161.

18 Tompkins, '"Said the Mistress"', 213–14.

19 Kay, *Lady of the Sun*, 80.

20 CPL, vol. 4, 96.

21 *Issues of the Exchequer*, Devon, 193–4.

22 CCR, Edward III, vol. 12, 440.

23 Dyer, *Standards of Living*, 31.

24 Ormrod, *Edward III*, 465.

25 A.G. Rigg, 'John of Bridlington's Prophecy: A New Look', *Speculum*, 63 (1988), 600.

26 Historians have debated whether this Diana does indeed refer to Alice or not (see, e.g., Rigg, 'John of Bridlington's Prophecy', 601), but the allusions certainly seem to have clear parallels to Alice's situation at this time.

27 Rigg, 'John of Bridlington's Prophecy', 600.

28 Ormrod, *Edward III*, 534.

29 Peter Crooks, 'Representation and Dissent: "Parliamentarianism" and the Structure of Politics in Colonial Ireland, *c.*1370–1420', *English Historical Review*, 125 (2010), 8–9.

30 Ormrod, *Edward III*, 536.

31 CPR, Edward III, vol. 15, 191, 229.

32 Ormrod, 'John Salisbury', 386.

33 His goods were seized alongside Alice's in 1377 as seen in the inventory mentioned. *Inquisitions miscellaneous IV*, 13–16; TNA E 199/26/1.

34 Tompkins, 'Goldsmiths' Mistery', 1384.

35 *Inquisitions miscellaneous IV*, 13–16.

36 See Richardson, '"Riding like Alexander"', 253–70.

37 *John of Gaunt's Register*, vol. 2, ed. Sydney Armitage-Smith (London: Offices of the Society, 1911), 194.

38 Although the date of birth of their first child, John Beaufort, is not certain, he might have been born in the winter of 1372–3: see Alison Weir, *Katherine Swynford: The Story of John of Gaunt and His Scandalous Duchess* (London: Vintage Books, 2008), 111.

39 Tompkins, 'Goldsmiths' Mistery', 1384–5.

40 *Foedera*, vol. 3:2, 989; CPR, Edward III, vol. 15, 347.

41 For example Holmes, *The Good Parliament*, 69; Ormrod, *Edward III*, 537; Mortimer, *The Perfect King*, 379; Helen Carr, *The Red Prince: The Life of John of Gaunt, Duke of Lancaster* (London: Oneworld Publications, 2021), 102–3.

42 Mortimer, *The Perfect King*, 379.

43 CPR, Edward III, vol. 15, 331.

44 CIPM 12, Edward III, no. 147; TNA C 135/194/5.

45 CPR, Edward III, vol. 15, 408; CCR, Edward III, vol. 14, 48.

46 CPR, Edward III, vol. 15, 338.

47 Tompkins, 'Mary Percy', 135.

48 TNA E 101/509/20.

49 Ormrod, *Edward III*, 537.

50 Ibid., 530–2.

51 E.g. Walsingham, *Chronicon Angliae*, 95–6.

52 *Foedera*, vol. 3:2, 996; Holmes, *The Good Parliament*, 68.

53 'Edward III: April 1376', PROME, membrane 3, item 17.

54 Tompkins, 'Goldsmiths' Mistery', 1388.

55 Ormrod, *Edward III*, 533.

56 TNA E 101/397/20 m3.

57 Tompkins, 'Mary Percy', 135.

58 CPR, Edward III, vol. 16, 180.

59 TNA E 101/397/20 m4.

60 CPR, Edward III, vol. 16, 153.

61 Bothwell, 'The Management of Position', 46.

62 CPR, Edward III, vol. 16, 154.

63 Ormrod, *Edward III*, 539–40.

64 Ibid., 544–5.

65 Ibid., 547.

Chapter 8

1 Ormrod, *Edward III*, 547; the *Chronicle of London* dates this tournament to 1374/5, but Ormrod argues that the tournament in fact took place in Edward's jubilee year.

2 *Chronicle of London, from 1089 to 1483*, ed. Edward Tyrrell and Sir N.H. Nicolas (London: Longman, Rees, Orme, Brown & Green, 1827), 70.

3 Ormrod, *Edward III*, 548.

4 Kay, *Lady of the Sun*, 116.

5 TNA E 101/397/20 m6.

6 George Frederick Beltz, *Memorials*, 10.

7 Ormrod, *Edward III*, 548.

8 TNA E 101/397/20 m6; Holmes, *The Good Parliament*, 68; Beltz, *Memorials*, 10.

9 'Edward III: April 1376', PROME, item 9, membrane 2.

10 Mortimer, *The Perfect King*, 383.

11 For an account of the meeting, see *The Anonimalle Chronicle, 1333 to 1381, from a MS. Written at St Mary's Abbey, York*, ed. V.H. Galbraith (Manchester: Manchester University Press, 1970), 85–9.

12 'Edward III: April 1376', PROME, introduction.

13 Ibid., item 15.

14 For example, in 1367 Edward had to take money from the ransom of John II of France to pay household debts: Ormrod, *Edward III*, 448.

15 *Anonimalle 1333 to 1381*, 87.

16 'Edward III: April 1376', PROME, introduction, item 27.

17 'Edward III: April 1376', PROME, item 17; Ormrod, *Edward III*, 554.

18 Chris Given-Wilson, *The Court and Household of Edward III, 1360–1377* (University of St Andrews, PhD Thesis, 1976), 198–9.

19 Translated in Tompkins, 'Goldsmiths' Mistery', 1382.

20 *Anonimalle 1333 to 1381*, 87, 89, 92.

21 'Edward III: April 1376', PROME, item 45.

22 Thomas Walsingham, *The St Albans Chronicle: The Chronica Maiora of Thomas Walsingham*, vol. 1, ed. and trans. John Taylor, Wendy R. Childs and Leslie Watkiss (Oxford: Clarendon Press, 2003), 45.

23 Walsingham, *St Albans Chronicle*, 46–9.

24 A discussion of the charges brought against Latimer and Lyons and whether they are likely to have been guilty can be found in Given-Wilson, *The Court and Household*, 196–216.

25 Ibid., 39.

26 Ormrod, *Edward III*, 558.

27 Mark Ormrod, 'The Trials of Alice Perrers', *Speculum*, 83 (2008), 370.

28 'Edward III: April 1376', PROME, items 17–30.

29 Gwilym Dodd, 'A Parliament Full of Rats? Piers Plowman and the Good Parliament of 1376', *Historical Research*, 79 (2006), 32–3.

30 Tompkins, 'Mary Percy', 148.

31 Ormrod, *Edward III*, 562.

32 *Issues of the Exchequer*, 199–200.

33 Walsingham, *St Albans Chronicle*, 57.

34 *Anonimalle 1333 to 1381*, 95.

35 Ormrod, *Edward III*, 562–3.

36 'A Mandate from Archbishop Neville to His Officials at York', in *Historical Papers and Letters from the Northern Registers*, ed. James Raine (London: Longman, 1873), 410–11.

37 *A Collection of All the Wills, Now Known to Be Extant, of the Kings and Queens of England Etc.*, ed. John Nichols (London: J. Nichols, 1780), 59–65.

38 CPR, Edward III, vol. 16, 364–5.

39 *Issues of the Exchequer*, 199–200.

40 CCR, Edward III, vol. 14, 443.

41 *Rotuli Parliamentorum*, vol. 2, 330b; *Foedera*, vol. 3:2, 1075.

42 *Chronicles of Froissart*, Brereton, 194.

43 Tompkins, 'Mary Percy', 135.

44 'Edward III: January 1377', PROME, introduction.

45 Ormrod, *Edward III*, 570.

46 Walsingham, *St Albans Chronicle*, 101.

47 'Edward III: January 1377', PROME, item 89.

48 *Anonimalle 1333 to 1381*, 103.
49 See testimony during the first parliament of Richard II: 'Richard II: October 1377', PROME, item 42.
50 Tompkins, 'Mary Percy', 141.
51 Ibid.
52 TNA E 101/397/20 m9; see translation in Tompkins, 'Mary Percy', 142–3.
53 TNA E 101/397/20 m20.
54 Cambridge University Library, EDR, G/1/2 f101v., translated in Tompkins, 'Mary Percy', 145.
55 'Edward III: January 1377', PROME, introduction.
56 Ormrod, *Edward III*, 573.
57 Mortimer, *The Perfect King*, 390.
58 Walsingham, *St Albans Chronicle*, 59.
59 CCR, Edward III, vol. 14, 485.
60 'Richard II: October 1377', PROME, item 42.
61 Ibid.
62 CPR, Edward III, vol. 16, 439–40, 444.
63 Beltz, *Memorials*, 11.
64 *Anonimalle 1333 to 1381*, 106.
65 Margaret Galway, 'Alice Perrers's Son John', *English Historical Review*, 66 (1951), 243–4.
66 Ibid., 245.
67 CPR, Edward III, vol. 16, 462.
68 Walsingham, *St Albans Chronicle*, 119.
69 CPR, Edward III, vol. 16, 477.
70 *The History of the King's Works*, vol. 1, 236.
71 TNA E 101/397/20 m11.
72 CPR, Edward III, vol. 16, 478.
73 Walsingham, *St Albans Chronicle*, 119.
74 *Chronicles of Froissart*, Brereton, 195.
75 Walsingham, *St Albans Chronicle*, 119.
76 Ibid., 63.
77 Members of Edward's family were at Sheen the day after his death: Chris Given-Wilson, 'The Exequies of Edward III and the Royal Funeral Ceremony in Late Medieval England', *English Historical Review*, 124 (2009), 263.
78 Walsingham, *St Albans Chronicle*, 119.
79 Given-Wilson, 'The Exequies', 268.
80 Mortimer, *The Perfect King*, 392.
81 Given-Wilson, 'The Exequies', 265–6.
82 For a detailed account of Edward's funeral, see Given-Wilson, 'The Exequies', 257–82.
83 *Chronicles of Froissart*, Brereton, 196.
84 Ibid., 195–6.

Chapter 9

1 Ormrod, 'Trials', 376.
2 'Richard II: October 1377', PROME, item 42.
3 Ibid.
4 Ibid.
5 Ibid.
6 Ibid., item 43.
7 CPR, Edward III, vol. 16, 180.
8 Walsingham, *St Albans Chronicle*, 169–71.
9 Paul Strohm, *Hochon's Arrow: The Social Imagination of Fourteenth-Century Texts* (Princeton: Princeton University Press, 1992), 95–103; Carmi Parsons, 'Family, Sex, and Power', 6–9.
10 'Richard II: October 1377', PROME, item 43.
11 E.g. *Inquisitions miscellaneous IV*, 1–5.
12 Bothwell, 'The Management of Position', 36n, 43.
13 *Issues of the Exchequer*, 209–10.
14 Bothwell, 'The Management of Position', 36n.
15 Dyer, *Standards of Living*, 31.
16 *Inquisitions miscellaneous IV*, 13 item 17.
17 Walsingham, *St Albans Chronicle*, 47.
18 See for example Gambier-Parry, 'Alice Perrers', 273; Ormrod, 'Trials', 373–4; Bryan Bevan, *Edward III: Monarch of Chivalry* (London: Rubicon, 1992), 143.
19 Benz St John, *Three Medieval Queens*, 83–4.
20 Ormrod, 'Trials', 379–80.
21 *Inquisitions miscellaneous IV*, 16.
22 CCR, Richard II, vol. 1, 43–6.
23 Ibid., 56.
24 R.G. Davies, 'Brantingham, Thomas', in *Oxford Dictionary of National Biography* (2004), accessed online at oxforddnb.com.
25 CPR, Richard II, vol. 1, 102.
26 Ibid., 42–3.
27 CCR, Richard II, vol. 1, 49–50.
28 CCR, Richard II, vol. 1, 160; CPR, Richard II, vol. 1, 98, 105, 124, 285, 324, 376.
29 TNA SC 8/41/2011.
30 Ormrod, 'Trials', 381, 385.
31 'Richard II: October 1378', PROME, introduction.
32 Ibid., item 36.
33 TNA SC 8/146/7279.
34 'Richard II: October 1378', PROME, item 36.
35 Ibid., item 37.
36 Ormrod, 'Trials', 387.
37 CPR, Richard II, vol. 1, 412.
38 Walsingham, *St Albans Chronicle*, 170–1.
39 Ormrod, 'Trials', 387–8; Tompkins, '"Said the Mistress"', 222.

40 CPR, Richard II, vol. 1, 503–4.

41 Ibid., 399.

42 Tompkins, '"Said the Mistress"', 206.

43 CPR, Edward III, vol. 16, 483; Walsingham, *St Albans Chronicle*, 108–11.

44 Ormrod, 'Trials', 388.

45 CCR, Richard II, vol. 1, 462–8.

46 Tompkins, '"Said the Mistress"', 221.

47 Tompkins, 'Mary Percy', 145.

48 Ibid.

49 Cambridge University Library, EDR, G/1/2, f. 101v. quoted in Tompkins, 'Mary Percy', 145.

50 TNA E 101/39/7 (4).

51 Dodd, 'A Parliament Full of Rats?', 40–3; Jean Froissart, *The Chronicles of Froissart*, ed. G.C. Macaulay (London: Macmillan & Co., 1895), 251.

52 *The Chronicles of Froissart*, Macaulay, 251.

53 Ibid., 255.

54 Ibid., 255–6.

55 Dodd, 'A Parliament Full of Rats?', 40–3.

56 Kay, *Lady of the Sun*, 186; Philomena Connolly, 'Windsor, William, Baron Windsor', in *Oxford Dictionary of National Biography* (2004), accessed online at oxforddnb.com; CPR, Richard II, vol. 2, 85, 246, 252; CCR, Richard II, vol. 2, 75.

57 'Richard II: November 1381', PROME, introduction.

58 CPR, Richard II, vol. 2, 327, 334.

59 Ibid., 364.

60 CIPM 16, Richard II, nos. 162–74.

61 CPR, Richard II, vol. 2, 447.

62 Tompkins, 'Mary Percy', 150.

63 'Richard II: November 1384', PROME, item 13.

64 CFR, Richard II, vol. 10, 66.

65 Arthur Collins, *Collins's Peerage of England; Genealogical, Biographical, and Historical*, vol. 3 (London: 1812), 653; Gambier-Parry, 'Alice Perrers', 272–3; Tompkins, '"Said the Mistress"', 208.

66 CPR, Richard II, vol. 2, 561–2, 566–7.

67 Ormrod, 'Trials', 389–90.

68 TNA SC 8/148/7358; Ormrod, 'Trials', 391.

69 Lopez, *The English in Portugal, 1367–87*, quoted in Tompkins, 'Mary Percy', 149.

70 Froissart, *Chronicles of England*, vol. 2, Johnes, 688–90.

71 CCR, Richard II, vol. 2, 501–2.

72 Ibid., vol. 3, 645–6.

73 Ibid., vol. 5, 48.

74 Ibid.

75 In her will, Alice gives Jane her manor of Gaynes and makes her her executor: Lambeth Palace Library, Reg. Arundel 1, f. 188–9.

76 TNA SC 8/22/1060; *Rotuli Parliamentorum*, vol. 3, 327b–28a.

77 'Richard II: September 1397, Part 1', PROME, item 68.

78   Ormrod, 'Trials', 391.

79   TNA SC 8/150/7459.

80   Tompkins, '"Said the Mistress"', 222–3.

81   Given-Wilson and Curteis, *Royal Bastards*, 136–7.

82   *Plea and Memoranda Rolls*, vol. 2, Roll A 18: 1372–3, 150–62.; TNA E 101/68/6/132.

83   CPR, Edward III, vol. 15, 374, 413–14.

84   Ibid., 420–1.

85   CCR, Richard II, vol. 3, 300–8, 350–62; TNA SC 8/213/10640.

86   TNA SC 8/290/14462.

87   CIPM 18, Henry IV, nos. 586–7. However, 'occupied' in this sense could just mean having ownership rather than a literal habitation so this is conjecture.

88   Lambeth Palace Library, Reg. Arundel 1, f. 188.

89   British Library, Seal CLXV.4: 1374; *Inquisitions miscellaneous* IV, 15; Lambeth Palace Library, Reg. Arundel 1, f. 188.

90   '*Dico in pariculo anime mee pro dictus Johannes nunquam hunc ius ad easdem*', Lambeth Palace Library, Reg. Arundel 1, f. 189.

91   For example CIPM 18, Henry IV, nos. 586–7 say that Alice died on 16 December 1399, which cannot be possible as that predates her will, and CPR, Henry IV, vol. 2, 395 says she died in the first year of the reign of Henry IV, which would be 1399–1400.

92   Lincolnshire archives, 1ANC2/A/18/10. The grant refers to Robert Skerne and 'Johanne Northland' and whilst this could refer to a man named John, as it has been indexed, given the context of the grant being a manor previously owned by Alice, then William Wyndesore, and now being granted to Robert Skerne, it seems more likely that this Johanne is Jane, Alice's daughter, under her married name.

93   Lambeth Palace Library, Reg. Arundel 1, f. 189.

94   Tompkins, '"Said the Mistress"', 223.

95   CPR, Henry IV, vol. 2, 421.

96   CCR, Henry IV, vol. 2, 381–6.

97   CIPM 18, Henry IV, no. 1192.

98   W.R. Powell (ed.), 'Upminster: Introduction and Manors', in *A History of the County of Essex: Volume 7*, ed. W.R. Powell (London, 1978), 143–53.

99   CCR, Henry IV, vol. 3, 227.

100 J.A. Roskell, *The House of Commons, 1386–1421* (Stroud: Sutton, 1992), 383.

101 Mill Stephenson, 'A List of Monumental Brasses in Surrey', *Surrey Archaeological Collections*, 29 (1916), 103–5.

Conclusion

1   *Knighton's Chronicle*, 197.

Bibliography

Abbreviations

CCR	Calendar of the Close Rolls
CFR	Calendar of the Fine Rolls
CIPM	Calendar of Inquisitions Post Mortem
CPL	Calendar of Papal Registers (Letters)
CPR	Calendar of the Patent Rolls
Foedera	Rymer's *Foedera*
PROME	Parliament Rolls of Medieval England
TNA	The National Archives

Primary Sources

British Library:
Seal of Alice Perrers, Seal CLXV.4: 1374

John Rylands University Library Manchester:
MS Latin 234

Lambeth Palace Library:
Reg. Arundel 1

Lincolnshire Archives:
1ANC2/A/18/10

The National Archives:
C 135/194/5
E 101/39/7 (4)
E 101/68/6/132
E 101/397/20
E 101/509/20
SC 8/22/1060
SC 8/41/2011
SC 8/104/S165
SC 8/119/5932
SC 8/146/7279
SC 8/148/7358
SC 8/150/7459
SC 8/213/10640
SC 8/290/14462
SC 119/5917

Annales Paulini, Chronicles of the Reigns of Edward I and Edward II, Volume 1, ed. William
  Stubbs (London: Longman, 1882).
The Anonimalle Chronicle, 1307 to 1334: From Brotherton Collection MS 29, ed. Wendy R.
  Childs and John Taylor (Leeds: Yorkshire Archaeological Society, 1991).
The Anonimalle Chronicle, 1333 to 1381, from a MS. Written at St Mary's Abbey, York,
  ed. V.H. Galbraith (Manchester: Manchester University Press, 1970).
Avesbury, Robertus de. *Adæ Murimuth Continuatio chronicarum ... De gestis
  mirabilibus regis Edwardi Tertii*, ed. Edward Maunde Thompson (London: Eyre &
  Spottiswoode, 1889).
Bel, Jean le. *Chronique de Jean le Bel*, Volumes 1 and 2, ed. Jules Viard and Eugène
  Déprez (Paris: Librairie Renouard, 1904).
The Brut; or, The Chronicles of England, Volume 1, ed. Friedrich Brie (London: Kegan
  Paul, 1906).
Calendar of Close Rolls, Edward II: Henry IV (London: HMSO).
Calendar of Fine Rolls, Edward II: Richard II (London: HMSO).
Calendar of Inquisitions Miscellaneous (Chancery) Volume IV 1377–1388 (London:
  HMSO, 1957).
Calendar of Inquisitions Post Mortem, Edward III: Henry IV (London: HMSO).
Calendar of Papal Registers Relating to Great Britain and Ireland, Volumes 2–4, ed. W.H.
  Bliss (London), accessed via British History Online.
Calendar of Patent Rolls, Edward III: Henry IV (London: HMSO).
Calendar of the Plea and Memoranda Rolls of the City of London: Volume 1, 1323–1364, ed.
  A.H. Thomas (London: HMSO, 1926).
Calendar of the Plea and Memoranda Rolls of the City of London: Volume 2, 1364–1381, ed.
  A.H. Thomas (London: HMSO, 1929).
Chronicle of London, from 1089 to 1483, ed. Edward Tyrrell and Sir N.H. Nicolas (London:
  Longman, Rees, Orme, Brown and Green, 1827).

Chronicon Galfridi le Baker de Swynebroke, ed. Edward Maunde Thompson (Oxford: Clarendon Press, 1889).

A Collection of All the Wills, Now Known to Be Extant, of the Kings and Queens of England Etc., ed. John Nichols (London: J. Nichols, 1780).

Crawford, Anne. *Letters of the Queens of England, 1100–1547* (Stroud: Alan Sutton, 1994).

Déprez, E. 'La mort de Robert d'Artois', *Revue Historique*, 94 (1907).

Eulogium (Historiarum Sive Temporis), Volume 3, ed. Frank Scott Haydon (London: Longman, 1863).

Foedera, conventiones, litterae, et cujuscunque generis acta publica …, Volumes 2:1–3:2, ed. Thomas Rymer (London: Joannem Neulme, 1739–45).

Froissart, Jean. *The Chronicles of Froissart*, trans. Geoffrey Brereton (Harmondsworth: Penguin Books, 1968).

Froissart, Jean. *The Chronicles of Froissart*, ed. G.C. Macaulay (London: Macmillan & Co., 1895).

Froissart, Jean. *Chroniques de J. Froissart*, Volumes 1:2, 4 and 7, ed. Siméon Luce (Paris: Mme Ve. J. Renouard, 1869–78).

Froissart, Jean. *Oeuvres de Froissart*, Volumes 2, 7 and 17, ed. Kervyn de Lettenhove (Brussels: V. Devaux, 1867–77).

Froissart, Jean. *Sir John Froissart's Chronicles of England, France, Spain, Etc.*, Volumes 1 and 2, ed. Thomas Johnes (London: William Smith, 1839).

Great Britain Exchequer. *Issues of the Exchequer: Being a Collection of Payments Made out of His Majesty's Revenue, from King Henry III to King Henry VI Inclusive*, ed. Frederick Devon (London: John Murray, 1837).

Historical Papers and Letters from the Northern Registers, ed. James Raine (London: Longman, 1873).

Issue Roll of Thomas de Brantingham, ed. Frederick Devon (London: John Rodwell, 1835).

John of Gaunt's Register, Volume 2, ed. Sydney Armitage-Smith (London: Offices of the Society, 1911).

Knighton's Chronicle 1337–1396, trans. G.H. Martin (Oxford: Clarendon Press, 1995).

Memorials of London and London Life in the 13th, 14th and 15th Centuries, ed. H.T. Riley (London: Longmans, 1868).

Mote, Jean de le. *Li Regret Guillaume, Comte de Hainaut*, ed. A. Scheler (Louvain: Imprimerie de J. Lefever, 1882).

Original Letters Illustrative of English History Etc., Volume 1, ed. Sir Henry Ellis (London: R. Bentley, 1846).

Parliament Rolls of Medieval England, Edward III 1328–Richard II 1397, ed. Chris Given-Wilson, Paul Brand, Seymour Phillips, Mark Ormrod, Geoffrey Martin, Anne Curry and Rosemary Horrox (Woodbridge: Boydell, 2005), accessed via British History Online.

Register of Edward, the Black Prince, Volume 4, ed. M.C.B. Dawes (London: HMSO, 1933).

The Register of Walter de Stapeldon, Bishop of Exeter, (A.D. 1307–1326), ed. Rev. F.C. Hingeston-Randolph (London: G. Bell & Sons, 1892).

Rotuli Parliamentorum, ut et petitiones, et placita in Parliamento, Volumes 2 and 3 (Great Britain: Parliament).

Scalacronica: The Reigns of Edward I, Edward II and Edward III, as Recorded by Sir Thomas Gray, trans. Sir Herbert Maxwell (Glasgow: James Maclehose & Sons, 1907).

Selby, Walford. *Life-Records of Chaucer* (London: Kegan Paul, Trench, Trübner & Co., 1900).

Testamenta Vetusta, Volume 1, ed. Nicholas Harris Nicolas (London: Nichols & Son, 1826).

Vita Edwardi Secundi: The Life of Edward the Second, ed. Wendy R. Childs (Oxford: Clarendon Press, 2005).

Walsingham, Thomas. *Chronicon Angliae, Ab Anno Domini 1328 Usque Ad Annum 1388*, ed. Edward Maunde Thompson (London: Longman, 1874).

Walsingham, Thomas. *Historia Anglicana AD 1272–1381*, ed. Henry Thomas Riley (London: Longman, 1863).

Walsingham, Thomas. *The St Albans Chronicle: The Chronica Maiora of Thomas Walsingham*, Volume 1, ed. and trans. John Taylor, Wendy R. Childs and Leslie Watkiss (Oxford: Clarendon Press, 2003).

The Wardrobe Book of William de Norwell: 12 July 1338 to 27 May 1340, ed. Mary Lyon, Bryce Lyon and Henry Lucas (Brussels: Palais des Académies, 1983).

Secondary Sources

Bárány, Attila. 'The Participation of the English Aristocracy in the First Phase of the Hundred Years' War, 1337–1360', *Hungarian Journal of English and American Studies*, 3, British Studies Issue (1997): 211–240.

Barber, Richard. *Edward III and the Triumph of England: The Battle of Crécy and the Company of the Garter* (London: Penguin Books, 2014).

Barber, Richard. 'Edward III's Arthurian Enthusiasms Revisited: Perceforest in the Context of Philippa of Hainault and the Round Table Feast of 1344', *Arthurian Literature*, 30 (2013): 55–74.

Beltz, George Frederick. *Memorials of the Most Noble Order of the Garter, from its Foundation to the Present Time Etc.* (London: William Pickering, 1841).

Bennett, Michael. 'Isabelle of France, Anglo-French Diplomacy and Cultural Exchange in the Late 1350s', in *The Age of Edward III*, ed. J.S. Bothwell (York: York Medieval Press, 2001) pp. 215–226.

Bennett Connolly, Sharon. *Heroines of the Medieval World* (Stroud: Amberley Publishing, 2019).

Benz St John, Lisa. *Three Medieval Queens: Queenship and the Crown in Fourteenth-Century England* (New York: Palgrave Macmillan, 2012).

Bevan, Bryan. *Edward III: Monarch of Chivalry* (London: Rubicon, 1992).

Bothwell, James. 'An Emotional Pragmatism: Edward III and Death', in *Monarchy, State and Political Culture in Late Medieval England: Essays in Honour of W. Mark Ormrod*, ed. Gwilym Dodd and Craig Taylor (York: York Medieval Press, 2020) pp. 39–70.

Bothwell, James. 'The Management of Position: Alice Perrers, Edward III and the Creation of a Landed Estate', *Journal of Medieval History*, 24 (1998): 31–52.

Braddy, Haldeen. 'Chaucer and Dame Alice Perrers', *Speculum*, 21 (1946): 222–28.

Brown, R.A., Colvin, H.M. and Taylor, A.J. *The History of the King's Works*, Volumes 1 and 2: The Middle Ages (London: Ministry of Public Building and Works, 1963).

Carmi Parsons, John. 'Introduction: Family, Sex, and Power: The Rhythms of Medieval Queenship', in *Medieval Queenship*, ed. John Carmi Parsons (New York: St Martin's Press, 1993) pp. 1–12.

Carmi Parsons, John. 'The Pregnant Queen as Counsellor and the Medieval Construction of Motherhood', in *Medieval Mothering*, ed. John Carmi Parsons and Bonnie Wheeler (New York and London: Garland Publishing, 1996) pp. 39–62.

Carmi Parsons, John. 'Ritual and Symbol in the English Medieval Queenship to 1500', in *Cosmos Vol. 7, Women and Sovereignty*, ed. Louise Olga Fradenburg (Edinburgh: Edinburgh University Press, 1992) pp. 60–77.

Carr, Helen. *The Red Prince: The Life of John of Gaunt, Duke of Lancaster* (London: Oneworld Publications, 2021).

Castor, Helen. *She-Wolves: The Women Who Ruled England before Elizabeth* (London: Faber & Faber, 2011).

Collins, Arthur. *Collins's Peerage of England; Genealogical, Biographical, and Historical*, Volume 3 (London: 1812).

Connolly, Philomena. 'Windsor, William, Baron Windsor', in *Oxford Dictionary of National Biography* (2004), accessed online at oxforddnb.com.

Crane, Susan. *The Performance of Self: Ritual, Clothing, and Identity During the Hundred Years War* (Philadelphia: University of Pennsylvania Press, 2011).

Crawford, Anne. 'The Queen's Council in the Middle Ages', *English Historical Review*, 116 (2001): 1193–1211.

Crooks, Peter. 'Representation and Dissent: "Parliamentarianism" and the Structure of Politics in Colonial Ireland, *c.*1370–1420', *English Historical Review*, 125 no. 512 (2010): 1–34.

Davies, R.G. 'Brantingham, Thomas', in *Oxford Dictionary of National Biography* (2004), accessed online at oxforddnb.com.

Davis, Virginia. 'William Wykeham's Early Ecclesiastical Career', in *European Religious Cultures: Essays Offered to Christopher Brooke on the Occasion of His Eightieth Birthday*, ed. Miri Rubin (London: University of London Press, 2020) pp. 47–62.

Devaux, Jean. 'From the Court of Hainault to the Court of England: The Example of Jean Froissart', in *War, Government and Power in Late Medieval France*, ed. Christopher Allmand (Liverpool: Liverpool University Press, 2000), pp. 1–20.

Devillers, Leopold. *Monuments pour servir à l'histoire des provinces de Namur, de Hainaut et de Luxembourg*, vol. 3 part 1 (Brussels: F. Hayez, 1874).

Dodd, Gwilym. 'A Parliament Full of Rats? Piers Plowman and the Good Parliament of 1376', *Historical Research*, 79 (2006): 21–49.

Dunn, Caroline. 'All the Queen's Ladies? Philippa of Hainault's Female Attendants', *Medieval Prosopography*, 31 (2016): 173–208.

Dyer, Christopher. *Standards of Living in the Later Middle Ages: Social Change in England, c. 1200–1520* (Cambridge: Cambridge University Press, 1998).

Fredell, Joel, 'Late Gothic Portraiture: The Prioress and Philippa', *Chaucer Review*, 23 (1989), 183–5.

Galway, Margaret. 'Alice Perrers's Son John', *English Historical Review*, 66 (1951): 242–246.

Gambier-Parry, T.R. 'Alice Perrers and Her Husband's Relatives', *English Historical Review*, 47 (1932): 272–276.

Gillespie, James L. 'Ladies of the Fraternity of Saint George and of the Society of the Garter', *Albion: A Quarterly Journal Concerned with British Studies*, 17 (1985): 259–278.

Given-Wilson, Chris. *The Court and Household of Edward III, 1360–1377* (University of St Andrews, PhD Thesis, 1976).

Given-Wilson, Chris. 'The Exequies of Edward III and the Royal Funeral Ceremony in Late Medieval England', *English Historical Review*, 124 (2009): 257–282.

Given-Wilson, Chris. 'The Merger of Edward III's and Queen Philippa's Households, 1360–9', *Historical Research*, 51 (1978): 183–187.

Given-Wilson, Chris. *The Royal Household and the King's Affinity: Service, Politics and Finance in England 1360–1413* (London: Yale University Press, 1986).

Given-Wilson, Chris and Curteis, Alice. *The Royal Bastards of Medieval England* (London: Routledge & Kegan Paul, 1984).

Gransden, Antonia, 'The Alleged Rape by Edward III of the Countess of Salisbury', *English Historical Review*, 87 (1972), 333–44.

Grant, Alexander. 'The St Bees Lord and Lady, and Their Lineage', Working Paper (Lancaster: University of Lancaster, 2013).

Green, David. 'Lordship and Principality: Colonial Policy in Ireland and Aquitaine in the 1360s', *Journal of British Studies*, 47 (2008): 3–29.

Harvey, John H. 'Mediaeval Plantsmanship in England: The Culture of Rosemary', *Garden History*, 1 (1972): 14–21.

Highfield, J.R.L. 'The Early Colleges', in *The History of the University of Oxford Volume 1: The Early Oxford Schools*, ed. J.I. Catto (Oxford: Clarendon, 1984), pp. 225–64.

Hollman, Gemma. *Royal Witches: From Joan of Navarre to Elizabeth Woodville* (Cheltenham: The History Press, 2019).

Holmes, George. *The Good Parliament* (Oxford: Clarendon Press, 1975).

Hunt, Edwin S. 'A New Look at the Dealings of the Bardi and Peruzzi with Edward III', *Journal of Economic History*, 50 (1990): 149–62.

Johnstone, Hilda. *The English Government at Work 1327–1336, Volume 1: Central and Prerogative Administration* (Cambridge, MA: Mediaeval Academy of America, 1940).

Kay, Frederick George. *The Lady of the Sun: The Life and Times of Alice Perrers* (London: Muller, 1966).

Keiser, George R. 'Through a Fourteenth-Century Gardener's Eyes: Henry Daniel's Herbal', *Chaucer Review*, 31 (1996): 58–75.

Lucas, Henry S. 'Diplomatic Relations between England and Flanders from 1329 to 1336', *Speculum*, 11 (1936): 59–87.

Lucas, Henry Stephen. *The Low Countries and the Hundred Years' War, 1326–1347* (Philadelphia: Porcupine Press, 1976).

Lutkin, Jessica. 'Isabella de Coucy, Daughter of Edward III: The Exception Who Proves the Rule', in *Fourteenth Century England VI*, ed. Chris Given-Wilson (Woodbridge: Boydell Press, 2010): 131–48.

Malden, H.E. (ed.) *A History of the County of Surrey: Volume 4* (London: Victoria County History, 1912).

McHardy, A.K. 'Paying for the Wedding: Edward III as Fundraiser, 1332–3', in *Fourteenth Century England IV*, ed. J.S. Hamilton (Woodbridge: Boydell Press, 2006) pp. 43–60.

Meulen, Janet van der. '"Sche sente the copie to her daughter": Countess Jeanne de Valois and Literature at the Court of Hainault-Holland', in *'I Have Heard about You': Foreign Women's Writing Crossing the Dutch Border*, ed. Suzan van Dijk (Hilversum: Verloren, 2004) pp. 61–83.

Michael, Michael A. 'A Manuscript Wedding Gift from Philippa of Hainault to Edward III', *The Burlington Magazine*, 127 (1985), 582–600.

Mortimer, Ian. *The Perfect King: The Life of Edward III, Father of the English Nation* (London: Vintage Books, 2008).

Newton, Stella Mary. 'Queen Philippa's Squirrel Suit', in *Documenta Textila: Festschrift für Sigrid Müller-Christensen*, ed. M. Flury-Lemberg and K. Stolleis (Munich: Deutscher Kunstverlag, 1981) pp. 342–48.

Orme, Nicholas. *From Childhood to Chivalry: The Education of the English Kings and Aristocracy 1066–1530* (London: Routledge, 2017).

Ormrod, Mark. 'Alice Perrers and John Salisbury', *English Historical Review*, 123 (2008): 378–93.

Ormrod, Mark. *Edward III* (London: Yale University Press, 2013).

Ormrod, Mark. 'Edward III and His Family', *Journal of British Studies*, 26 (1987): 398–422.

Ormrod, Mark. 'The Personal Religion of Edward III', *Speculum*, 64 (1989): 849–77.

Ormrod, Mark. 'Queenship, Death and Agency: The Commemoration of Isabella of France and Philippa of Hainault', in *Harlaxton Medieval Studies XX: Memory and Commemoration in Medieval England*, ed. Caroline M. Barron and Clive Burgess (2010) pp. 87–103.

Ormrod, Mark. 'The Royal Nursery: A Household for the Younger Children of Edward III', *English Historical Review*, 120 (2005): 398–415.

Ormrod, Mark. 'The Trials of Alice Perrers', *Speculum*, 83 (2008): 366–96.

Ormrod, Mark. 'Who Was Alice Perrers?' *Chaucer Review*, 40 (2006): 219–30.

Patourel, John Le. 'The Treaty of Brétigny, 1360', *Transactions of the Royal Historical Society*, 10 (1960): 19–39.

Penman, Michael A. 'The Scots at the Battle of Neville's Cross, 17 October 1346', *Scottish Historical Review*, 80 (2001): 157–80.

Phillips, Rod. *Alcohol: A History* (Chapel Hill: University of North Carolina Press, 2014).

Powell, W.R. (ed.) 'Upminster: Introduction and Manors', in *A History of the County of Essex: Volume 7*, (London, 1978) pp. 143–53.

Richardson, Amanda. '"Riding like Alexander, Hunting like Diana": Gendered Aspects of the Medieval Hunt and its Landscape Settings in England and France', *Gender & History*, 24 (2012): 253–270.

Rigg, A.G. 'John of Bridlington's Prophecy: A New Look', *Speculum*, 63 (1988): 596–613.

Rose, Susan. *The Wine Trade in Medieval Europe 1000–1500* (London: Bloomsbury Academic, 2011).

Roskell, J.A. *The House of Commons, 1386–1421* (Stroud: Published for the History of Parliament Trust by Alan Sutton Publishing, 1992).

Sekules, Veronica. 'Dynasty and Patrimony in the Self-Construction of an English Queen: Philippa of Hainault and Her Images', in *England and the Continent in the Middle Ages: Harlaxton Medieval Studies VIII*, ed. John Mitchell (Stamford: Shaun Tyas, 2000) pp. 157–74.

Shenton, Caroline. 'Edward III and the Coup of 1330', in *The Age of Edward III*, ed. J.S. Bothwell (York: York Medieval Press, 2001) pp. 13–34.

Shenton, Caroline. 'Edward III and the Symbol of the Leopard', in *Heraldry, Pageantry and Social Display in Medieval England*, ed. Peter Coss and Maurice Keen (Woodbridge: Boydell Press, 2008) pp. 69–81.

Shenton, Caroline. 'Philippa of Hainault's Churchings: The Politics of Motherhood at the Court of Edward III', in *Family and Dynasty: Harlaxton Medieval Studies IX: Proceedings of the 1997 Symposium*, ed. Richard Eales and Shaun Tyas (Donington: Shaun Tyas, 2003) pp. 105–21.

Slater, Laura. 'Defining Queenship at Greyfriars London, c.1300–58', *Gender & History*, 27 (2015): 53–76.

Smith, Kathryn A. *The Taymouth Hours: Stories and the Construction of the Self in Late Medieval England* (London: The British Library and University of Toronto Press, 2012).

Staniland, Kay. 'Clothing and Textiles at the Court of Edward III 1342–1352', in *Collectanea Londiniensia: Studies in London Archaeology and History Presented to Ralph Merrifield*, ed. Joanna Bird, Hugh Chapman and John Clark (London and Middlesex: Archaeological Society, 1978) pp. 223–34.

Staniland, Kay. 'The Great Wardrobe Accounts as a Source for Historians of Fourteenth-Century Clothing and Textiles', *Textile History*, 20 (1989) pp. 275–81.

Staniland, Kay. 'Medieval Courtly Splendour', *Costume: The Journal of the Costume Society*, 14 (1980): 7–23.

Stephenson, Mill. 'A List of Monumental Brasses in Surrey', *Surrey Archaeological Collections*, 29 (1916) pp. 79–139.

Strohm, Paul. *Hochon's Arrow: The Social Imagination of Fourteenth-Century Texts* (Princeton: Princeton University Press, 1992).

Tompkins, Laura. 'Alice Perrers and the Goldsmiths' Mistery: New Evidence Concerning the Identity of the Mistress of Edward III', *English Historical Review*, 130 (2015): 1361–91.

Tompkins, Laura. 'Mary Percy and John de Southeray: Wardship, Marriage and Divorce in Fourteenth-Century England', in *Fourteenth Century England X*, ed. Gwilym Dodd (Woodbridge: Boydell Press, 2018) pp. 133–56.

Tompkins, Laura. '"Said the Mistress to the Bishop": Alice Perrers, William Wykeham and Court Networks in Fourteenth-Century England', in *Ruling Fourteenth-Century England: Essays in Honour of Christopher Given-Wilson*, ed. Rémy Ambühl, James Bothwell and Laura Tompkins (Woodbridge: Boydell Press, 2019) pp. 205–25.

Tuchman, Barbara. *A Distant Mirror: The Calamitous 14th Century* (London: Macmillan, 1979).

Vale, Juliet. 'Philippa [Philippa of Hainault]', in *Oxford Dictionary of National Biography* (2010), accessed online at oxforddnb.com.

Vale, Malcolm. *The Princely Court: Medieval Courts and Culture in North-West Europe* (Oxford: Oxford University Press, 2003).

Warner, Kathryn. *Philippa of Hainault: Mother of the English Nation* (Stroud: Amberley Publishing, 2019).

Weir, Alison. *Katherine Swynford: The Story of John of Gaunt and His Scandalous Duchess* (London: Vintage Books, 2008).

Woolgar, C.M. *The Senses in Late Medieval England* (London: Yale University Press, 2006).

Index